Global Labour Studies

Work & Society Series

GLOBAL LABOUR STUDIES

Marcus Taylor and
Sébastien Rioux

polity

First published in 2018 by Polity Press

Polity Press
65 Bridge Street
Cambridge CB2 1UR, UK

Polity Press
101 Station Landing Suite 300
Medford, MA 02155 USA

ISBN-13: 978-1-5095-0406-0
ISBN-13: 978-1-5095-0407-7(pb)

A catalogue record for this book is available from the British Library.

Typeset in 10.5 on 12 pt Sabon by
Servis Filmsetting Ltd, Stockport, Cheshire
Printed and bound in Great Britian by Clays Ltd, St Ives PLC

For further information on Polity, visit our website:
politybooks.com

Contents

Acknowledgements

Our greatest intellectual debt goes to labour scholars who, through research, fieldwork and theoretical and conceptual developments, have shaped global labour studies. Amy Williams and Jonathan Skerrett from Polity deserve special thanks for their commitment, help and support throughout the project. We also acknowledge the contribution of two anonymous reviewers who provided us with positive and constructive criticisms. At a more personal level, we thank Susanne Soederberg and Sibel Ataoğul for their profound help and support. Nicholas Bernards and Josh Travers kindly provided useful feedback on sample chapters.

Chapter 1
Introduction: Thinking Global Labour Studies

It's a slightly chilly late September day and we are sitting in a café in downtown Montreal. While chatting and occasionally typing on our laptops, we each sip a cup of steaming black tea. This moment of consumption appears as an isolated act, something we might do on a daily basis without giving it a passing thought. For our part, we simply chose from an extensive list of excellent teas, paid the cashier and thanked the server when the hot mugs arrived at our table. Our actions, it seemed, were localized. After all, they took place in a small corner of a café in a backstreet of Montreal. And yet, through the simple activity of buying tea we are immediately yet unknowingly inserted as one nodal point within a dense web of productive activities that link thousands of people across continents. Although the leaves in our cups are predictably silent about their path from production to consumption, it turns out that they were grown in the Sri Lankan highlands half a world away. If you run a quick Google search, you'll see that these tea plantations have a rather idyllic appearance, with lush green foliage flowing down across picturesque hillside terraces. Owing to humid subtropical temperatures and a fertile soil that is amply watered by seasonal monsoons, the region provides excellent conditions for cultivating *Camellia sinensis*, the bush from which all tea is produced. This was certainly the impression of the nineteenth-century British colonial authorities who imported tea plants from China and conscripted thousands of indentured labourers from India to start the first commercial tea operations in Ceylon, now the nation of Sri Lanka. Fast-forwarding 150 years, these plantations have risen to become one of the biggest tea exporting sites in the world.

Putting the serene vistas of the Sri Lankan terraces to one side, we can start to map out the complex network of labouring relationships that collectively turn the leaves of a hillside shrub into a marketable commodity distributed to consumers via shops and restaurants many thousands of miles away. Tea, of course, is not an unduly complex commodity, yet the sheer variety of actors involved in this process is notable: from female tea pickers on the plantations, to various workers in the local companies where the tea is dried and processed into teabags, through to managers in international corporations that buy the bulk tea and market it to stores globally. Together, these agents – each with different roles, interests and degrees of power – have collectively shaped the journey of tea through its sequential stages of production, distribution and consumption. In so doing, they form part of a chain of lives and livelihoods that spills over a vast geographical terrain, stretching from the terraces of Sri Lanka to an unassuming café on another continent. Importantly, each actor has an unequal ability to shape the conditions under which they participate in the network. This affects not only the relative gains such as wages or profits that they accrue, but also the type and level of risks they face from their participation.

The tea leaves swilling in our cups, for example, are picked by a predominantly female workforce that is descended from Tamil indentured labourers imported by the British well over a century ago. These workers have spent generations assiduously labouring for poor pay and under arduous working conditions on the terraced hillsides. While tea picking is largely portrayed as women's work, men from the local villages typically look for jobs in the processing companies that transform the raw leaves into finished teabags. Despite their long hours, jobs on the processing side tend to be slightly better paid and have less punishing working conditions in comparison to the pickers. These inequities indicate how the division of labour in the tea industry is highly gendered. Women disproportionately occupy lower paid, more arduous and less secure tasks and, as a result, experience a strong degree of marginalization with very little power to challenge their conditions of work or pay. Although they actively seek to improve conditions for themselves whenever possible, many women tea workers strive to ensure that their children gain sufficient educational achievements to pursue other paths of work, far away from the plantations on which they themselves often feel trapped.

The production of tea, of course, does not begin and end upon the terraces. It is filtered through the regulatory structures and political power of firms, states and other organizations, each of which exerts its own influence on how tea is made, including the conditions of workers at the foot of the industry. Although the lowly status of pickers is contested by the activities of workers and supportive non-governmental organizations (NGOs) that seek to improve conditions within the sector, both plantation owners and processers have often been resistant to such initiatives. Noting the strong international competition in the tea industry – with rival plantations in Assam, Fujian and other parts of Asia – they decry the potential adverse impacts on profitability that substantive wage rises would entail. The plantations themselves form the lowest link in a chain of companies headed by retailing corporations that market the tea internationally. The tea processors occupy a middle tier: buying leaves from the plantations before selling the processed product onwards to the retailers. At the top of the chain, these retailers actively seek to ensure that their suppliers provide low-priced yet high-quality goods so as to maintain their market share and profit line. Most consumers in distant markets, they note, are more interested in the price tag and flavour than in the social conditions of workers on plantations. At the same time, the Sri Lankan government has also provided an extremely facilitating environment for the plantations and processors owing to the status of tea as an important export crop.

Through this cursory glance at the journey of a simple teabag, we can lift the lid on an intricate web of labouring activities and livelihood struggles that link production in the hills of Sri Lanka to the consumption of a warm beverage in Montreal. We've noted diverse power relations at play – between workers with limited options and employers seeking cheap labour; between genders; between different tiers of firms – and we've taken note of the different connections and networks that cross space, to link producers and consumers across the globe. There are many more steps we could add to make this web more complete. Think about the activities of transportation, advertising, retailing and even the post-consumption question of who deals with the waste. All of a sudden, it becomes clear that a teabag is never just a bag of tea! It is a nexus point for a complex array of relations between thousands of people labouring in different corners of the world.

Why Global Labour Studies?

As an academic field, global labour studies seeks to map out precisely these kinds of relationships in order to analyse their contrasting implications for the actors involved at each node. By exploring the interconnections that link the production, circulation and consumption of goods and services, we seek to open up essential questions concerning who is producing what, for whom, under what conditions and with what long-term effects. This makes global labour studies an extremely useful way of engaging some of the most pressing concerns facing us in the present era. Several compelling issues stand out. First, the networks that link production, distribution and consumption have become increasingly intricate, creating a more unified global economy that is able to produce vast amounts of diverse commodities and distribute them across long distances. Looking out at any university food mall, for example, you can easily discern the globality of contemporary production and consumption. You'll find a mix of foodstuffs for sale, with ingredients sourced from around the world: from fresh bananas to ramen noodles to cans of Pepsi. Electronic goods are also in clear display, such as cellphones and laptops designed in North America, Japan or Europe, but most likely assembled in East Asia. Even the standardized tables and seats we're sitting on turn out to have been produced in locations ranging from Mexico to Indonesia.

That this zone of consumption is a meeting place for commodities from all over the world seems very natural and we likely don't give it much thought. That said, when we reflect a little more deeply, the logistics involved in making all this happen on a daily basis suddenly appear breath-taking. Take, for example, that fresh-sliced mango in the package sitting next to the bananas. Less than forty-eight hours ago that fruit was hanging from a tree in central Brazil. After being picked, it was transferred by van to a refrigerated facility where a workforce of 184 Brazilians can process close to 200,000 mangoes per hour. There, the workers cut, skinned, sliced and diced the mango before sealing it away in its own personal plastic container. Once stacked in crates, those containers were loaded onto planes in São Paulo airport and then shipped outwards and onwards to retailers across Europe and North America. From tree to table across the length of a continent in just two days – now that's fast food![1]

Despite this incredible productivity, however, the workforce that underpins the global economy is stratified by vast inequalities in income and working conditions both within and between countries. A quick glance at working conditions in the Brazilian fruit picking and processing sector, for example, shows how low paid and arduous such occupations are. Under conditions of intense competition for contracts with European and North American supermarkets, juice producers and other fruit retailers face strong downward cost pressures. These constraints are frequently transmitted onto those at the very bottom: i.e., the labourers who have little power to shape the terms of their employment. In the orange picking sector, workers are typically paid by volume so they must collect a huge amount of fruit per day in order to make a minimum wage. They do so by working long hours on temporary contracts in difficult conditions, wrapped in cloth despite the heat to protect themselves from the blazing sun, yet nonetheless exposed to a range of chemicals used in production.[2] In short, the social context of precarious labour in Brazil is intimately connected to the fresh fruit sitting in our university food mall.[3] In this respect, we need not only to understand who has the opportunity to enter into relatively well-paid and secure work, but also how different forms of employment sustain uneven patterns of consumption at a global scale.

By exploring the tangible processes that create astonishing levels of wealth alongside persistent poverty, global labour studies offers crucial tools to better decipher the ways in which individuals and households work towards a more materially secure life, while also highlighting the many barriers and constraints to such outcomes. To do this, global labour studies provides a framework to better understand the structures and forces that shape lives and livelihoods across the globe. This is done explicitly in order to seek more equitable and sustainable forms of production, distribution and consumption in our increasingly interconnected and rapidly changing world. Examining these questions requires us to ask how goods are produced and exchanged through the daily activities of people who work, communicate, cooperate and conflict within diverse and contrasting circumstances. For this task, we use a series of concepts and approaches drawn from fields that include political economy, sociology, geography and development studies. Building upon these foundations allows us to understand what we might term 'economic life' outside the quantitative reductions of mainstream economic analysis.

This kind of quantitative economic analysis certainly has its place in our understanding of the world, but it must be kept in its place. It would no doubt be possible, for example, to transform the processes that underpin the production of Sri Lankan tea into a set of dollar values regarding gross domestic product (GDP), trade flows, per capita income and so forth. Yet to do so would be to produce a decisively weak brew. We would immediately rule out understanding the complex social and political dynamics that operate between plantations and their workers; between genders in production; between the international tea companies and their localized suppliers; and between those who consume goods and those who make them. In short, we would turn a blind eye to all the social, geographical and political processes through which the global economy functions on a day-to-day level. This book, in contrast, seeks to excavate precisely those processes and bring them to light. Before we can move on to that task, however, two definitional questions need to be addressed. What do we mean when we refer to 'labour' and why is it prefaced by the term 'global'?

What is the 'Labour' in Global Labour Studies?

To grasp the significance of the term labour we can helpfully compare it to the related idea of work. In formal terms, work can be described as the conscious application of physical and mental energies necessary to produce something. The thing being produced might be a tangible item like a handcrafted guitar, an intangible good such as a piece of computer code that exists virtually, or a service such as sweeping a kitchen floor. In all cases, work is the deliberate expenditure of energy necessary for a productive activity. Now, whereas you might say that you worked really hard on designing a piece of art or writing an assignment, you are unlikely to term this as labour. The reason for this is that labour is a broader category that captures not only the purposeful expenditure of energy, but also the social context under which such work is performed.

The concept of labour therefore opens up a broader set of questions and issues than simply the physical and mental exertions involved in work. Consider, for example, how we talk about 'slave labour' rather than 'slave work'. We do this to highlight the deeply uncomfortable proprietary relationships in which one individual has legal possession of others and compels them to toil on their behalf. Similarly, we term the work performed by children outside basic household tasks 'child labour' as a way to highlight the ethical questions inherent in putting children to work. Finally, the idea of 'wage labour' encapsulates how our ability to work has become a commodity that we sell to an employer in exchange for a wage. So when we talk about labour, we are deliberately engaging a set of questions around who is performing work for whom, under what conditions, and how such work fits within the wider production of goods and services at a society-wide level.

To talk about labour is therefore to put work as a productive activity in its social context. As the following chapters elaborate, we find a vast diversity of forms of labour at a global level. We often think of work in terms of waged labour in which workers sell their ability to work for a wage and – potentially – other benefits such as social security. However, there are many forms of labour, including self-employment through to forced or coerced labour. We follow up on these issues at length in further chapters, but it's helpful to highlight a few key common issues that global labour studies must address.

Workforce

It seems obvious, but for work to happen there must be workers. Yet workforces do not simply exist. Rather, they must be produced and reproduced. This means that a key task of global labour studies is to understand how workforces with specific skills, attributes and characteristics are created and put to work, both on a daily and a generational basis. Without doubt, questions of education and training are key to making workforces, but we must also think of the relative rights that workforces enjoy regarding pay, conditions, security and so forth. For example, the presence of low-skilled workforces, composed primarily of rural migrant women, that were expected to do large amounts of forced overtime work at times of peak consumer demand was an important factor behind the growth of light manufacturing industries in southern China during the 1990s.[4] So a key question concerns how these workforces are created, mobilized and put to work.

Workplace

Work always occurs somewhere – whether in a factory, an office, a marketplace or the back room of someone's home. Different workplaces are structured by different kinds of technology, but also distinct relationships between workers and their employers. Bicycles, for example, can be made in a state-of-the-art factory in California or in an informal workshop in the backstreets of Bangkok. The end product might not be too different, but the process through which work occurs – including the activities, hours, conditions and compensation of work – will be worlds apart. We therefore need to consider how different workplaces shape, and are shaped by, the social contexts of work. This leads us directly to a third domain of study.

Regulating institutions

Productive work is essentially a collective activity involving the combined efforts and energies of a workforce. Whether in an office or a factory, these collective activities will be regulated by institutions.

Institutions are conventions that govern behaviour, including formal rules, such as government stipulated laws enforced by courts, and informal rules, such as the shared norms about accepted behaviour in an office. When we think about key institutions that regulate the production and distribution of goods and services, government authority is evidently a key factor. States typically regulate the minimum level of wages, the details of contracts, worker rights and social benefits, and the conduct of workplace relations such as collective bargaining and dispute reconciliation. The state, however, is not the only regulatory institution. Firms themselves regulate relationships within the organization through various types of incentives and punishments, including under the rubric of 'corporate social responsibility'. In other work contexts, particularly those characterized by an absence of effective state regulation, it can be informal networks that shape work relations, including in small family businesses or community associations of street vendors.

Cooperation and conflict

One of the paradoxes of global labour studies is that the production, distribution and consumption of goods requires intense cooperation and generates enduring conflicts. As we noted in the example above, the passage of tea from bushes in Sri Lanka to cups in Montreal requires the cooperation of multiple actors, from pickers to processors to marketers to retailers. Producing any commodity is a collective process that involves coordination and cooperation. At the same time, however, it is also a process riven with conflicts of interest: from gender inequalities over the division of jobs; conflicts between workers and management over wages and conditions in both fields and factories; tussles between large corporate wholesalers and small processing companies over the price of bulk tea; and, potentially, conflicts between activist consumers demanding socially responsible products and retailers seeking to keep prices down. This duality of cooperation and conflict is a key thematic of global labour studies and arises repeatedly across the following chapters.

What's the 'Global' in Global Labour Studies?

When we attach the adjective 'global' to 'labour', we do so to explore how lives and livelihoods in any one part of the world are intimately connected to processes ongoing in others. In this sense, using the term global is not to suggest that there is some exterior global realm or level that exists 'out there' in a global space distinct from the local or national. On the contrary, as the example of the Sri Lankan teabag demonstrated, the global is very much present here and now in our localized, everyday relations and lived spaces. Each of the activities involved in producing, distributing and consuming that tea was local – in the sense that they happened somewhere specific – yet each was also global in that they were closely connected through processes occurring across continents. In short, the relationship between the global and the local is not one of opposition. Rather, we must seek to understand the conditions under which localized actions have impacts on a global scale.

As a result, the global in global labour studies is an invitation to analyse what forms of interconnection exist, how are they established and reproduced, what scale they operate on and to whose benefit they function. Although we sometimes think in terms of a heavily globalized world, we need to keep a close eye on the unevenness of such connections. As the historian Fred Cooper puts it, structures and networks may shape certain places and make things happen with great intensity, yet their impacts may tail off sharply elsewhere.[5] As a result, within global labour studies there are some key modes of interconnection that we need to consider.

Markets

We often hear talk about how global markets create an important form of interconnection between peoples through trade. Yet to operate on a world scale, markets must first be made global. For this to happen, they need a dedicated set of institutions and technologies to underpin them and no shortage of political determination to maintain them. The market for wheat, for example, is currently heavily globalized with political agreements in place to allow the movement of grain between borders and an infrastructure of transportation and storage in place to facilitate its travel across vast distances. As a result, a fall in production owing to a localized drought in the American Midwest is quickly transmitted onto prices at a global scale, affecting the price of bread across continents. In contrast, the market for labour is strongly constrained. As we shall see in chapter 8, the movement of people is actively controlled and migrants are frequently unable to legally work in countries they may move to. The degree of globality of markets, therefore, is politically grounded, open to contestation, and is something that must constantly be reproduced over time.

Firms

Most firms in the world are extremely small: from tiny workshops to street-side food stalls and corner shops. In terms of numbers, these businesses make up the vast majority of the world's enterprises and are for the most part localized in their operations. At the other end of the spectrum, transnational corporations are emblematic of globalization. Owing to their expansive scale, such firms shape the contexts of production, work and consumption therein, linking lives and livelihoods across space. Walmart, for example, is the world's biggest multinational in terms of sales and has established extensive supply chains that source massive amounts of goods from across the world into its many thousands of stores. It was estimated that Walmart alone accounted for 10 per cent of Chinese exports, many of which are produced under typically austere working conditions.[6] This has often led critics to assert that Walmart has played a lead role in facilitating a 'race to the bottom', depreciating labour standards on a global scale. From its perspective, Walmart would claim that it has fashioned an incredibly efficient division of labour, uniting producers and consumers through its state-of-the-art logistics in a way that provides jobs at one end and ever cheaper goods at the other. Either way, the role that the firm plays in coordinating a global production network that links quite simply millions of workers and consumers across national spaces is of extreme importance, and we examine this in detail in chapter 4.

International organizations

We argued above that regulating institutions are crucial to shaping the social contexts of work. In this respect, a number of key international organizations play a pivotal role in extending regulation at a global scale. Consider how the World Trade Organization (WTO) creates a system of rules and regulations governing trade and investment that applies to all 164 member states, providing a degree of conformity of such regulations on a global scale. To be clear, not all countries uniformly apply WTO regulations and there are vast differences in the ability of different countries to shape WTO agendas, to challenge its rules and regulations, and to make motions against other countries under its protocols. While the WTO provides trade regulations, the

International Labour Organization (ILO) has a mandate precisely to promote decent working conditions at a global level. It does so by producing conventions on workplace rights that it invites its 187 member countries to sign up to. Unlike the WTO, however, the ILO has no direct power to enforce its conventions even though the vast majority of countries have ratified them. As this indicates, different international organizations have vastly uneven levels of influence to shape the world of work at a global level, with the protection of trade and investment rights much more closely guarded than worker rights despite formal recognition of both.

Social networks

As all users of Facebook know, building social networks across long distances has never been easier. And while it might be easy to dismiss such networks as simply a means to share the latest cute cat video, we should not underestimate how informal social networks can facilitate flows of money, information, goods and authority across contexts that strongly influence the world of work. For example, rural to urban migrants often use informal networks to gain information to help connect them to potential employers. Equally, such social networks within migrant communities can also be used to pass money back to families without recourse to the formal banking system. On a different scale, informal social networks are frequently key to international labour rights movements which seek to link the struggles of workers in a specific factory with consumer activist groups in the West. In short, social networks are an important way in which the challenge of distance is overcome.

Global Labour Studies

This brief discussion of the terms 'labour' and 'global' primes our discussion for the following chapters where we begin to unpack and analyse the changing world of work. On this basis, the next chapter turns to how we should go about doing global labour studies. It begins to put together a toolkit of concepts that can help us examine and explain the social contexts of work and the forms of interconnection that produce an increasingly unified division of labour on a global scale, while also reproducing stark differences and inequalities of opportunity and outcomes.

Further reading

As a field of enquiry, global labour studies can be traced back to debates over the New International Labour Studies movement of the 1980s. You can read these approaches in foundational texts such as Ronaldo Munck's *The New International Labour Studies* (London: Zed Books, 1988) and Robin Cohen's *Contested Domains: Essays in the New International Labour Studies* (London: Zed Books, 1991). More recently an important attempt to update these themes was provided by Edward Webster, Rob Lambert and Andries Bezuidenhout in *Grounding Globalization: Labour in the Age of Insecurity* (Oxford: Blackwell, 2008).

Chapter 2
The Toolkit of Global Labour Studies

In the previous chapter we defined global labour studies as the study of work in its social context. To grasp what we mean by this, consider the case of Raj, a software engineer from Bangalore in India who currently holds a H-1B visa that allows him to work temporarily at an IT firm in Silicon Valley. He got this visa by paying an Indian contracting company to use its networks in the United States to seek out potential employers. Successful in this pursuit, Raj's visa is valid for an initial three years and is renewable for a further three if his employer lobbies on his behalf. In the meantime, Raj is to all extents and purposes bound to that firm, with extremely limited opportunities to shift his visa to work for a different company. Further, although his wife, Priti, and their daughter have accompanied him to California, Priti is explicitly denied the right to work in the United States under the conditions of the visa, despite her university degree in psychology.

For Raj, the H-1B visa is both an opportunity and a burden. On the one hand, there is a possibility that, with his employer's firm support, he may be able to renew the visa and eventually apply for the Green Card that would allow the family to remain in the country permanently. Raj is therefore strongly tied to his employer, who holds the key to his visa renewal and, therein, his hope to remain permanently in the United States. A power relation emerges between these actors, in which temporary hires like Raj are expected to work very long hours at pay levels typically some 15–30 per cent below the industry norm. Only by conforming to these conditions does Raj have a chance of maintaining his employer's support for the visa renewal. More likely, however, once Raj has completed his three years of work for the US company, either his employer will seek a visa for a new temporary worker or the state will turn Raj's renewal application down and he and his family will return to India to rejoin the Indian software sector. There he will hope to translate his employment experience in the United States into leverage within the crowded Indian job market.[1]

This brief example illustrates the complexities of studying labour in its social context. It shows how we need to pay close attention to the connections and institutions that link together labouring activities across space. It pushes us to analyse how such relationships shape the distribution of opportunities, benefits, costs and risks between actors. In this instance, we get a hint of the important networks that source workers into jobs through contractors who work closely with US firms to place temporary Indian workers into the American IT sector. We also see how institutions, such as the H-1B visa itself, strongly shape the relationships and conditions operating within the workplace. The outcomes are evidently complex and uneven. For Raj, the H-1B visa undoubtedly represents an opportunity in which he was prepared to invest heavily. Yet in the immediate future it keeps him locked into a dependent relationship with his employer who expects intense work in return. For Priti, the conditions of the visa mean setting aside her own career aspirations for up to six years, creating a strong gender imbalance in career opportunities within the marriage. For the employer, the visa programme allows the creation of a labour segment that is typically caught in a dependency relationship that encourages disciplined work at a cost below labour market rates for full-time workers from within the United States. There is no doubt that American companies benefit strongly from these relationships and many argue that they are key to their continuing global competitiveness. Others point out that such disposable temporary workers – who account for up to 30 per cent of new hires – depress wages and conditions across the sector, leading to a downgrading of work and pay.

This microcosm of work in its social context illustrates how we might sharpen our analysis by more explicitly confronting questions of power, networks, space and livelihoods. For instance, you'll note how in the above example there is a clear power relationship between Raj and his employer, and also potentially one between Raj and Priti. Yet what exactly do we mean by power, what forms does it take, and how is it exercised? Equally, we can also see how networks shape livelihoods across space. But again, we might first ask what we mean by networks and livelihoods: how do they take shape and for what ends? Answering these questions forces us to rely on more precise concepts about power, networks, space and livelihoods to make our assumptions explicit and consistent. Given that the questions posed in global labour studies are multifaceted, we need to integrate insights

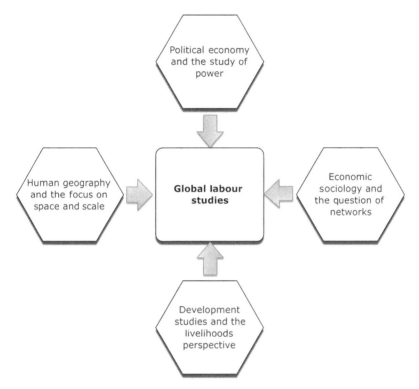

Figure 2.1 Global labour studies

from across disciplinary traditions to build a suitable analytical toolkit. Four influential perspectives are noteworthy and we explore these below (see Figure 2.1): (1) political economy and the study of power; (2) economic sociology and the study of networks; (3) human geography and the analysis of space; and (4) development studies and the livelihoods perspective. The following sections map out concepts stemming from these four influences and talk about how we might usefully synthesise them into a coherent framework.

Political Economy and the Study of Power

Much of what is written in the tradition of global labour studies is rooted in the framework of political economy. Unlike contemporary economics, political economy is not focused on creating ideal-type mathematical models to help explain real world events. Rather, it seeks to understand qualitatively how the relationships and institutions through which goods are produced, distributed and consumed have taken shape over time, and how the risks and rewards involved in such processes are distributed among actors. Take, for example, the question of markets. While economists tend to see markets as a natural way of organizing economic life that operate according to a universal principle of supply and demand, political economists reject such assumptions. They argue instead that markets are socially constructed through a range of supporting institutions, including money, property rights, state regulations, the presence of suitable workforces, shared behavioural norms and cultural values. Given that all the latter vary greatly across contexts, how markets work will shift according to the character of these supporting institutions. An informal market selling foodstuffs in Johannesburg, for instance, will operate very differently from a financial market based in New York or London. On this basis, political economists approach markets by asking how and why any given market has been created. What institutions and actors structure its operations? What power imbalances exist within it and what forms of agency are required to reproduce it over time?

Whether they are trying to understand the operations of a rice market in rural India or the informal labour market in the restaurant sector of Barcelona, political economists will start by conceptualizing how its unique structure of actors, institutions and social relations have taken shape. On this point, political economists are very clear: actors make history, but they do not do so in conditions of their own choosing. A smallholder farmer in rural Indonesia, for example, is manifestly less able to shape rice markets than a large European supermarket chain determined to increase its flexibility and profits by expanding within the subcontinent. Should the Indonesian government suddenly ban foreign retailers from operating within its borders, the resources and institutional capacities at the disposal of the supermarket chain would count for little. As a result, everyday actors from corporations to bureaucrats to worker organizations to smallholder farmers are aware that they must actively seek to shape the contexts in which they operate. Put simply, they seek to accumulate and exercise power. The study of power therefore stands as a pivotal focus of political economy. For our purposes, power can be usefully thought of in terms of the relative capacity of social actors to shape the context in which they and others interact. More powerful social agents are ones that have a greater ability to shape their own opportunities and those of others around them. Conversely, weaker social agents have their conditions set from elsewhere.

To elaborate, consider the following. When a municipal official in Cusco, Peru, tells an informal street vendor to move her stall away from a lucrative selling location outside a major bank on pain of being arrested or fined, this is an example of power relations over who can use public space. For the official, the street seller is emblematic of an unruly informal economy that lowers the prestige of the area and detracts from the modernity of the city. Conversely, for the vendor, finding a suitable location to sell goods is a major determinant of her livelihood. Failure to be able to effectively plead with or bribe the official to allow her to occupy this space and continue to sell means a greatly reduced ability to earn a living. Potentially, she might be able to assert her right to sell goods in this location through a legal challenge, but such an action would necessitate having resources, time, knowledge and contacts that she simply does not possess. Given this level of relative disempowerment, her best hope might be some form of collective action. If enough street sellers repeatedly establish themselves in this location, they might be able to force officials to accept their presence for fear of a wider social mobilization or political protest.[2]

This focus on power as a relation between actors in a given context is central to global labour studies. Power is typically exercised for two reasons. First, actors deploy power to ensure that a larger set of gains, profits or resources flow to them. Second, they also do so in order to displace risks or costs onto others. In this way, the exercise of power is simultaneously enabling or facilitating for some, and constraining or disabling for others. Power is fundamentally relational. It allows some actors to systematically seize opportunities and, at the same time, it reduces the ability of others to shape their respective conditions or to avoid costs being placed upon them. A firm like Walmart, for example, exercises power over smaller suppliers that depend upon the retail giant for contracts. While Walmart is renowned for offering 'everyday lower prices' to its customers as a key element of its profitability, to do so it has garnered a reputation of squeezing suppliers, who are expected to find ways to deliver products at ever cheaper unit costs. Given the concentrated market share that Walmart holds, many suppliers view the threat of losing their contract as a sizeable problem. As a result, they feel compelled to bear the brunt of Walmart's cost cutting and find ways to meet the larger company's demands. The power that Walmart holds, backed by the threat of moving business to a competitor supplier, is therefore a way of displacing costs onto suppliers while reaping the benefit from such efficiency gains. It is possible that both firms will ultimately benefit, although they are unlikely to do so equally given the strong power imbalance that structures the market.[3]

The exercise of power takes different forms and it is useful to focus on three overlapping types in turn. The first can be thought of as direct power. This form of power manifests itself in the immediate relationship between two or more parties in which one actor is able to directly compel another into a specific course of action, through force, persuasion, payment or threat of punishment. Direct power often translates into an explicitly coercive type of relationship. Korean textile factories operating in China in the 1990s and early 2000s, for example, became renowned for deploying a militaristic work discipline in which male production managers would enforce incredibly intense working conditions upon largely female workforces through a mixture of verbal threats and instant punishments, such as deducted wages, confiscated documents and the ultimate threat of being fired. This represents the systematic exercise of direct power across the workplace in order to increase productivity and profitability. Given that factory owners habitually delayed wage payments – meaning that workers were typically owed two months of back wages – being fired implied not only the loss of future income but also the forfeit of wages already earned. Factory owners used these direct power methods to enforce a particularly intensive application of work.[4]

If direct power is explicit and often coercive, a second form of power is more subtle yet arguably more important. Indirect power refers to the ability to shape the institutional context in which actors operate in a given domain. Put simply, certain actors have more influence to set the 'rules of the game' in a manner that is advantageous to their own interests. Indirect power is therefore actualized not through direct coercion, but through creating institutions, constitutions, formal norms and informal rules of behaviour. In the working of labour markets, for example, regulations set the conditions on which employers may hire, fire and otherwise use the workers they employ. If employers are able to lobby for a more flexible set of regulations that enable them to quickly fire workers without needing to pay severance, they are able to increase their ability to respond to market changes and will also have greater control in the workplace, where the threat of dismissal will be more acute. Workers, on the other hand, will see a decrease in their security and find themselves more exposed to market fluctuations.

Our final type of power – sometimes overlooked – is symbolic power, which refers to the ability to shape how things are represented and interpreted. Being able to frame an issue in a particular way greatly affects how it is understood, analysed and resolved (or potentially left unresolved). It shapes who has legitimacy or expertise to speak to an issue, affects how people view their own status within society, and defines what counts as normal and justified or exceptional and illegitimate. Of particular interest within global labour studies is how specific types of work are represented as being suited to certain social groups. For example, when the labour-intensive assembly zones known as 'maquiladora industries' were being established in northern Mexico as export platforms into the United States, a struggle broke out over the representation of an ideal worker. Factory managers universally sought to establish the idea of a passive, young, disciplined woman as the archetypal worker for this industry. This was done for two reasons. First, it was a means to attract investment by project-ing a compliant workforce to foreign firms. Second, in consolidating an image of maquiladora workers as diligent and passive women, managers sought to use this norm to police workplace relations by disciplining or firing those who did not conform. As a result, imposing the image of the maquiladora worker as a passive female was a key strategy in shaping the industry even though the women who were hired actively contested such representations. This led to many bitter struggles and some peculiar outcomes. As sociologist Leslie Salzinger notes, one manager in the factories she studied sought to make up for a shortage of women workers by hiring effeminate gay men as substi-tutes. For this manager, the representation of maquiladora labour as uniquely feminine work was to be maintained at all costs.[5]

Economic Sociology and the Question of Networks

If political economists have made major contributions to under-standing how power shapes the social contexts of work, economic sociology has made a parallel impact based on its interrogation of social norms and networks. To grasp the importance of economic sociology's contribution, it's helpful to briefly contrast its conceptual-ization of how economies operate to that of mainstream economics. For the latter, individuals and firms are assumed to act in a univer-sally strategic way. Whether buying a good or entering a contract for a specific service, they are assumed to calculate their options and choose the one that makes the most economic sense in terms of future returns. In this framework, agents are isolated and their interactions largely accidental. It is simply a matter of strict economic rationality – i.e., the pursuit of optimal benefit or profits – that deter-mines who does business with whom.

For economic sociologists, these kinds of assumptions about how people behave are strongly questionable. In the real world, most economic transactions occur between people who know each other to a greater or lesser extent. As a result, their interactions are not simply governed by an unflinching cost-benefit analysis. Rather, they are shaped according to a social context of shared norms, values and habits. These do not necessarily follow a narrow economic rationality but represent a wide range of mutual expectations about how people should interact that are shaped at a broader, societal level. Indeed, as economic sociologists emphasize, when people do make decisions based on short-term profit-orientated mentalities, this is itself a cultural disposition that must be explained rather than assumed.

In their insistence that society matters, economic sociologists argue that we must consider closely the social and cultural contexts in which all economic transactions are embedded. The concept of embedding is important to this aim because it captures how individual choices and actions are set within prevailing norms and values operating at a societal level. Put simply, all economic action is embedded within a cultural context. Whether we are analysing interactions in a marketplace, a factory, a corporation or a family farm, we need to understand how prevailing social norms influence the ways in which people act and the decisions they make. While an economist might assume that individuals act in ways that are narrowly rational and self-serving, economic sociologists would emphasize that such decision-making may well be strongly influenced by powerful social norms such as deference and reciprocity, trust and duty, obligation and caring. The latter may be established at the level of family and kin or at a broader level of community or society that shapes our shared values and perceptions.

For economic sociologists, one particular manifestation of this role of embedding is the importance of networks as a key feature of material life. A network corresponds to an enduring set of relationships or social ties between actors that reinforce shared expectations and a degree of reciprocity between participants. Such ties can be relatively weak – for example, a loose network of college graduates who keep in touch on Facebook. However, they can also be extremely strong – such as a close kinship group that meets in person frequently and has strongly engrained values of mutual support. As the empirical studies of economic sociologists reveal, such networks are widespread and form a basic foundation of everyday life. We can find such networks present across the world of work: from the shantytowns of Ulaanbaatar through to the corporate boardrooms in Silicon Valley. In the former, networks based on kinship often provide a vitally important means for marginal groups in Mongolia's capital city to access food and other goods from rural areas.[6] In the latter, groups of executives can become closely linked by social ties in which they share information and strategies about regulatory changes over a weekly round of golf.[7]

For economists, these networked relations and the social ties they rest upon would stifle efficient economic activity because they dampen the ability of agents to make rational decisions based on purely economic criteria. What economic sociologists have shown, however, is that networks can be vital for promoting stability and addressing key problems in the organization of economic life. They do so because repeated interactions that consolidate shared norms help to build trust and familiarity that can be vital for doing business, solving problems and making ends meet. Networks can therefore facilitate the flow of goods, services, information and other important assets among participants. Moreover, the trust that networks create can enable collective problem solving and promote forms of reciprocal behaviour that are greatly valuable yet might be impossible outside a networked context. As a result, if networks are strong and their values are widely shared among members, actors will frequently seek to maintain the network and their position within it even at the personal cost of avoiding more immediately profitable courses of action.

Networks are therefore central to understanding the social contexts of labour. As an example, consider how migrants from rural India use networks to overcome significant livelihood challenges when they reach urban centres. Migrants frequently have no access to formal social entitlements or services – from healthcare to banking to housing – and need to work in a social setting that is alien to them, occasionally in languages that are not their own. In order to access the goods, services and information that are vital to survival, migrants depend heavily upon networks. Alongside such tangible access to housing and employment, networks also provide a means of circulating the tacit yet essential cultural knowledge about how to deal with new employers, landlords and officials who can be resolutely hostile to or exploitative of migrants. As David Mosse and collaborators have noted in their study of migrants from Bihar state in East India, this means that the quality of household networks greatly shapes migratory experiences.[8] In tracing the livelihoods of migrants from rural villages in northern India, they show how a household's position in village-based networks strongly affects the relative success of migrants in job hunting, including their potential income and working conditions. Better networks translate into better contacts and opportunities, and less dependence on exploitative middlemen. As a result, rural households invest considerable resources in maintaining and improving their networks from year to year.

It is important to emphasize that networks are not intrinsically good or bad. While embedded relationships may promote a degree of stability, longevity, mutual dependence and trust, these qualities do not necessarily lead to socially beneficial outcomes. On the one hand, depending on the relative power of the actors, networked relations can also be constructed upon and reinforce hierarchies in which the greater dependency of some upon the network can lead to their relative exploitation within it. Some networks may exclude women, as in the idea of the 'old boys' club' that can strongly limit the ability of women to gain positions of authority within workplaces. On the other hand, the ends that networks are put to can be socially injurious. For example, networks may facilitate corruption, particularly when a close network encompasses both business executives and the state functionaries that are meant to regulate them. The character and purposes of each network must therefore be assessed on its own terms. What is clear, however, is that networks matter. Having strong networks is a type of power: membership facilitates access to assets that outsiders are excluded from. It is of little surprise, therefore, that both individuals and firms invest considerable resources and energies in building their networks.

Human Geography and the Analysis of Space

Human geographers are interested in the ways in which spatial dynamics are key to social relations. Economic development and labour relations, to take only two examples, occur in space and should be understood accordingly. But what is space and how should we understand it? One productive way to approach the issue is to follow geographer David Harvey's threefold definition of space as absolute, relative and relational.[9] Absolute space is the physical and material space where all natural processes and human activities take place. Mountains, cities, oceans and highways are examples of physical objects populating absolute space. These objects can also be the aggregate of other objects, such as the way cities are composed of buildings, households, shopping malls and so on. Absolute space can be measured, rationalized and represented in different ways such as maps, architectural plans, cadastres or globes. For global labour studies, absolute space is the space of goods, money, factories, work offices, tools, machineries and work processes. It is also the area of private property, state borders, economic zones of production and consumption.

The idea of relative space adds an important twist to absolute space. Consider how, from the perspective of absolute space, the distance between Davao and Manila in the Philippines is fixed. That fixed absolute space, however, means very different things relative to whether I cover it by plane (978 kilometres) or by car (1,476 kilometres). Moreover, the construction of a new private highway between the two cities will shorten the relative space compared to driving on the old road, so long as you can afford to use it. In this way, the concept of relative space helps us bring questions of power and access into the discussion. For a Filipino farmer in Davao looking to migrate to the capital Manila to find work, the relative space between the two locations might seem a considerable obstacle. For a businessman looking to close a deal, it might be as simple as hopping on a plane. As such, relative space is undoubtedly influenced by the quality of roads, infrastructures and public transportations, as well as the availability and frequency of organized transportation. It also changes through technological shifts which contribute to 'time–space compression'. From snail mail to phone line to cellphone, and from sailing ship to car to aeroplane, technological developments continuously diminish the 'friction' of space and constantly reshape relative space. Pivotally, relative space also depends very much on who has access to these ways of crossing space, meaning that relative space and our earlier discussion of power are closely related.

Taking this point further, our third category, relational space, highlights the dynamic ways in which collective ideas, experiences and practices materialize from our spatial existence. As an example, consider Mae Sot in northwest Thailand, a thriving export-processing zone where some 200,000 predominantly female migrant workers from Myanmar cross the border to labour in garment and textile factories. In moving into this new and closely controlled space, at least 95 per cent of them have no legal status and almost all of them are paid below the minimum wage. The lax enforcement of labour regulations and the prohibition of non-nationals from joining unions have exacerbated the problems facing such workers. Threats of denunciation to the authorities – leading to deportation – are recurrently used to control migrants, and it is standard practice for employers to deduct a sum to bribe the police and prevent raids from their wages. Such problems are further compounded by the lack of facilities nearby for the workers to shop in, which gives the factory the capacity to sell them overpriced goods at 20 per cent monthly interest.

Despite this strong degree of marginality, the experience of labouring within this oppressive space catalysed some migrant workers towards collective action. Through a spontaneous mobilization, the workers in one factory forced the employer to sign a contract that made the factory the first one to pay minimum wages without deductions. In this case, the shared experiences of 400 workers who had been collected into the tight factory space acted as a powerful incentive for self-organization. It goes without saying that low wages, oppressive working conditions and little control over their lives had fuelled tensions and conflicts between them and the management. Yet there was no leadership and the action had not been organized from above. Rather, out of a clear sense of a common experience of oppression, the workers simply decided that enough was enough and walked out together. Moreover, this shared expression of solidarity and power within the spatial confines of the factory reinforced their determination in having their demands met. This is relational space, the flow of ideas, experiences and practices arising from our social and spatial existence.[10]

This conception of space is particularly relevant for global labour studies. The workplace is spatially organized as it contains workers and work processes within specific places. Yet workspaces are located somewhere (e.g., home, office, factory) and are therefore positioned in relation to other places (e.g., daycare, household, school, grocery store, subway station, roads, bike path). Individuals might privilege specific living and working areas according to the configuration and accessibility of services, or they might be ready to commute to live in a specific neighbourhood or be able to own a house. Moreover, the relational nature of space and of its impact on labour depends on a series of complex phenomenon such as uneven geographical development, political expediency and environmental degradation. Work environments are social, political and economic spaces whose very existence and organization are intimately connected to broader processes. Investing in new technologies, relocating production to a different country or expanding production by hiring more people are deeply spatial business decisions based on the availability of skilled workers, transport and shipping facilities, and markets. And like in the case of Mae Sot, workers' collective sense of exploitation and injustice can lead to confrontations over working conditions.

Human geographers also use the notion of scale as a complement to their consideration of space. We often think of scale in a linear fashion, getting progressively bigger, in which any specific scale encompasses – and therefore determines – the lower levels ranging from the individual body up to the household, on to local, regional, national, international and global scales. While this perspective is a useful starting point, we should resist the urge to reduce scale to a series of fixed spatial areas. A more complex approach would recognize that social phenomena are always the result of interacting scales. As an example, surveying the fridge for your breakfast while coffee is brewing, you opt for a bowl of yogurt with fresh berries and pineapple. What seems like a banal, localized event in fact hides great scalar complexity. While the berries give you a taste of what is locally produced and available at this time of the year, the milk from which the yogurt is made comes from national dairy farms that are protected from international competition through import quotas. Your pineapple from Honduras and your coffee from Costa Rica were made available through the combined work of distant producers and regional traders operating within global supply chains and under international trade agreements. Your breakfast is a multi-scalar project – quite literally, there is a world of labour in front of you.

Because social phenomena are also spatial phenomena, notions of space and scale are deeply connected with those of power and networks. This means that power, as the relative capacity of social actors to shape the context in which they and others interact, hinges upon the relative capacity to shape the space in which social actors interact. For example, construction firms and developers will have a greater ability to shape urban development policies than slum dwellers and squatters. Moreover, this capacity to shape urban space and create investment opportunities is likely to rely on more or less established networks of developers, investors, politicians and citizens having an interest in municipal development.

Development Studies and the Livelihoods Perspective

The approaches we've surveyed so far tend to focus on the big questions of power and production, with an important emphasis on governments, corporations and labour markets at a macro-level. These are expressly important issues, but global labour studies requires us to understand the social contexts of labour from the bottom up by focusing on the activities of individuals and households who encounter both constraints and opportunities in their everyday struggles to both survive and prosper. To this end, a focus on livelihoods forms a fourth analytical perspective that we can draw upon to help fill out and provide nuance to our analysis.

Livelihoods approaches became very popular within the field of development studies in the 1990s as a way to understand both the opportunities and the constraints that households face while trying to make ends meet. Robert Chambers, one of the original contributors to the livelihoods perspective, argued that many government policies that aimed to benefit marginal households failed because they were based on ill-founded assumptions about how households actually mobilized resources and put them to use. For Chambers, livelihoods analysis offered a way to build from the bottom up by mapping how households strategically make decisions about their assets in an ongoing attempt to secure reliable income streams.[11] In this respect, livelihoods approaches seek to understand the complex ways that households actively put together a livelihood strategy using the limited assets they possess. For example, most households in the developing world pool multiple forms of income-generating activities undertaken by different household members. These might include various options for seeking work, including in local labour markets, migration to urban centres or even migration internationally. It might also include petty commercial activities, such as buying locally produced goods to sell informally at regional markets or devoting a certain amount of the household's labour to subsistence or commercial agriculture either on family owned or rented land. Households might focus on one or two of these strategies, while also keeping other options open in case the former do not pan out.

The emphasis here is on agency: how households and the individuals within them seek to strategically manage their resources in order to take advantage of opportunities and avoid potential risks. By tracing out a livelihood strategy from the ground up, the perspective moves towards a descriptive analysis that often portrays a complex web of activities and interactions that highlights the sheer diversity of ways in which people make ends meet. That said, a livelihoods focus only makes sense in the context of questions of power, networks and space as set out above. The relative ability of a household to maintain a viable livelihood strategy will depend on its level of power, the quality of its networks, and so forth. There are clear political dimensions to this. Households not only seek to put together secure and stable livelihoods; they often seek to alter the conditions under which they must do so through individual or collective action. They may do so by joining or challenging existing networks, political groups or social movements or starting new ones. Moreover, decisions within a household should in no way be assumed to be egalitarian or fair. As generations of feminist scholars have shown, strongly gendered power relations frequently affect the distribution of labour, resources and opportunities within the household. Women are often expected to do a majority share of the unpaid labour associated with the day-to-day running of the house, including child raising, cleaning and food preparation. They are often also expected to either join the waged labour force in some capacity or, in many parts of the global South, engage in agricultural labour or informal sector activities in order to add a further income stream.

Caveats aside, livelihoods approaches can provide impressive detail regarding the texture of everyday lives in diverse settings. Livelihoods analysis brings into focus how households negotiate with employers, state officials, merchants, financial lenders and neighbours in complex and contingent manners. The work of Jonathan Rigg, Tuan Anh Nguyen and Thi Thu Huong Luong, for example, maps out in rich detail the livelihoods of thirty households in urban Hanoi, Vietnam. By illustrating the shrewd ways in which these marginal households navigated difficult political economic challenges, these studies remind us how individuals exercise agency in the pursuit of stability and security despite unforgiving circumstances with meagre resources. They also reveal the small margins and uncontrollable elements that separate relative success and harsh failure at the bottom of the job market. In moving from the micro-level upwards, they make clear just how important questions of power and networks are in fashioning secure livelihoods in difficult conditions.[12]

Finally, the application of a livelihoods perspective need not be limited to contexts in the global South despite its origins within the field of development studies. On the contrary, the approach provides a perspective that travels well across settings. Consider how many households in the urban centres of North America and Europe might combine working at several jobs with potential flows of other income – from backyard gardening to social assistance claims – to ensure a livelihood in a manner not dissimilar to the urban residents of Hanoi noted above. Common questions over livelihood strategies can therefore be found across contexts, particularly given the current significant expansion of more precarious and temporary work in the industrialized countries of the West, as we examine in chapter 5.

Towards an Integrated Perspective

The above sections have set out how understanding labour in its social context requires us to draw upon an interdisciplinary perspective in order to highlight elements of power, networks, space and livelihoods. In combining the insights from these four perspectives, the integrated framework gives us a series of analytical tools that we can employ to help guide our study of more specific cases and issues. Having this diverse range of analytical tools is particularly useful because it allows us to approach issues from a range of angles and entry points in order to understand the complex processes that drive them. One word of caution is necessary. Although we now have a toolbox full of useful concepts, we need to remain keenly aware that the analytical tools provided by global labour studies do not in themselves provide any answers. Rather, they offer ways to ask important questions and help us orientate ourselves towards a strong and grounded analysis of pressing social issues. Our obligation as analysts is to proceed reflexively, using these concepts as guiding tools to make sense of the complexities of the world around us while recognizing the inherent limitations and blind spots of our own analysis. Let us start this process by examining how labour forces are made, reproduced and put to use.

Further reading

Political economy and the study of power can, of course, be traced back to classic works such as those of Karl Marx and Max Weber, and a succinct account is provided by Derek Sayer in *Capitalism and Modernity* (London: Routledge, 1990). A concise guide to network thinking within the field of economic sociology is David Knocke's *Economic Networks* (Cambridge: Polity, 2012). For deepening your understanding of space, David Harvey's essay 'Space as a key word' appears in his book *Spaces of Global Capitalism: Towards a Theory of Uneven Geographical Development* (London: Verso, 2006). Finally, the essential guide to livelihoods approaches is Ian Scoones's *Sustainable Livelihoods and Rural Development* (Halifax: Fernwood Press, 2015).

Chapter 3
Labour Regimes

Selina Begum is a 23-year-old Bangladeshi seamstress who was tragically caught up in one of the worst industrial disasters of the past decade. Employed in a garment workshop on the sixth level of the Rana Plaza building in Dhaka, she remembers vividly the day the floor collapsed beneath her and the walls fell inwards. Fears about the building's structural integrity had made her and many coworkers unwilling to enter the factory that morning. Regardless, under pressure to meet contract deadlines with Western brands, the owners threatened apprehensive employees with fines or sacking if they refused to enter. Soon after work started, the collapse occurred, trapping her for some six hours before rescue workers pulled her out. More than 1,000 of her colleagues perished, and another 2,500 were injured. Yet just months after recovering from the physical injuries, and still shaken by the trauma of the incident, Begum began searching for work in the very same garment sector. 'We're poor', she said. 'I have to work to survive. Unless I go to work at the factory, who will feed me?'[1]

Although her narrow escape from the Rana Plaza disaster was an exceptional occurrence, Begum's readiness to re-enter the garment labour market is typical of many young women who have recently moved into Dhaka from rural areas. Working as cutters, seamstresses and ironers, this workforce is formed from an estimated 3.6 million predominantly female labourers who collectively produce clothes for retailers worldwide. These days, all the top brands source from Bangladesh, including Gap, Benetton, Walmart, and Marks and Spencer. This labour-intensive industry is powered by a constant flow of young women into the factories where they are expected to work long and intense hours – an average of eleven hours a day, six days a week – for wage rates that are among the lowest in the region. It is not simply cheap labour, however, that makes Bangladesh a nodal point in global garment production networks. It also rests on how workforces can be used within production: their discipline and motivation, their readiness to work in a focused manner over long hours, their relative flexibility to take on overtime at short notice on top of already long working weeks, and the ability of firms to easily shed labourers at slack periods of the garment production cycle.

A workforce with such flexible characteristics, however, does not emerge out of thin air. Rather, it must be produced and reproduced through a range of social institutions and processes that shape the availability of workers, their relative costs and, more specifically, their conduct and expectations about work. In much of the literature on the global economy, these social and political dynamics of how workforces are produced, mobilized and utilized are conspicuously ignored. In mainstream economics, for example, labour is typically assumed to be a technical 'factor of production'. Workers are presumed to simply exist, waiting to be hired. As a result, the process of work is viewed a bit like baking a cake. You mix together a pinch of capital, a scoop of technology, a sprinkle of management and a generous helping of workers out of the packet. Stir well, and production proceeds accordingly creating a steady stream of outputs.

Reality, however, is more complex. Although it may be convenient for economists to assume that suitable workers exist ready and waiting to be hired, neither firms nor states suffer from such myopia. On the contrary, they are keenly aware that labour forces with specific characteristics, dispositions, attributes and skills must be actively produced and mobilized as a cohesive, hierarchically structured and socially integrated workforce. The reason for this is relatively simple: how labour is produced strongly shapes how labour can be used. It therefore impacts heavily upon the competitiveness of firms and regions. By asking the seemingly innocuous question 'how are workforces produced?', we can open an essential window onto the social foundations of the global economy.

Producing Workers

To grasp how important this process of producing workers is, consider the following hypothetical question. If you were to magically substitute a class of Western undergraduate students into the seats of their equivalent age factory-working Bangladeshi counterparts for a month of 'work experience', how long would it take before production ground to a halt? Very quickly, one imagines. This would not be because the students couldn't learn the tasks involved in garment production. After all, many of the young Bangladeshi women have no specialized skills prior to arriving at the factory. Rather, it is because Western students would likely be unable to conform to intensive eleven-hour working days of closely monitored stitching in a hot factory with limited breaks and demanding production schedules. They would resist and quite probably rebel against working under such conditions because they clash with their expectations of what counts as legitimate work. Such rejection would, in part, result from the feeling that they have better options available and therein a degree of power with which to contest the imposition of arduous labour. Quite clearly, substituting equivalent bodies into the workplace is not enough to ensure a cohesive workplace. This is because labouring is not simply a technical process. It is also a political and social one in which norms about the nature and conduct of work and the power relations between employers and employees are fundamental influences on how work proceeds.

In this respect, producing workforces with a full package of suitable skills, aptitudes and dispositions is an extremely complicated business involving a wide range of overlapping social institutions and processes. If we wanted to dig deeper into the production of workers within the Bangladesh garment industry, for example, we would need to consider factors such as the hiring strategies of employers with their strong preference for women labourers who are viewed as more controllable owing to patriarchal norms across Bangladeshi society; the lax state regulations on hiring practices, worker rights and wages; the socially constructed norms about how a textile worker behaves both inside and outside the factory; the livelihood strategies of households that frequently rely on sending younger female members to factories for cash income; and the activities of collective worker organizations and other forms of political representation that contest conditions within individual workplaces and the sector at large.

One useful concept to help us pull together such disparate elements into a more unified framework is that of the labour regime. As sociologist Frederic Deyo puts it, a labour regime refers to the mechanisms through which labour is socially reproduced, mobilized and motivated for economic ends, and utilized in production.[2] The labour regime concept therefore gives us four linked moments of producing a workforce, as set out in Figure 3.1, starting with the moment of reproduction, travelling through mobilization and motivation, and

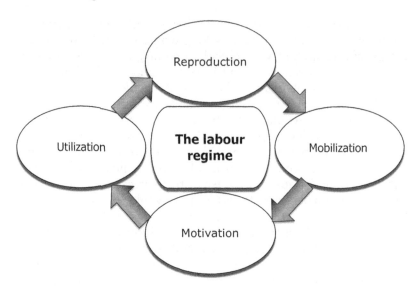

Figure 3.1   The labour regime

ending with the utilization of labour. This gives us an expressly useful research tool for examining how workforces are produced in practice.

Reproduction: Households and the State

The economic anthropologist Karl Polanyi famously labelled labour as a fictitious commodity.[3] In using this term, Polanyi sought to capture how labour circulates as a commodity – i.e., something that's bought and sold on a market – despite it not being produced for such a purpose. Put more simply: your mother and father didn't make you in order to produce a worker, yet seeking employment on labour markets is a role that you will most likely have to take on. For Polanyi, the significance of the fictitious commodity concept was that it emphasized how the production of labour relies on a wide range of relationships and processes that are outside the realm of the market. The first and most immediate domain where the reproduction of labour takes place is the household. This is where children are born, raised and socialized, and where they learn the norms and basic dispositions that will be essential to them as future workers. The household is also the place where workers rest, eat, sleep, wash and find emotional support and companionship. Despite being roundly ignored in much of the economic literature, the household and relationships within it are the fundamental building blocks of the economy.

Although the household is critical to these processes, in many countries the state also plays a major role in the reproduction of labour. As we shall see in greater detail in chapter 5, the period following the Second World War was characterized by a more interventionist approach of the state in organizing social reproduction. Especially but not exclusively in the West, governments put in place welfare programmes with the intention of providing workers with greater social and economic security. This 'social wage', as it came to be known, was based on state provisions such as healthcare, as well as measures that socialized risk such as pension programmes, unemployment insurance schemes and social safety nets. Moreover, the state played a key role in the development of the labour force through education. These two domains – the private realm of domestic work and the public realm of public service work – provided the main structures through which the reproduction of labour was secured.

As several generations of feminist political economy have indicated, the roles and responsibilities of social reproduction are pervasively assigned along gender lines. The concept of gender is a way to engage the socially constructed differences in the rights, roles and responsibilities that are assigned to people on the basis of their sex. In this respect, both historically and in the present, women are overwhelmingly seen as the primary caregivers within the household, which frequently leads to an uneven division of household responsibilities over reproductive care. Throughout the 1960s and 1970s, the women's movement challenged the view of the household as the natural place of women. At the same time, many argued that, despite being unvalued in monetary terms and rendered invisible to policymakers focused on waged labour, domestic labour should be recognized for what it is: unpaid work. German ecofeminist Maria Mies, for example, argued that the exploitation of women was intrinsic to the functioning of the global capitalist economy. She viewed the unpaid work appropriated from women as the basic social foundation upon which larger economic structures were built. Without patriarchy, she claimed, capitalism quite simply couldn't work. As such, she recognized that the economy relies on essential contribution of unpaid domestic workers, who daily and generationally reproduce the workforce.[4]

Three recent trends in contemporary social reproduction are particularly important. First, the ascendency of neoliberal policymaking dedicated to expanding the role of markets within society has profoundly reshaped the nature, place and dynamics of reproductive work as households are increasingly engaged in market relations. Take food, for example. More meals are prepared and eaten out of the home than ever before, and food delivery, especially with apps connecting consumers directly with local food restaurants, is increasing. Even groceries and supermarkets have reconsidered their business model by offering a growing selection of ready-made food. Other service providers such as dry-cleaners and laundromats are also part of this trend. The marketization of social reproduction has not only happened in the formal sector of the economy, but is part and parcel of vast and expansive networks of informal street sellers in the global South, where millions of vendors ply the streets or attend unplanned markets selling prepared food or offering services that are essential to the reproduction of urban populations (see chapter 6).

The second notable change concerns the re-privatization of social reproduction, especially in the global North. The decline of the welfare state under neoliberalism means that elements of social reproduction such as childcare, which were once undertaken or subsidized by the state, have been increasingly transferred back to families who must either undertake them or purchase them as commodities. The net result is the transfer of reproductive work back into the private sphere of the household or the market. This creates a double burden for many women who, in addition to shouldering most of the unpaid domestic labour, also need to earn a wage in the formal economy.

Finally, the redistribution of housework constitutes a third dimension of the manner in which reproductive work is being transformed. With the help of 'guest worker' schemes and other forms of temporary worker programmes, an increasing number of states now allow more affluent households to hire an overseas maid or a nanny – many of whom are from the global South and the former Soviet Union – to help with the domestic chores. While this opens some opportunities for migrant employment, it also effectively redistributes one woman's domestic burden onto another one.

What is notable about these trends is the extent to which they uphold a sexual division of labour. While the commercialization, re-privatization and redistribution of housework have transformed who, where and how reproductive labour is performed, it is still women who perform the bulk of it either in the household or as employees in the labour market, such as daycare workers, teachers, nurses, old-age home workers and so forth. The major difference is that, in addition to the sizeable amount of unpaid domestic work undertaken primarily by women in the household, we now must add the under-paid reproductive work of women and migrant workers locked into the lowest rung of the labour market as care workers.

Mobilization: Labour Markets and Segmentation

The term mobilization asks us to focus on how potential workers are drawn into specific occupations or jobs, therein becoming a work-force. Often this is seen to be a simple outcome of the labour market wherein job seekers with distinct skills and employers with particular needs come into contact and sign a labour contract. While labour markets are certainly a key institution in capitalism, it is important to note that much contemporary work occurs outside such market exchanges. As noted above, vital reproductive labour in both the household and community is typically done on a voluntary, reciprocal or coerced manner without a formal market relationship. Likewise, various types of self-employment and familial labour within small firms provide a significant source of employment, particularly in the informal economies of the global South (see chapter 6), and much agricultural labour – particularly in Asia, Africa and parts of the Americas – occurs on self-owned or rented small plots (see chapter 7). Finally, there are many forms of forced labour present globally in which work is rendered primarily through explicit coercion rather than market exchange (see chapter 9).

Furthermore, when considering hired labour, it is important to remember that there is no such thing as 'the labour market' in the singular. What we encounter in the real world is a multiplicity of distinct markets for different types of labour, with each structured by different regulations, networks and forms of social hierarchy.[5] As we set out below, these factors are critical determinants of who gets which jobs, for what pay and under what conditions. The term commonly used to express these divisions is 'labour market segmenta-tion'. To visualize segmentation, you might think of labour markets like segments of an orange, with entry into each segment shaped by different qualifications and professional criteria; place-specific norms and livelihoods; social divisions of class, gender, ethnicity and age; the role of social networks that source workers into jobs; and the role of the state and other agencies in regulating contracts, condi-tions and wages. Importantly, while movement within a segment is possible, transferring from one segment to the next is much more difficult. For workers, getting trapped in less-desirable segments of the orange typically means less secure employment with poorer pay and conditions. This can entrench social inequality within and across populations.

So what causes labour market segments to form? Certainly, skills and training are important vectors of segmentation because these attributes shape the bargaining power of workers. If a particular type of skilled labour is in short supply, then the power balance between employer and potential employee for setting a contract is quite different from more plentiful unskilled labour. In the software industry in Bangalore, India, for instance, the competition between firms to attract and retain highly skilled computer systems engineers and programmers results in relatively good salaries alongside promises of plush working environments and in-house facilities such as gyms, childcare centres and quality food courts. In contrast, the service workers who staff those gyms, childcare centres and restaurants are part of an entirely different labour market segment wherein a surplus of potential workers means that they have comprehensively less power vis-à-vis employers, particularly in the absence of strong state regulation of conditions.[6]

Segmentation is not, therefore, simply a question of supply and demand based on skills or qualifications. The segments of the labour market and the conditions within them are also shaped by the nature of state regulations, types of social discrimination, collective group bargaining and the formation of networks that link particular people to jobs. In virtually all countries, labour markets are regulated by the state, which sets the basic parameters for the hiring process and the subsequent contracts. These criteria range from minimum wage rates, regulations over weekly hours of work, mandatory holidays and leaves, workplace insurance, pensions and other social benefits and the precise conditions under which an employee can be laid off (see chapter 5). Notably, state regulations often treat different types of labour differently, therein providing varied degrees of contract security and unemployment benefits to distinct segments of workers. In the United States, for example, the reforms to social security legislation over the 1990s and early 2000s were deliberately designed to compel low-income workers to seek and accept work in order to be able to qualify for basic benefits, no matter how poor the wages and conditions of the jobs on offer. These regulations served to consolidate a segment of extremely vulnerable low-income workers – with a strong overrepresentation of black women – seeking work in tenuous and low-paid service sectors from cleaning to work in hotels or restaurants.[7]

In other cases, segmentation occurs precisely when state regulations are ignored or circumvented. The informal sector – which provides for the majority of employment in Asia, Africa and Latin America – is characterized by the absence of such regulation (see chapter 6). This means that for the majority of the world's workers, a regulated labour contract is a distant dream. In other settings, the rules may exist on paper but are only partially implemented or enforced. In southern China during the boom years of labour-intensive production, for example, the formal labour laws that guaranteed workers an encompassing set of rights were systematically ignored by employers and largely unenforced by complicit state officials, particularly for rural migrants entering industrial production or the construction industry. Indeed, migration is often a strong vector of labour market segmentation as some types of migrants find themselves acutely vulnerable to poor working conditions (see chapter 8). This is because migrants typically have restricted access to jobs and rely on a limited range of networks to channel them into certain labour market segments in their new location. Sociologist Simon Clarke's extensive study of labour markets in post-Soviet Russia, for example, demonstrated clearly how the density of social networks exerted a powerful impact on the ability to get a desired job in conditions of falling wages during a period of socioeconomic turbulence. Notably, better networks were closely associated with more affluent social classes who could invest and reciprocate in building such ties, thereby reinforcing existing social hierarchies.[8]

Labour market segments typically coalesce around class, race and gender distinctions, and play a key role in reproducing and entrenching social inequalities within societies.[9] Consider, for example, the experiment put together by sociologist Devah Pager, who enrolled two pairs of entry-level job seekers in Milwaukee and gave them résumés with identical profiles and qualifications. On paper, all four were indistinguishable high school graduates with the only difference being that two of the applicants were white and two were black. Then Pager introduced a second twist. She sent them all out to apply for the same positions, having instructed one each of the white and black job seekers to tell their potential employers that they had a nonviolent drugs possession charge on their record. The results were striking. Not only did the white applicant with a clean record receive double the number of call backs than the otherwise identical black applicant, but the white applicant with a drug charge also received more call backs than the black applicant with a clean record. In short, a white applicant with a drugs conviction was seen as more employable than an identically qualified black applicant with no record.[10] The overall impact of such discrimination is to push black job seekers into lower segments of the US labour market, a trend that is starkly represented in aggregate national jobs data.

Gender frequently acts as another vector of segmentation. In most parts of the world, specific jobs and occupations are commonly held to be typically 'men's work' or 'women's work'. Consider how care occupations – from nurses to childcare workers to primary school teachers – are largely construed as feminized work. This does not mean that only females work in these sectors. There are, of course, male nurses, kindergarten teachers, and so forth. Yet the professions as a whole are symbolically represented as feminine because care work is seen to extend out of women's unpaid labour in the home. These segments have typically been devalued and accompanied by poorer wages and conditions in comparison to other occupations with comparable skillsets and work demands and do indeed tend to be staffed predominantly by women.[11] Similarly, up to 85 per cent of jobs in the Bangladeshi garment industry mentioned above are taken by women, most of which involve labour-intensive, low-skilled tasks. In contrast, men still primarily take supervisory positions. Despite claims by factory managers that women have more 'nimble fingers', the reason for specifically hiring female workers is not because they are innately more suited to that form of labour but rather because they are subject to a different level of disciplinary power owing to their gender. It is this degree of disempowerment that textile industries – from Bangladesh to Mexico and beyond – have projected as a desirable trait for their workforces because employers require intensive labour for long hours at low pay.[12]

To be clear, many authors have argued that work in labour-export industries can also be beneficial for young women, offering a route towards personal liberty because the ability to earn a wage is seen as an important lever of social power. Women's employment therefore potentially offers greater influence within the household and can open up access to new spaces and relationships that were previously inaccessible.[13] These are expressly important points and speak to the importance of examining cases using the kind of approach that livelihoods analysis offers, in which the aspirations and agency of individual protagonists can be examined and considered.[14] That said, while some women can indeed find a valued source of empowerment within paid labour, it is important to also recognize that employers systematically create feminized labour market segments as a strategy to bring down costs, reduce their long-term commitment to workers and intensify labour. It is no accident that Selina Begum, the young Bangladeshi women with whom this chapter opened, felt she had no choice but to find another job in the garment sector despite being nearly killed in a traumatizing industrial accident. That is a powerful indication of labour market segmentation at work.

Motivation: Discourses of Labour

So far we've looked at how workers are reproduced and mobilized. One further aspect is that a labour regime also rests on what workers think. This is because, as economic geographers Neil Coe and Philip Kelly have argued, workers are political actors capable of a range of individual and collective forms of agency that can embrace, resist or reject change. We noted this factor above when considering how Western university students and equivalent age Bangladeshi garment workers are likely to have sharply divergent ideas about what is legitimate work. In short, making a workforce is partly a process of shaping how workers perceive their roles. States, firms and workers frequently seek to articulate shared understandings about what work should entail, what is legitimate within the workplace and how work fits into a broader social context. Coe and Kelly, for example, examined how the Singaporean state played an integral role in promoting a powerful discourse about the need for labour to make sacrifices to ensure national competitiveness and the collective betterment of the nation as a whole. This discourse – a form of symbolic power – was used to help pave the political grounds for public sector reforms that reduced labour rights, while also being calculated to send a clear message to foreign investors that Singapore held a vision of work relations that made it an attractive investment location.[15]

That producing workforces involves this cultural dimension has been long understood. Eminent social historian Edward P. Thompson, for example, highlighted how the transition to a capitalist industrial society in Britain entailed a dramatic shift in the way that people thought about time. In contrast to an agrarian work-cycle, in which daily rhythms and seasonal changes governed how and when people worked, Thompson charted how the new industrial machine in eighteenth-century England required the precise organization and synchronization of workers to regularize production and maximize output. This intensive restructuring of working habits necessitated a cultural shift in which workers were variously taught and compelled to respect time measured in minutes and hours in order to perform specific actions at precise times with utmost regularity. Although fiercely resisted, Thompson mapped how the imposition of what he terms 'time-discipline' both inside and outside the workplace was central to building a culture of industrial work.[16]

Thompson's emphasis on imposing time-discipline in industrial Britain may now look somewhat dated, but the processes he highlighted are still very much present in contemporary global labour. In her study of export-orientated manufacturing in southern China, sociologist Mary Gallagher noted a sign hanging prominently at the entrance to one of the factories she was studying. Its message was clear: 'Time is Money, Efficiency is Life.' In the factory, this discourse of efficient personal time management was enforced through attempts to inculcate a shared sense of personal reasonability among workers for precise time management, supplemented with severe fines for workers who were not punctual or did not adopt the strict time regulations of the assembly lines.[17]

Workers, it must be noted, rarely accept such representations at face value. Indeed, they often challenge and contest the ways in which they are represented by management or the state by seeking to assert their own collective representations of their identity as a workforce. As Leslie Salzinger notes in her detailed ethnographic study of women workers in the maquiladora zone in northern Mexico, ideas of gender, of what a female workforce should look like, and the kinds of labouring conditions it should accept, were bitterly contested within the workplace. Women workers actively sought to challenge the representation of women as docile and subordinate as part of a protracted struggle for better wages and conditions across the industry.[18]

Utilization: The Workplace and Strategies of Labour Control

At this point in the labour regime, we've looked at how workforces are produced, mobilized and motivated. The climax of this sequence is utilization – i.e., the deployment of labour for the production of goods or services. A key tool to open up this final quadrant of the labour regime is a deceptively simple yet extremely important concept: that of labour power. The concept of labour power refers to an individual's capacity to work over a given period of time. An employer might hire a seamstress in a Cambodian apparel factory to work eleven hours a day, six days a week. This means that they have hired her labour power for sixty-six hours over the period. That said, quite how she works during that time is still to be determined. Will she work hard in a dedicated fashion or seek to subvert intensive work? Will she use efficient labouring practices and technology to maximize productivity, or resist the constraints this imposes upon her? And will she collaborate productively and efficiently with other workers, or cause problems in the workplace?

Here we can grasp the importance of the labour power concept. Employers don't buy work per se; rather, they buy the employee's capacity to work over a period of time. They must then find ways to turn that potential into as large a quantity of realized work as possible. This transformation of labour power into realized work is known as the labour process. The stakes are high because the productivity of any enterprise depends on an efficient labour process. Failure to get employees to work collectively in a focused and intensive manner will ultimately compromise the profitability of the firm vis-à-vis competitors. As a result, from textile factories to call centres, employers spend considerable time and money working out the best way to turn labour power into realized work.

This concept of labour power helps lift a lid on a fundamental tension in most workplaces: employers and employees will frequently conflict over the organization of work. Office workers, for example, might check their Facebook pages multiple times during the day, but employers are likely to see this unsanctioned use of office time as a barrier to converting potential labour into realized labour. They will therefore seek to stop it, for example by installing monitoring software onto office computers to prevent unauthorised Internet use. Indeed, turning an employee's capacity to work into realized labour requires varied forms of management strategies and the exercise of both direct and indirect power within the workplace. These tensions within the labour process often emerge around three pivotal issues:

1 *The length and intensity of work.* Although an employer hires the worker for a specific number of hours or days, how many breaks – either sanctioned or unsanctioned – will she take within that period? Will she be expected to extend work beyond the paid hours, either *pro bono* or for compensated overtime? And will the worker spend those hours working in a dedicated way, or at a low pace, chatting with coworkers or focusing on issues outside work?

2 *The timing of work.* Is the employee prepared to work at times when the employer wants her to – including overtime – in order to maximize coordination with other workers or to meet fluctuating demands for orders? Are workers prepared to remain off the books at low-demand times? Notably, the idea of a nine-to-five

job that prevailed in some sectors of advanced industrialized countries appears increasingly passé as employers seek ever more flexible usage of labour. Indeed, the introduction of 'zero-hour contracts', whereby the employee works only when called upon, represents an extreme, yet increasingly common, scenario in the United Kingdom.

3   *The specific tasks performed and the use of technology.* Tension can also surface over the specific tasks undertaken within work. What tasks are deemed necessary or acceptable for workers (e.g., questions of safety, cleanliness or cultural reservations about performing certain tasks)? For example, an employer might prefer an employee to use a specific technology to improve productivity, yet employees might object to using certain tools, techniques or processes either because they are not familiar with them, because they restrict their autonomy over the work they perform, or because they make work boring. More worryingly, employers may pressure workers to perform work in dangerous conditions – as indeed we saw at the start of this chapter – which workers may or may not have the power to resist.

The mechanisms adopted to ensure that labour capacity is turned into performed work together comprise what is called labour control. Such mechanisms are often very complex, and the human relations departments of larger companies spend considerable time focusing on developing more efficient forms of labour control. Part of the complexity of this issue is that management must consider not just how single individuals work within the firm, but also how the labour force works collectively as a synchronized whole to operate – ideally – as a finely tuned machine. A key question facing any firm, therefore, is what strategies can help create a workforce that functions in a disciplined, efficient manner with due cooperation in order to maximize productivity. This will have the effect of turning the labour power into realized labour manifested in goods or services. Particularly in low-skilled labour-intensive industries, this involves finding ways to limit the potential for individual or collective resistance to the imposition of work.

Types of labour control vary greatly between workplaces and geographical spaces. As a starting point, it is useful to follow three ideal types highlighted by industrial relations scholar Richard Edwards.[19] The first of these is 'simple control', which he considered as the exercise of direct power in the workplace, such as immediate supervision, surveillance and coercion of workers. This could be a case of the manager looking over the worker's shoulder or, more coercively, the presence of on-the-spot fines and other penalties imposed for failure to meet work targets. In exercising simple control, supervisors are expected to discipline the workforce towards intensive work habits. Constant supervision can incur high costs for employers, particularly if workers are not well motivated and resistant to the drudgery of low-skilled labour. Although Edwards saw it as a historically dated form of labour control, simple control continues to be widespread, primarily in smaller firms, technologically less sophisticated workplaces or workplaces where workers have limited protection from either self-organization or state regulation. Sociologist Ching Kwan Lee, who herself worked in an export-oriented factory in Shenzhen, southern China, labelled this form of labour control as 'localistic despotism', in which the authority of managers over their closely selected workforce of young female migrants was militaristic and operated with the complicity of local political authorities.[20] The workdays were regimented, with extreme workplace discipline including closely controlled bathroom and rest breaks and the verbal abuse of managers towards those perceived not to be working with sufficient intensity. At times of peaks orders, workers would be expected to work sixteen-hour shifts for several days or face dismissal.

The second type of control identified by Edwards is 'technical control'. Here, technology sets the character and pace of work. Many factories are now heavily automated, with new materials coming down the production line at a pace that forces the worker onto a schedule set by the machinery itself. While we might think of technical control as operating in modern factory settings, it has a much wider remit. In many call centres, for example, an advanced form of technical control exists whereby computer systems source a new call directly to the call worker once they have ended the prior one. In such circumstances, the intensity of work is governed by technological means so that the rhythm of work is written into the structure of the workplace. While potentially expensive for employers, owing to the necessary investment in workplace technologies, this mode of control has the advantage of de-personalizing the dynamics of control and resistance implicit in the simple control model.

The third type of labour control that Edwards highlighted is 'bureaucratic control'. In this instance, a series of rules and regulations govern the workplace offering structured pay rises, opportunities for personal advancement and other incentives for good performance and hitting productivity targets. The key idea here is that the rules governing work are clearly stipulated, agreed upon and mutually enforced, inducing a high degree of self-motivation and self-discipline. For Edwards, this often took the form of a bureaucratic agreement between the employer and a union as a representative of the employees. However, there are other forms of bureaucratic control. Sales clerks at many electronics retail stores often find themselves on commission in which their overall pay and potential for promotion is affected by how many sales they can turn over during their work hours. 'Recognition and rewards' programmes provide additional incentives for good performance and loyalty to the organization.

In practice, workplaces tend to be structured by combinations of all three types of labour control to create an integrated structure of incentives and compulsions. Close surveillance – often now undertaken by video cameras – can work alongside a series of individualized rewards for workers deemed to surpass production targets. At the same time, prevailing forms of labour control are also shaped by worker responses. In particular, the potential for collective agency as manifested in worker associations such as unions can greatly shift the balance of power within the workplace. As an example, consider the comparative study of conditions in textile factories located in Vietnam and China undertaken by Anita Chan and Hong-zen Wang. Though these factories were owned and operated by the same Taiwanese firms and made comparable textiles for global supply chains, the authors were surprised to find that the form of labour control in each location was markedly different. To be clear, workers in both sets of factories were expected to work intensively for relatively low wages. Nonetheless, the Chinese factories were characterized by a militaristic form of simple labour control that included widespread abuse of workers on the factory floor, regular forced overtime and habitually unpaid wages. In contrast, the Vietnamese factories located around Hanoi and Ho Chi Minh City were characterized by a somewhat 'softer' form of labour management where flagrant abuses were notably less present.[21]

The authors noted how these differences in workplace labour control related to a broad range of factors shaping the labour regime. In particular, they highlighted how militaristic labour control was closely related to the institutional discrimination against rural–urban migrants in China, who were deprived of full citizenship rights once they left their administrative homes in rural areas. They also flagged the trend of forcing Chinese workers to live in onsite dormitories situated in the very grounds of the factories at which they were employed. This gave firms an exceptional degree of control over the social reproduction of their workers. Labour was kept at close quarters so it could be subjected to close control and surveillance, and quickly moved in and out of production to meet intensive cycles of demand. Finally, given the stronger degree of trade union autonomy in Vietnam, the authors noted that state authorities in Vietnam were less likely to systematically ignore labour rights violations owing to the political pressure of collective labour organizations.

Chang and Wang's study drives home the importance of examining how all facets of the labour regime interact to produce workforces of a distinct nature. We shouldn't think of a labour regime as a singular mechanism, but rather as a series of overlapping social processes that, together, shape how workforces with specific characteristics are produced and utilized. It also contradicts the idea that there exists a homogenous body of cheap and disciplined labour across the developing world. On the contrary, it demonstrates how the utilization of labour is embedded within distinct labour regimes that shape the production, mobilization, motivation and utilization of labour. This point about the importance of understanding local specificities is similarly reinforced by Philip Kelly's comparative study of labour control and contestation in three different Southeast Asian factory sites. As Kelly noted, the three labour regimes located in Malaysia, Indonesia and the Philippines differed significantly despite the commonality of producing low-skilled workers for ostensibly similar labour-intensive factories.[22]

Labour Regimes in Motion

The concept of the labour regime offers us a useful tool for breaking down the production of workers into more easily identifiable processes and is therefore a helpful way to organize empirical case studies of work, labour and livelihoods and how they fit into the global economy. One further point should be stressed: labour regimes are rarely static and are often highly unstable. This is because they take shape and evolve through the actions of states, firms, workers and consumers whose interests frequently collide. States typically look to improve regional competitiveness by ensuring a disciplined and flexible labour force while simultaneously seeking to ensure political and social stability by mediating or repressing conflicts. Firms seek profitability above all, and this means that they must seek to balance the creation of an efficient collective workforce with keeping costs low. Workers, for their part, are often caught between the need for a job – particularly a secure and stable one – and the pressures to work intensively and efficiently within the workplace. This reinforces a point made at the very start of this chapter: labour is intrinsically political. Indeed, many authors refer to the processes of imposing, regulating, negotiating and contesting workplace dynamics as the politics of production.[23] What the labour regime approach makes clear, however, is that such dynamics of compromise and contestation are not formed purely in the workplace itself, but by the labour regime as a whole. How workers are reproduced, mobilized and motivated is essential to how they are utilized and the degree to which they may accept or contest particular work arrangements.

Further reading

Jamie Peck's classic, *Work-Place: The Social Regulation of Labour Markets* (New York: Guildford Press, 1996), offers an integrated perspective on labour market segmentation, labour regimes and the politics of production. Feminist Silvia Federici provides a challenging examination of the connections between gender, social reproduction and labour market inequities in *Revolution at Point Zero: Housework, Reproduction, and Feminist Struggle* (Oakland, CA: PM Press, 2012).

Chapter 4
Global Production Networks

In the North American academic setting, one commodity reigns supreme. As lecturers, we encounter it most strikingly in the classroom where we often peer outwards at a sea of signature silver rectangles, each with its own illuminated brand shining back at us. Apple's MacBook Pro, it would seem, has risen to become the laptop of choice for students and professors alike. While many of us depend on them, only a small minority could say with any degree of confidence that they know who produces them, where and how. At first blush, it would perhaps seem self-evident to say that Apple makes the MacBook Pro as evidenced by that iconic brand indelibly tattooed upon their casing. Yet, upon closer inspection we find that Apple as a company does not make a single component within the laptop nor does it assemble the final product. Instead, Apple focuses solely on the design and branding activities while outsourcing all the direct production aspects to an expansive range of subcontracted companies. This means that the production of the screen, the hard drive, the camera, the audio unit, the battery, memory card and a multiplicity of other parts is spread across a network of close to 200 companies on a global scale. So while Apple designed the product in California and a Taiwanese-managed company assembled the laptop in southern China, its component parts were themselves sourced from multiple independent companies linked together as part of a global production network.

What seemed to be a simple question leads to a surprisingly complex answer. No single company or workforce makes a MacBook Pro – rather, it is produced collectively by a dense network of firms. Apple certainly plays the primary role in shaping this network and its activities, yet independent firms undertake each specific aspect of production. As we'll see below, orchestrating the production of thousands of laptops on a daily basis requires a lead firm like Apple to exercise considerable power and control over the network as a whole. Like all firms, Apple is driven to maximize profits and shareholder value. It will seek to leverage the best possible costs for component parts within the supply chain. This entails imposing rigorous demands upon suppliers and their workforces regarding the price, quality and delivery times of components. Alongside the exercise of power, however, Apple must also promote a strong degree of cooperation and trust with suppliers. The network must facilitate not only the flow of products, but also shared knowledge and problem solving necessary to deal with the uncertainties of producing technologically complex goods.

This dynamic interplay between control, cooperation, power and trust makes global production networks a rich topic for study. While the laptop example is emblematic of how contemporary global production networks operate, similar forms of networked production facilitate the manufacture of an encompassing range of commodities – from bicycles and refrigerators through to blue jeans and tennis shoes. Engaging global production networks is therefore crucial to understand how commodities are created and how this impacts upon working conditions within production. In the sections that follow, we use our focus on power, networks, space and livelihoods to prise open global production networks and to link them into discussion of the labour regimes approach from the previous chapter.

Making Production Networks

As the MacBook Pro example reveals, contemporary capitalism is predicated upon an enormously complex organization of production in which a great number of diverse and spatially separated workforces are drawn into a collective process to produce and distribute goods. Strategies to integrate labouring activities across space are not new, and an integrated global division of labour has been taking shape over centuries. The industrialization of Britain and Western Europe, for instance, rested on the importation of a vast array of inputs from colonies in Africa, Asia and the Americas (see table 4.1). While such goods had long been traded in small quantities, the colonial era saw a dramatic increase in the scope and scale of their production and

Table 4.1   Key colonial commodities

Southeast Asia	India	Caribbean	Africa	Latin America
Tin	Cotton	Sugar	Sugar	Gold
Rubber	Jute	Bananas	Tobacco	Silver
Rice	Tea	Lumber	Cocoa	Sugar
Palm oil	Sugar		Nuts	Rubber
Coffee	Opium		Diamonds	Cotton
	Grains		Gold	Coffee
	Spices		Rubber	Wheat
			Copper	Meat

consumption, a process that required new labour forces to be created in colonial zones to work in plantations and mines. This form of economic integration lead to the formation of a colonial division of labour in which the colonized countries became exporters of raw materials and agricultural goods, while colonizers focused on the production of manufactured goods.

By the later decades of the twentieth century, this colonial division of labour had evolved as a number of developing world countries actively produced a growing number of industrial goods not only for domestic consumption but also for export. In some cases, such as Mexico's export promotion zones on the northern border with the United States, this export-orientated production was focused on basic industrial goods such as toys, textiles and low-end electronics, and was driven by US companies shifting facilities abroad to cut costs. In others, such as the East Asian Tigers – Hong Kong, Singapore, South Korea and Taiwan – domestic companies aided by national government support expanded production of more complex industrial goods such as cars, computers and large consumer items for regional and international markets. Together, these trends pointed to the growing importance of developing world countries as expanding hubs for labour-intensive production, a process that required the development of new labour regimes to produce the large quantities of industrial workers in countries where industrial production had previously been relatively limited.

The present global division of labour represents a continuation and deepening of such patterns. One notable characteristic of contemporary global production networks is that firms increasingly focus not on producing a finished good, but on specializing at a much more finely graded level: creating component parts or services that form only one element of the final commodity. This division of productive functions into specialized and self-contained units is called modularization. Instead of a single firm attempting to bring all the various labouring processes together under one roof, the production process is splintered into numerous subtasks to be distributed across a range of independent companies. Importantly, this allows firms to locate specific moments of the production process in regions with desired labour regimes. For example, the extraction of the labour-intensive operations within industries such as electronics and textiles and their relocation to countries located primarily in the global South are often highlighted as pivotal dynamics of global production networks. Through modularization, production can be situated in locations where the local labour regimes produce workforces that can be mobilized for long periods of intensive work at relatively low costs.

Within global production networks, the coordination of the network as a whole is often undertaken by what is termed a lead firm, which plays the primary role in shaping the network's organization and operations. Viewed as market leaders, lead firms tend to have significant brand recognition and are heavily invested in the design and marketing of their products. According to sociologist Henry Yeung, exemplary lead firms would encompass Apple, Sony and Philips in consumer electronics; Toyota and General Motors in automobiles; Gap and Nike in clothing and footwear; Hewlett-Packard and Motorola in information and communication technology (ICT); Citicorp and HSBC in banking; and Hilton and Marriott in the hotel sector.[1] We might also consider the role of large retailers – supermarkets such as Loblaws or Tesco and stores such as Walmart or Costco. While the latter do not typically manage the production of specific goods themselves, they play a substantive role in the distribution side of global production and exercise considerable influence over production networks for low-end goods and foodstuffs.

The degree to which modularization of production can take place, however, rests on a number of factors. The first is a technical question concerning information: how easy is it to give precise specifications to another firm to ensure that the parts or components they provide are made exactly to specification? This is known as codification and expresses the degree to which information about production can be accurately shared with another firm and operationalized by them. The stakes in codification are very high. Even very small variations in a produced component can have large unintended effects when assembled in a final product. In the electronics industry, for example, ultra-precise codification is vital because a component that either doesn't fit seamlessly into a motherboard or doesn't work to the most exacting specifications is likely to be useless or, worse, could undermine the final product. Similarly, in the fashion industry codification questions revolve primarily around sizing, trim and colours. The bottom line is that if information about a product cannot be easily set out, transmitted, understood and put into practice, then there are significant barriers to the degree of modularization that can occur.

The second factor affecting modularization is the relative ability of the network to respond flexibly to problems and resolve unexpected issues. Producing sophisticated goods is not a simple business particularly if a product needs to be developed, altered or changed during its lifecycle. As a result, the degree of modularization faces considerable constraints if it hampers flexibility and adaptability. With strong pressure to constantly release new models of consumer goods at regular intervals – the smartphone is a particularly apt example – companies often continue to troubleshoot issues in the latest design well after its release. This occurred famously in the case of Apple's iPhone 6 display, which, despite being a technical improvement, seemed vulnerable to scratching and cracking. This problem required an immediate shift in design even as mass production continued apace.

The third factor is reliability and control. To outsource production of a key component is to place a great deal of trust on a partner firm within the network. Any failure to deliver on time or to produce good-quality components can bring the entire production process to a halt. For example, when a number of Thai factories producing parts for Toyota were shut down as a result of flooding in 2011, this created a huge lag in production for Prius and Camry models. A shortage of key components meant that the final assembly of the full models was impossible, bringing production to a halt and creating bottlenecks in other parts of the production network. Floods, of course, may present an unanticipated event beyond any company's control. That said, delays for whatever reason – whether technical problems in the factory, striking workers, or shortages of raw materials – will have an impact upon other companies in the network. Lead firms will necessarily devise strategies to avoid such risks or overcome them rapidly should they occur.

When we consider these aspects together, it becomes clear that modularization may well improve efficiency – in part by allowing production networks to tap into specific labour regimes that can lower costs or improve efficiency – but it also raises considerable problems of coordination and control at a global scale. These are not merely technical questions. They are also questions of how a network functions in its social and political dimensions. To understand these production network dynamics, it is useful to draw upon economic sociology's analysis of networks and political economy's focus on power relationships.

Social Embedding in Global Production Networks

Given the complexity of coordinating production across a network of firms, building embedded relationships can provide important advantages to lead firms. As we examined in chapter 2, networks are formed out of repeated transactions between social agents to create more durable ties through the generation of shared norms and expectations. Within global production networks, the latter are important because they can curb the tendency of actors to operate in a narrowly self-interested fashion. By building norms of trust and reciprocity and facilitating communication between otherwise independent firms, embedded ties can smooth the flow of information between agents, improve its speed and quality, and therein facilitate joint problem solving activities. These attributes are particularly useful when firms need to work flexibly and adapt to changing circumstances or address unforeseen challenges in production.[2]

Embedded linkages can therefore provide the foundations for more robust interfirm organizational relationships that aid the development of more sophisticated production techniques for products of increasing complexity. On this basis, despite the time and effort necessary to build them, cultivating embedded ties can be an important strategy for firms to lower the costs of doing business. This is one reason why global production networks are not always driven by firms seeking simply the lowest price for components. Instead, lead firms can build long-term relations with some suppliers that might provide a component or service at a slightly higher cost, but offer other advantages on the side of communication, joint problem solving and other forms of flexibility enabled by an embedded relationship.

That said, as economic sociologists are keen to point out, there may also be significant downsides to networked relations if they constrain actions and close off opportunities. For example, a personal network characterized mainly by kinship and other ties may improve trust and reliability, yet it can also serve to insulate actors from alternative sources of information or goods that might be extremely important. At the same time, the reciprocity necessary for networked building can sometimes force agents to make poor decisions that are undertaken to reproduce the network but potentially at considerable expense, particularly if the networked partner is performing poorly. It is in this respect that sociologist Brian Uzzi talked of a 'bliss point' where firms would combine what he termed 'arm's-length' ties – i.e., one off, market-based relationships – with 'embedded' relationships based on close ties, reciprocity and trust. In his study of small fashion industry firms in New York, Uzzi suggested that successful firms were precisely defined by arrangements that allowed them to seek the benefits of both networked and marketized relationships.[3]

An example of this phenomenon is when Apple decided to shake up its production networks by moving some assembly functions for its flagship iPads and iPhones away from its longstanding Taiwanese partner Foxconn to a new company called Pegatron. On the one hand, Apple appeared to be looking to hedge its considerable dependence on Foxconn, explore potentially cheaper competitors, and therein keep its suppliers on their toes. Pegatron, it should be noted, was renowned for a highly disciplinary form of labour control that went beyond Foxconn in imposing intensive work on factory labourers as a means to lower costs.[4] On the other hand, this shift of supplier wasn't entirely a leap into the unknown. Apple's chief executive Tim Cook had a direct personal contact with the owner of Pegatron meaning that there remained a form of embedded ties between the new partners. The shift had mixed results. Pegatron indeed offered lower production costs, yet initially proved unable to handle the volume of iPad minis required by Apple or deal effectively with late changes to design. Notably, faced with an emerging bottleneck, Apple shifted some production of the iPad mini back to its established partner, Foxconn, with which it had stronger embedded linkages.[5]

Putting the Power into Global Production

Although social embedding is clearly important to the operation of global production networks, it is necessary to avoid being seduced by the emphasis on relationships of trust, coordination and mutual problem solving that paints interfirm relationships in rather harmonious colours. While global production networks do involve relations of trust and reciprocity, there is also a fundamental tension in their operation. As profit-maximizing entities, each firm intrinsically seeks to maximize its own returns from its role in the network. Lead firms, for example, are acutely aware that keeping costs low across their supply chains is central to generating a high rate of profit necessary to satisfy their shareholders. This means that they will use their power over the network to ensure that the functions they specialize in are richly rewarded, while costs elsewhere are kept low. At lower ends of the network, producers will strive where possible to meet their own expectations of profit rates while seeking opportunities to improve their standing within the network. As a result, global production networks are not simply about positive sum interactions between firms, but also competition within the network over how the total value produced is distributed between firms. This raises important questions of power and hierarchy among firms that shapes not only what each firm might be able to claim, but also the impacts upon their respective workforces.

For many lead firms, their power over the chain stems from their closely guarded control over the retail, branding and design functions. It is important to recognize that markets for key commodities are often not fully competitive but are instead oligopolistic, in that a limited number of key firms dominate sales. Consider, for example, how many distinct brands there would be if an entire class of students were to put their sports shoes on the table. We'd wager that there would be only a handful of brands – a classic case of oligopoly. Such oligopolies are notable for two key reasons. First, competition between oligopolistic firms is often partial, with each firm aware that it can maintain high profits by tacitly refusing to engage in strong price competition. Second, with a firm control over market share, oligopolistic firms are able to exert strong downward cost pressures throughout their production networks since they are the gatekeepers to retail sales.[6] For branded firms whose goods are instantly recognizable – Reebok and Nike are good examples – control over market share provides considerable power over subordinate firms that have no independent ability to access such markets.

As a result, although contracting for a major international corporation may offer significant opportunities for smaller producers, they inevitably enter a lopsided relationship characterized by strong power imbalances. A medium-sized textile firm in Cambodia, for example, is far from an equal partner with major international fashion retailers. With the latter holding dominant positions in marketing, design and technology, they are uniquely well placed to shape the rules of interaction across the network as a whole, while also exercising considerable direct power in their one-on-one negotiations with subcontracted firms. As Dennis Arnold and Toh Han Shih have noted, heavy competition from producers in Bangladesh and China led to many Cambodian textile producers sidelining earlier government attempts to foster relatively strong labour rights within the sector and, instead, promoting cost-cutting through the flexibilized hiring of workers on short-term contracts.[7] As this shift in the Cambodian labour regime indicates, for some subordinate firms, power imbalances across production networks lead to rampant discounting, whereby producers seek to cut costs to a minimum in order to maintain contracts. Unsurprisingly, this often has extremely negative impacts upon workforces and is strongly associated with the idea of a 'race to the bottom', in which labour and environmental standards are sacrificed under heavy competition.

It is notable here that while oligopolistic conditions at the top end of global production networks tend to moderate competition, no such constraints exist at the bottom. Those firms that might seek to escape such a vicious cycle may have ambitions to absorb some of the more profitable functions within the network into their own operations – a process known as upgrading. Those firms that have greater leverage within a network owing to the importance or complexity of the roles they play are better able to set their own prices for the goods they produce or the services they render. They are also less likely to be replaced by a competitor firm, which can provide greater security for workforces. As sociologists Jennifer Bair and Marion Werner have detailed in the Mexican jeans industry, the upgrading of producers from the simple tasks of assembly to full-package manufacturers has been extremely uneven, creating both winners and losers. Where successful, it can generate higher-quality jobs and spin-off benefits to other local firms helping to catalyse a process of regional development. Such successes, however, are far from assured and, even when accomplished, are potentially prone to collapse, as occurred when a change in international regulations governing textile exports pulled the rug from underneath a number of key Mexican producers in the mid-2000s, generating significant layoffs.[8]

The most significant recent expression of industrial upgrading in global production networks has probably been the rise of a handful of large manufacturing firms based in major developing countries that take on a complete range of production functions for lead firms. The sports shoe company Yue Yuen is one of the most striking examples. In fact, you've almost certainly worn a pair of shoes made by Yue Yuen, although its name will not have been the official brand inscribed on the shoe. A Taiwanese company, Yue Yuen directly undertakes production for lead brands through a combination of using its own factories and subcontracting to smaller Chinese producers. Its facilities demonstrate an impressive economy of scale. By 2010 its Dongguan factories in China incorporated some 27,000 workers making shoes for Nike and other leading brands. Notably, its facilities tend to be technologically more advanced than smaller producers, with higher productivity owing to the deployment of specialized lean-production methods. This means that Yue Yuen is prepared to pay a small premium to its workers to assure stability of employment and avoid disruptions to production schedules that could otherwise occur, as, for example, in the run-up to leading sporting events when the volume and timing of delivery are critical. To maintain flexibility, however, Yue Yuen also subcontracts to smaller suppliers which operate under a considerably more austere production regime using disciplinary labour regimes at the factory level.[9]

The concentration of production functions by companies such as Yue Yuen speaks to a further aspect of power relations within global production networks. Conflicts over the distribution of value are only part of the matter. A second vector of power relations forms around the distribution of risks. Markets for many consumer commodities can be rather volatile, with shifting levels of demand and fluctuations in styles. Part of the attraction of having extensive production networks with subcontracted firms is the ability to displace the risks of, for example, a drop in demand onto other firms. It is generally much easier to cut ties with subcontracted firms within a network than with in-house workers who often cannot be made redundant without some form of compensation. In this respect, subcontracting arrangements give the lead firms great flexibility to deal with market flux, while loading the risks onto smaller firms – and their labour forces – lower down the hierarchy (see box 4.1). As we noted in chapter 2, this displacement of risk is a key element of contemporary power relations.

Typologies of Network Governance

When we combine our emphasis on both power and embedded relations, we start to appreciate some of the diversity of organizational forms across global production networks. A number of analysts have pointed to five main ways that integration occurs across networks.[11] Labelling these linkages as different types of 'value chains', each is characterized by a different degree of social embeddedness and power relations between networked firms (see table 4.2). To be clear, a production network for any given commodity is unlikely to be characterized by a single type of value chain and its associated governance structure. Rather, a production network will typically display a combination of different types of value chains depending on the specific tasks performed by individual firms and the complexity

Box 4.1 Subcontracting in the Chilean paper industry

In the Chilean forestry sector, larger firms subcontract specific tasks to smaller firms, not simply for reasons of cost effectiveness but also to create a 'mattressing effect' in which risks can be pushed further down the network. In this case, the big paper producers cultivate a tiered network in which they subcontract work to a lower level of smaller firms; these smaller firms then subcontract specialized tasks out to a second level of firms of their own choosing. In this way, pyramids of hierarchical subcontracting take shape that rest on relations of dependency running from the central contractor down to sublevels, forming the 'mattress' that cushions the higher levels from adverse shocks by allowing them to easily shed firms at the lower levels in the event of slackening demand. The risks of market fluctuation are simply passed down the chain. Notably, this means that labour is extremely precarious at the lower ends of the network, where workers typically have temporary contracts and face the constant fear that decisions made further up the chain – over which they exercise no control – will result in their unemployment. Such a structure, it should be emphasized, was greatly abetted by the extremely flexible regulations about firing workers created by the Chilean state during a long period of dictatorial rule.[10]

of the functions they perform. Importantly for our purposes, different types of value chains may also have implications for the types of labour regimes that produce workers and impact upon the conditions of employment.

The first form of governance is a market value chain. This represents what many economists assume to be the standard relationship wherein independent firms agree to a one-time business contract for a given product of service. We are likely to see this kind of market relationship in relatively simple production settings where a high degree of standardization of components or a very simple final product means that modularization is simple and easy. The lead firm does not need to convey complex information to the producer, nor does it need to actively problem shoot production processes owing to changing designs. As a result, a closer coordination between the firms is unnecessary. Although the firms may choose to renew the contract after its completion, there is no embedded relationship here. The firms have no lasting ties to each other and the costs of switching to another supplier or contractor are negligible.

These relationships are typically driven by price: lead firms choose suppliers that offer the best cost price for the component, although quality of product and reliability of delivery will also impact such

Table 4.2 Types of production network governance

Governance type	Degree of embedding	Power relations	Labour regime
Market	Very low – each party is not tied to future transactions	No direct power relationship, although large firms can use their concentrated market share to drive supplier prices downwards	Supplier maintains flexible labour regime
Modular	Medium – each party has some investment in the long-term relationship	Supplier is in a subordinate position, but embedded ties mean that it is less vulnerable to being replaced	Supplier may invest in higher-quality, permanent workforce alongside more flexible workforce
Relational	High – each party is somewhat dependent upon the other	More equitable given the mutual dependence and the strong need for cooperation in product design, production	Supplier requires high-quality dependable labourers and will offer perks to attract and retain them
Captive	Variable – costs for exiting relationship low for lead firm, high for subcontractor	Highly unequal, with the captive firms dependent on the lead firm for contracts, knowledge and technology	Disciplinary, flexibilized labour regime to cut costs
Hierarchy	Complete	Direct bureaucratic control between subsidiary parts of the multinational corporation	Uses distinct labour market segments across space, but stronger degree of formalization and conditions typically present

decisions. The power relations that may prevail are therefore strongly determined by the level of market control that a lead firm possesses. A dominant market player will have more power with which to dictate prices to suppliers: consider in this respect how a large supermarket chain will switch between suppliers of products purely on the unit cost of the product on offer. As a result, suppliers often resort to undercutting each other's price by cutting costs – a process termed 'discounting' – by intensifying labour to keep costs low and maintain competitiveness. Maintaining an extremely flexible labour regime that can easily absorb or shed workers as demand changes can be a pivotal part of a firm's strategy to consolidate its position within production networks.

A second governance type is the modular value chain. Here we see a greater degree of embedding between firms because a more complex production process requires a greater amount of design information to be transferred. Although modularization has reduced the complexity of the production process, some of the information necessary for production might remain difficult to codify or may be variable over time, requiring a supplier with capacity to offer flexibility. As a result, a closer degree of coordination, monitoring and problem solving is necessary as compared to the market form of governance. It is likely that, through these relationships, a measured degree of trust may arise alongside the ability to collectively manage the inevitable challenges thrown up by fluctuating production needs. The costs of switching away from the relationship are greater than in the market governance mode, but are not necessarily prohibitive so long as other potential suppliers can offer the same capacities. As a result, the power of lead firms over suppliers remains considerable despite the greater capacity of the latter. Given the greater importance of embedded relationships and specialized knowledge within the firm, these types of firms may cultivate labour regimes that retain a core of better skilled workers who expect a higher level of work security.

Relational value chains represent a third and highly embedded type of governance. In this case, the complexity of products requires a high degree of specialist knowledge that likely cannot be codified into simple instructions. As a result, both firms must communicate about design and production process and are strongly reliant upon the skills and abilities of the other firm. They therefore must collaborate continually in a context where maintaining a strong relationship is vital to both sides. The chance for hierarchical power relationships to form between the two firms is far smaller because both have a degree of dependency upon the other. These kinds of relationships are most prominent in the production of complex goods, where technological sophistication limits modularization and in which there is a far smaller pool of firms with the requisite abilities. On the labour side, it is likely that these firms seek to attract more highly skilled workers and therein may offer significant benefits to retain and motivate their workforces.

At the other end of the scale, captive value chains are characterized by extreme inequalities. Lead firms use their financial and technological advantages to institutionalize dominant relationships with suppliers who are left dependent upon the former. This dependency – which often means that captive firms operate at extremely thin profit margins – is exercised through a strong reliance upon the lead firm for production technologies and/or market access. Such firms are often concentrated in low-skill, labour-intensive industries and are inevitably price-takers, with little power to influence the terms of agreements. They typically exist through cost-cutting, often with worrying consequences for labour rights and environmental standards. Perhaps counterintuitively, there may be a certain degree of embedding involved in such relationships as the ties of dependency mean that the subordinate firm remains as a long-term yet extremely unequal partner operating for the benefit of the lead firm. In such unequal arrangements, the captive firm will typically seek to displace costs and risks downwards onto its labour force by maintaining a heavily disciplinary and flexibilized labour regime.

The final governance type is that of a hierarchal value chain. This refers to a situation where a lead company directly owns and controls subsidiaries that make component parts or provide vital services. Here we are talking about multinational corporations whose operations are integrated across national boundaries. Very often, this level of integration occurs when the corporation needs to exercise a particularly exacting control over the production process in order to ensure the synchronization of production and a high quality of output. In such cases, potential coordination problems inherent to distributing tasks across a network of independent firms may present too great a risk. These risks may involve worries over copyright infringement or safeguarding valued technology from competitors, but may simply stem from a need to precisely control the timing of a complex production process. Notably, some corporations – car manufacturers such as Volkswagen being a good example – will maintain core production functions within the company and its subsidiaries, while using a variety of the above forms of network governance to source more peripheral parts for production.

Putting Analysis into Practice

Producing typologies of value chain governance may seem a quirky pursuit, so what 'value added' does it provide? To address this, let us consider a practical application. In 2013, the *Financial Times* reported a series of momentous changes in the industrial zones of coastal China. Cities such as Shenzhen, Guangzhou and Dongguan lie at the heart of the Pearl River Delta, a region often termed the 'workshop of the world' owing to its concentration of labour-intensive manufacturing. As the newspaper reported, the city of Dongguan alone made almost a third of the total global Christmas toys, as well as 20 per cent of the world's sweaters and 10 per cent of its running shoes. By 2013, however, manufacturers in the region faced a significant problem: fewer migrants were arriving from rural China to work in coastal factories. As a consequence of this slackening labour supply, the cost of labour began to rise rapidly, with no end in sight. With wages doubling over five years, this added cost quickly ate into the competitiveness of suppliers located in the Pearl River Delta, forcing them to consider cost-cutting solutions.[12]

Although these firms were faced with a common problem, the *Financial Times* noted how they reacted in distinct ways to these rising labour costs. Some lead firms and large subcontractors started to source from smaller companies in Laos, Cambodia and other parts of Asia, where considerably cheaper labour costs prevailed. While this switch to new suppliers in cheaper labour zones might seem an obvious solution, many companies did not follow this route. Instead, some persuaded their Chinese suppliers to move factories inland to rural China as a way to access Chinese workers despite increasing wage costs. Others simply remained with suppliers in the Pearl River Delta region despite the increased wages. What could explain these three different reactions by companies to the shared problem of rising labour costs? This is a complex question, and our focus on power and embeddedness can help provide some of the answers. It directs us to consider how types of network governance shape the reactions of producers to changing external conditions. It also requires us to consider how such networked relations are situated within prevailing labour regimes.

First, the leading brands that moved their production to Cambodia and Laos are likely to be producing low-technology goods with a strong degree of standardization that require few embedded linkages between firms to solve problems. Basic textiles and toys, for example, are the kinds of goods that can be relatively easily produced by suppliers without the need for close linkages with a lead firm. As a result, these chains are likely to be characterized by market forms of network governance in which switching costs are few, facilitating the rapid move away from the Pearl River Delta and into Southeast Asia, where a new disciplinary labour regime with cheaper labour costs can maintain low unit prices. For lead firms in these production networks, Chinese suppliers could simply be discarded once new suppliers had been located with suitable production facilities and an intensive labour regime.

Second, those lead firms that pushed their suppliers to move inland are more likely to have some form of embedded links to these firms. Their products are probably more sophisticated, requiring a more elaborate form of coordination between firms, and therefore making lead firms somewhat reluctant to end the relationship. As such, these are potentially modular value chains with the embedded relationships. Pushing these suppliers to move inland is a way to recreate a labour regime that had collapsed in coastal China while maintaining the embedded linkages between the firms that facilitate the production process. Alternatively, such linkages may be representative of captive chains in which lead firms are keen to maintain existing power relations that might ensure a cheap and compliant supplier. Once again, cutting ties completely would end a useful form of dependency, so forcing the supplier to shift inland to access cheaper labour might offer the best of both worlds.

Third, those suppliers that remain in Dongguan despite rising labour costs are likely to be part of modular or relational value chains. Here we find a high degree of embeddedness in which trust, technological aptitude and mutual problem solving are key to producing a more sophisticated class of commodity. Lead firms are unwilling to relinquish such relationships because the benefits gained from this embeddedness – e.g., flexible problem solving, reliable delivery of goods, ability to quickly change products to new demands or react to change demand quantities – overshadow the rising labour costs. In this sense, the importance of trust and the quality of labour mean that it is worth paying the extra cost, including a supplement to attract appropriate workers. In this respect, the Dongguan labour regime has shifted greatly, but lead firms see the advantage of working with it, rather than moving production.

As the above example makes clear, it is important to consider the dynamic interplay between global production networks and labour regimes. To this end, we have mapped out how global production networks take shape with a keen eye on the forms of embedding, power relations and governance structures that bind them together. While embedded relationships may be ones of relative equality, longevity, mutual dependence and trust, they can also reinforce hierarchy, power asymmetries and the uneven appropriation of value across the network. These power relations that stratify global production networks have differentiated impacts upon workers within these networks. For workers who are able to position themselves in firms at the lead end of global production networks, the conditions of work can be more secure and well remunerated. At the bottom end of global production networks, however, strong competition between firms to maintain their position often results in the production of highly flexible labour regimes as a way of cutting costs and lowering risks. In this respect, it is notable that the global division of labour indeed divides labour – putting barriers between workers in structurally similar positions that can often prevent the common pursuit of labour rights both within and across borders. We return to this question directly in chapters 11 and 12.

Further reading

The collection assembled by Jennifer Bair in *Frontiers of Commodity Chain Research* (Stanford: Stanford University Press, 2009) provides a strong overview of both mainstream and critical approaches to global production networks; while a systematic and integrated perspective is provided in Neil Coe and Henry Yeung's *Global Production Networks: Theorizing Economic Development in an Interconnected World* (Oxford: Oxford University Press, 2015). Angela Hale and Jane Willis offer a concise overview of key themes in gender and global production in *Threads of Labour: Garment Industry Supply Chains from the Workers' Perspective* (Oxford: Blackwell, 2005).

Chapter 5
Formal Work in Transition

Daniel was born in 1952 in a small village in rural Québec, Canada. At the age of 10 his parents sold the farm and moved to nearby Montreal, where his dad took a job in a factory while his mom stayed at home to take care of the children. The oldest of ten children, Daniel dropped out of school at 16 to earn a wage as part of the household's livelihood strategy. The following year he joined the same factory as his father to work as a unionized steelworker, where he would enjoy a relatively high income, a stable and full-time job, an enviable company-based pension and health benefits for him, his wife and their two children. Only once was Daniel unemployed – a short period of four months in 1994 – and he was subsequently able to retire after more than 40 years of service on a secure defined benefits pension. Such an experience of regulated employment, relative job security and accordant social benefits typified formal work in the post-war era.

This story, a commonplace one at the time, now appears exceptional. In present day Canada, it would be virtually impossible for a 17-year-old unskilled worker without a high school degree to find working conditions remotely close to those achieved by Daniel. A typical male worker in the 1960s could anticipate working for an average of four employers by the time of his retirement. Today, the same worker could easily have had nine employers before even reaching the ripe age of 30. Put simply, the landscape of labour has shifted fundamentally. For a new generation of workers in Western countries, temporary contracts, part-time employment, lower than average wages, and limited social benefits and opportunities for advancement are part of the 'new normal'. Even though they are better educated than their parents, many are discovering that the nature and meaning of work has profoundly changed over the last few decades and they will struggle to match the lifestyle and security that their parents once took for granted. Good work that is well paid and secure still exists, but it is increasingly seen as the preserve of a fortunate minority rather than the majority.

So what is driving these changes and what implications do they hold for the future of labour? To begin to answer these questions, this chapter examines what formal work is, how it emerged and why it presently appears to be in a process of significant erosion in many Western countries. Our focus here is primarily on the advanced industrial countries of the West, yet we set the rise and partial demise of formal sector work in its global context. With specific reference to the internationalization of production, shifting political ideologies concerning the role of employment within society, and technological change, we ask whether we are on the cusp of an era of 'post-formal' work.

What is Formal Work?

In its simplest terms, formal work is any paid work relationship that is regulated by the state. There are, of course, various aspects of work that can be regulated, many of which we set out in chapter 3. For instance, the formalization of paid labour requires that there is a contract between employer and employee setting out the key requirements and expectations of each party. This can include the length of the contract, hours worked per week, pay rates, overtime provisions and the conditions under which an employee can be dismissed. Government regulations may provide conditions and basic requirements for all those points of negotiation. Minimum wages, for example, place a floor under which pay cannot fall. Statutes over dismissal will regulate how much advance notice an employer must give before terminating a contract and what kind of severance pay might be required. More extensively, the formalization of work might also include obligations regarding the responsibility of employers to provide social benefits to employees, from sick leave to pensions, maternity leave to health insurance.

As we saw in chapter 3, the kinds of conditions imposed by formalization may vary significantly across different segments of the labour market. Historically, the expansion of formalized work had been an ongoing process in many Western countries since the industrial revolution. In industrializing Britain, for example, social struggles over worker rights resulted in several milestone pieces of legislation, such as a series of Factory Acts in the early 1800s that gradually outlawed the use of child labour and set up independent commissions to enforce such regulations. In the second half of the nineteenth century, under continual pressure from the labour movement and allied social reformers within the political system, further statutes were passed limiting the working day to ten hours and regulating a range of health and safety conditions within workplaces. At the time, this normalized working week of sixty hours was considered a significant breakthrough for industrial workers, although the formalization of the weekend in the twentieth century would reduce that further. Presently, the ILO suggests that a working week of forty-eight hours should be considered a maximum justifiable expectation. For context, however, consider that the current corporate social responsibility initiative of electronics manufacturer Apple attempts to ensure that its suppliers in Asia do not surpass a sixty-hour working week for employees, indicating that hours beyond this are the norm within such globalized industries (see chapter 11).

Despite the slow emergence of formalized work in advanced industrialized countries, by the early 1900s most Western workers would still have perceived the employment conditions that we traced out for steelworker Daniel with considerable envy. In the early twentieth century, that level of protection over wages, employment rights and social security was unheard of outside very privileged sections of the workforce. So how did these formal rights covering a wide spectrum of the working population take shape and what goals did they serve?

Fordism, the Welfare State and the Expansion of Formal Work Relations

Many current norms about employment relations emerged after the Second World War when a much more extensive degree of formalized work developed primarily – but not exclusively – in advanced industrial countries. The conditions underlying this expansion were unique in historical terms. In the three decades following the war, Western economies, including Japan, experienced relatively strong and consistent economic growth, increased labour productivity, rising real wages and declining social and economic inequalities (see Figure 5.1). At the same time, the period also corresponds with the last major agrarian transformation in the West (see chapter 7), as millions of farmers like Daniel's parents migrated to urban areas

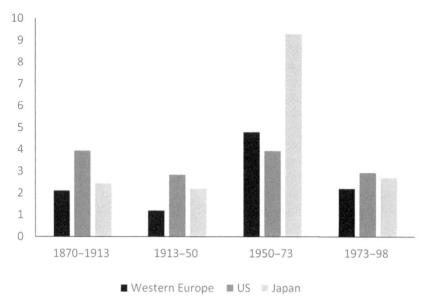

Figure 5.1 Rate of growth of per capita GDP (annual average compound rate), 1870–1998
Source: data from Angus Maddison (2003), p. 263

to work in manufacturing and service sectors in the expectation of finding stable, long-term and relatively well-paid employment. More generally, this unprecedented period of prosperity was accompanied by a more equal distribution of the products of work than earlier periods.

To understand what was driving these trends, we might begin in the factories of the industrialized United States, where the social and technological contexts of work were undergoing a notable shift. This transformation has been forever linked to the name of one particular industrialist – Henry Ford – who, in the early decades of the twentieth century, pioneered a dramatic change in the way that cars were produced. By introducing automated production lines, a much more focused division of labouring tasks, highly specialized tools for production and interchangeable mass-produced parts, Ford became the figurehead for a new breed of factories across the industrial heartlands of America. Ford's key idea was that integrating technological advances deep into the labour process could greatly increase productivity. To do this, he sought to break down the various steps necessary to make a car into small, specialized tasks which could then be fused back together as part of a flowing automated process. The aim was to create a factory in which workers formed synchronized parts of an efficient automated industrial machine.

As an integral part of this shift, Ford introduced a new labour regime into the automobile industry with major implications for how work-forces were reproduced, mobilized, motivated and utilized in produc-tion. One of Ford's crucial points was that mass production needed to be matched by mass consumption to provide markets for expanded output. He therefore argued that workers should have a greater share of the value produced so that they could become consumers of the same cars they spent their days building. Additionally, to integrate and motivate them within a fast-paced automated factory, he envisaged giving them more hours for leisure as a counterpart to intensifying their labour on the job. This led in 1914 to Ford announcing a stand-ardized five-dollar wage for an eight-hour day for all assembly line workers. This revolutionary move – effectively doubling the wage rate of line workers – not only appeared to recognize that workers needed time to rest from the heightened pace of modern production, it also linked increased productivity to better working conditions and social development. The ills of an older industrialism based on poverty-level wages and extensive working hours, Ford contended, should be con-signed to history as a blockage to the scientifically informed pursuit of increased productivity, profits and social advancement.

The flipside of such improvements, however, was that Fordism introduced new divisions within the workforce and imposed new forms of labour control. Whereas skilled workers had traditionally exercised a degree of autonomy within their immediate work environ-ment, the mass production of standardized goods called instead for semi-skilled workers with little to no control over the labour process. Fordism therefore invoked a transformation in power relations between an emerging class of managers, who controlled the design and pace of production, and workers subjected to the routinized and heightened pace of work.[1] These methods often provoked strong confrontations with labour organizations that sought to preserve control over the workplace. In the United States, Fordist managerial-ism was often implemented by mobilizing relatively disempowered immigrant workforces who accepted reduced autonomy in exchange for the promise of social mobility and relative economic prosperity. In Europe, the presence of stronger labour organizations and craft tradi-tions made this transition a bitterly contested one and led to the crea-tion of the political conditions under which labour unions retained a strong influence over workplace relations.

Fordism therefore originated as a form of class compromise that reshaped labour relations in modern industries. In exchange for accepting a transformation of work involving deskilling, automation, pervasive supervision and managerial control, workers stood to gain from stable employment, rising real wages based on productivity gains, collective bargaining and social benefits such as healthcare, social insurance and company-based pensions. These kinds of labour rights and social entitlements would become central to formalized work relations, greatly expanding the earlier legislation governing basic work conditions. Although Fordist practices emerged within the automobile industry, these principles came to be generalized across most leading industrial sectors and further afield. They therefore exerted a strong influence over how people conceived of the roles, rights and responsibilities of labour. In the decades after the Second World War, Fordism came to represent a broader social pact built upon the relationship between waged labour and household livelihoods, setting new norms for employment contracts, wages, social benefits and consumption trends.

Key to the generalization of Fordism was a new industrial relations system that emerged as a way to enshrine this social compromise at a political level. In many Western countries and some developing ones, tripartite alliances between employers, unions and the state emerged as a more cooperative form of organizing industrial relations. By incorporating labour into a social pact with business and the state, the intention was to provide the social stability needed for productivity growth that would benefit all parties. Given that unions were once outlawed as terrorist organizations in many Western countries, the legal recognition of the right to collective bargaining marked a dramatic transition. As part of this shift, the state in both North America and Europe became more involved in regulating labour relations, including the length of the working day, the right to strike, health and working safety at work, a minimum wage, conditions of work and overtime. Here we see precisely the consolidation and generalization of what we term formal work across many – but not all – economic sectors. Such was the spread of secure work with benefits that it became referred to as the Standard Employment Relationship and a template against which all other forms of employment would be judged.

The interventionist ethos of extending formalization meshed well with the broader economic philosophy of Keynesianism that dominated government thinking following the Great Depression which started in the 1929. Keynesianism is centred on the notion that sustaining aggregate demand within a national economy is key to maintaining strong and stable growth. British economist John Maynard Keynes argued that, although the production of goods and services should remain firmly in the hands of the private sector, the state must play a key management role, especially during economic downturns. In situations of high unemployment and low demand, he argued, it was up to the state to stimulate the economy and create the right conditions for investment to take place. Large state-funded infrastructure projects such as roads, bridges, ports and public buildings create jobs and consumption, which in turn will produce an economic environment conducive to investment. When the economy is stabilized and growing again, the state can step out and reimburse accumulated deficits through taxes generated by economic activities. Conversely, if the demand for goods and services is too high, the state can raise taxes to cool economic activity and control inflation. Importantly, Keynesian thinking strongly emphasized the central importance of labour to economic stability and growth. Sustaining consumption was seen to be best served by promoting full employment because workers provided the markets for produced goods. As a result, Keynesians tended to approve of the spread of formalized work with stable and durable contracts, and also of unemployment insurance and other social rights.

A third outcome of the class compromise represented by Fordism was the expansion of the welfare state. Through a series of institutions and programmes such as unemployed insurance, social assistance, maternity leave, food security schemes and public pensions, the state was charged with the role of shielding workers from market instability. The provision of this social safety net was therefore also in line with the Keynesian idea of sustaining aggregate demand by supporting workers in times of need and guaranteeing them an income during times of economic hardship. These direct social protections were complemented by further indirect interventions in the labour market through historically unprecedented investments in public education, skills formation and the democratization of higher education. As a result, heightened social mobility and declining economic inequalities became increasingly common during the peak of welfare expansion in the 1960s and 1970s.

Notwithstanding many positive impacts of formalization and welfarism, the benefits were not uniform and many people remained excluded. Even in the heartlands of industrial capitalism, not all workers fell within the regulated sectors and benefited from the social pact. Michael Harrington revealed that chronic poverty was the reality for some 40–50 million people in the United States at the height of the Fordist period.[2] It was the recognition of the structural nature of poverty for millions of workers – heavily concentrated among African Americans, women and youngsters – that led to the development of the segmented labour market theory discussed in chapter 3.³ At the same time, Fordism also encapsulated a set of gender norms that were strongly patriarchal. The ideal Fordist household typified a gendered social order reliant upon three complementary institutions: the husband's waged labour to provide for the needs of the family; the wife's unpaid domestic labour and care work for the members of the household; and the state's social wage in the form of welfare programmes and social security. This meant that, outside the Fordist ideal, those women wishing or needing to work – and many working-class women found waged labour an absolute necessity to maintain the household livelihood – encountered strongly segmented labour markets that pushed them into marginal employment sectors with low wages and few benefits.

While we have so far focused on the industrial West, the consolidation and expansion of formal sector work also occurred in a number of non-Western countries. In the communist countries of the Soviet Union, Eastern Europe and China, the norm of guaranteed work with accordant social benefits was enshrined as a constitutional right. Secure work was therefore guaranteed as part of citizenship, although job mobility was typically strictly limited and political allegiance to the party state was non-negotiable. The so-called 'iron rice bowl' in communist China, for example, was a form of bureaucratic job allocation that tied a worker to a particular work unit (*danwei*), which functioned not only as a lifelong source of employment, but also as a system of social welfare providing social goods including housing, healthcare, education and childcare. Given the wider context of job insecurity in many developing world countries, guaranteed employment and security laid an important marker for the rest of the world, where it greatly influenced debates over what work should look like. Notably, in the context of Cold War antagonisms, the existence of an alternative to capitalism undoubtedly impacted on the willingness of Western states to expand formal sector coverage and welfare rights.

Elsewhere, in Africa, Asia and Latin America, a more limited formal sector often consolidated around the tentative emergence of industrialization from the 1930s onwards. Across much of Latin America, for example, formalization was typically restricted to government jobs, state-owned enterprises and modern branches of industry. This tended to create strong labour market segmentation between the small formal sector and the mass of the population working in agriculture and the informal sector (see chapters 6 and 7). Nonetheless, government-promoted expansion of industrialization across the postwar period created the political grounds for expanding formalization as a means to both promote social stability and to fashion a stronger domestic consumer class. In countries such as Argentina and Mexico, formal sector workers' unions were incorporated into a durable social pact with the state that granted limited wage rises in return for political stability. This highly embedded form of unionism was often termed corporatism, wherein unions sacrificed political independence for the promise of a share of productivity growth for their members. At times when the economy was growing, such conflicts could generally be smoothed over through redistributive policies. In times of economic turmoil, however, social struggles might erupt into confrontations, violence and repression.[4]

The Crisis of Fordism and the Rise of Neoliberalism

While social conflicts often emerged most acutely in the countries of the developing world, all forms of Fordist compromise came under strong pressure from the mid-1970s onwards. This was a period of considerable economic turmoil at a global level, in which the 'golden age' of consistent economic growth turned into bouts of stagnation and crisis. Under these conditions, the social pact underpinning Fordism quickly unravelled (see Figure 5.2). When we consider transformations in the nature and expanse of formal work, two closely related trends stand out. First, we discuss technological and organizational changes in workplaces and the transition towards new forms of organizing economic activity across borders through global production networks. Second, we highlight the emergence of neoliberalism as the

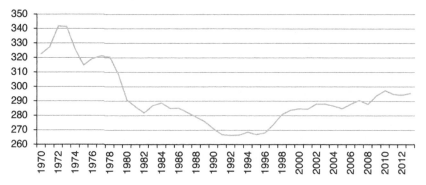

Figure 5.2   Average weekly earnings in private non-agricultural industries in the USA, 1970–2013 (monthly data seasonally adjusted), 1982–4 dollars
Source: Economic Report of the President, 2014, p. 384

dominant political ideology shaping policy practice at a global level. Together, these trends have shifted the power relations involved in work, rescaled labour markets and changed the ways that individuals seek employment and households put together livelihood strategies.

A useful starting place to capture these transformations is to return to the car factories that we saw had once been paragons of increasing productivity allied to Fordist labour regimes. By the 1970s, however, those older methods were being quickly supplanted by new technologies, managerial practices and labour regimes. This time, the avatar of transformation was not to be found in the United States, but in Japan, where Toyota's adoption of lean production methods pioneered a whole new approach of just-in-time production. The latter deployed new information technologies and robotization to reduce flow times within production, enhance inventory control and management, and lower the number of employees while increasing the rhythm of work. The quest for flexibility in production, it seemed, had arrived as the harbinger of competitiveness in a global economy and other car producers scrambled to implement these new technologies within the workplace.

It is significant that the Toyota model was first implemented in Japan, which had some of the most formalized labour markets on the planet; flexible production could be reconciled with secure employment. In the 1970s, however, Toyota increasingly modularized the labour-intensive moments of its flexible production process and relocated them to plants in East and Southeast Asia, creating a global production network through which they could access different labour regimes. By embedding its flexible production systems into the human fabric of cheap and flexibilized labour, Toyota created a strong competitive edge across the industry. As a result, labour market segmentation was transferred from a national to a global scale. A preserve of extremely well-paid technical jobs around design and engineering remained in Japan, while low-skilled, labour-intensive segments took shape elsewhere in developing countries.

This trend highlights the growing disparity between the spatial mobility of capital and the relatively fixed nature of labour that underscores a key power differential in global labour. The ability of firms to offshore or outsource their productive activities has been strongly advanced through trade liberalization, in part by overseeing the growth of legally binding bilateral and multilateral free trade agreements such as Mercosur and the North American Free Trade Agreement (NAFTA). By lowering trade barriers, such as import quotas and tariffs, member states seek to facilitate the trade of goods and services between them, and this hastened the formation of ever more specialized global production networks with different productive functions distributed across workplace sites and their accordant labour regimes (see chapter 4). For workers, this meant that geographically separated labour forces were put in a position of competing for jobs, as their capacity to attract or retain capital investments or contracts was tied to the maintenance of a labour regime composed of lower wages, limited benefits and flexible work. These trends led critics to declare a 'race to the bottom' in which the relocation of labour-intensive production outside of the advanced industrial countries led to a continual downward pressure upon wages and conditions, shattering the social pact of formalization.

Neoliberalism, Labour Market Flexibilization and Workfare

By the late 1970s, the political dynamics that had provided the social pact with legitimacy were fraying. With Keynesian-inspired policies seemingly no longer able to sustain dynamic growth, an alternative and explicitly anti-state intervention policy paradigm asserted that growth and welfare improvements were better achieved by promoting market competitiveness, trade liberalization and privatization. The authoritarian government of Augusto Pinochet in Chile in the mid-1970s first implemented this neoliberal paradigm, where it appeared to be an outlier to Keynesian normalcy. By the early 1980s, however, it became increasingly dominant at a global level, marked by the election of neoliberal advocates such as UK prime minister Margaret Thatcher in 1979 and US president Ronald Reagan in 1980. Subsequently, structural adjustment programmes implemented by the International Monetary Fund (IMF) and World Bank globalized neoliberalism across much of the developing world in the 1980s and into the former Soviet Union after the collapse of communist rule at the close of the decade. Notably, even the social democratic bastions of continental Europe have, since the 1990s, become increasingly neoliberal in key areas of financial and trade policy.

In contrast to the Fordist compromise, neoliberals stressed that such labour market regulations were profoundly counterproductive, as they limited innovation and competitiveness by constraining the ability of businesses to respond flexibly to market signals. In a globalizing economy, neoliberals contended, firms need to be able to set wage rates and hire and fire workers according to the dictates of the market without being bound by the regulations of the state or the power of labour unions. By restricting the ability of firms to achieve competitiveness, burdensome regulations and excessive job protection slow aggregate growth, overall employment and wage levels. Neoliberals therefore offered a politically powerful argument against expansive formalization. Their proposed solution was to undertake a process labelled labour market flexibilization, which entailed retrenching governmental constraints on employers regarding mandatory length of contracts, severance pay, minimum wages and payment of benefits. Formalization, in short, would be stripped back to become a set of minimum conditions around hours and work practices freed from the restrictions and obligations imposed during the Fordist period. Even if it meant that some workers would suffer falling wages and worsening conditions, labour market flexbilization was nonetheless argued to ultimately benefit the collective welfare of all workers by promoting economic growth.[5]

From within global labour studies, this argument has been treated with considerable suspicion. Unregulated labour markets are assumed to gradually reach equilibrium – termed labour market clearing – as market forces harmonize supply and demand so that all willing workers can find employment at a wage rate equivalent to their contribution to productivity. As we've seen in the previous chapters, however, labour markets and employment relationships are characterized not simply by supply and demand, but by power relationships between unequally situated social agents. Deregulating labour markets gives employers considerably more power in setting the terms of contracts. At the same time, different strata of employees enjoy vastly different levels of power with which to negotiate the conditions of their employment. Those with valued assets and strong networks are far better placed to find positions in a more lucrative and stable segment of the labour market (see box 5.1). For others without such power, finding a good job can be an exacting and elusive process, which is captured by the growth in precarious forms of temporary and part-time work, piecework and contractual employment. The proportion of contingent workers in the United States, for example, rose from 30.6 per cent of the workforce in 2005 to 40.4 per cent in 2015.[6]

Viewed from the perspective of uneven power relations, we can understand why labour market flexibilization can result in heavy segmentation of labour markets. For example, in the United States during the Fordist compromise period between 1948 and 1973, productivity increased by 96.7 per cent and hourly compensation for production and nonsupervisory workers kept pace with a comparable rise of 91.3 per cent. From 1973 to 2014, however, productivity growth of 72.2 per cent far exceeded the hourly compensation rise of a mere 9.2 per cent.[7] This indicates a deep stagnation of wages across the post-Fordist period despite the contribution of workers to increased productivity. Second, the data also reveals a further important facet of flexibilization. The category of production and nonsupervisory workers incorporates around 80 per cent of the labour market and excludes those in managerial or executive positions. When those top segments of the labour market are included, wages rose by 42 per cent over the period. While this is still below productivity gains – indicating that corporations and shareholders have been extracting the lion's share of wealth produced – it also indicates how privileged sectors of the US labour market have been better able to safeguard or expand their incomes. The end result has been a far more unequal society in which wealth is increasingly concentrated at the highest echelons.

These profound changes in employment relations have not gone unchallenged, yet falling unionization rates and annual strike statistics indicate the new power dynamics of employment relations (see chapter 12). An important part of this power shift has been the transformation of welfare that has accompanied labour market flexibilization. For many advanced industrial countries, this is often

---

Box 5.1   Paying for qualifications

As education increasingly becomes a commodity, gaining access to skilled labour market segments is now tightly linked to the ability to afford a university degree. For those students who do not come from affluent households, the options are to either to forgo higher education or to enter into considerable debt. A 2016 report from the British National Union of Students (NUS) on the impacts of the 2012 reforms, which allowed UK universities to charge up to £9,000 per year for an undergraduate degree, found that 52 per cent of 2015 graduates aged 25 or under and 47 per cent of all graduates were back living with their parents and taking casual jobs to pay off loans.[8] In the context of mounting student debt, rising living costs and declining government support, about 55 per cent of full-time 2015 employed graduates were earning less than £20,000 per year, and more than 80 per cent less than £25,000. Britain is not alone. In the United States, the class of 2015 was the most indebted in the history; the average debt of those taking on student loans almost quadrupled between 1993 and 2015 to reach $35,000.[9] Such trends are not yet universal, however. In Denmark, where education is considered a public good, university education is free and students get about $900 per month to study, allowing the vast majority to graduate without debts.

discussed in terms of a shift from welfare to workfare. Whereas welfarism is typically characterized by entitlement-based programmes, voluntary participation and eligibility-based benefits, the workfare state marked a shift towards market-oriented policies based on time-limited cash benefits, restrictive eligibility rules, strict work requirements for welfare recipients, as well as mandatory job search and job training programmes to improve employability. To gain benefits under workfare means continually demonstrating the willingness to take paid employment, no matter how poor the wages, contract or conditions. Eschewing the principle of social rights and entitlements, workfare emphasizes personal responsibility and obligation and enshrines market insecurity as an individual failure rather than a social problem. The primary goal of the workfare state is therefore to enforce market participation, not provide social insurance.

In theory, the neoliberal logic of labour market flexibilization presumes that jobs are available to those who are forced to leave the welfare rolls. In practice, however, the workfare state has contributed to a dramatic intensification of competition for jobs at the bottom end of the labour market. Because workfare reforms tend to undercut existing conditions by delivering a cheap, unstable and contingent labour force to employers, they have been central to the flexibilization of the labour market under neoliberalism. As part of this transition from welfarism to workfarism, social benefits tend to be reduced and become more difficult to obtain and harder to retain. In parallel, as documented by sociologist Loïc Wacquant, the rise of workfarism in the United States is directly related to the increased incarceration rates of the poor.[10] Amidst growing economic insecurity, the decline of collective bargaining and the retrenchment of the welfare state, law and order agendas have been on the rise, resulting in a criminalization of poverty and the growing incarceration rates of marginalized populations.

The Rise of a 'Precariat'?

Labour market flexibilization and workfare policies in areas such as the United States, Canada, the United Kingdom and Western Europe have not ended the preserve of secure, well-paid jobs. There is still immense wealth produced within these economies, as indicated by the strong productivity rises noted above, and some jobs are extremely well remunerated. What these trends have done, however, is to create a more pronounced segmentation of labour markets, with formalized jobs harder to access. Economists Lawrence Katz and Alan Krueger, for example, reported that nearly 95 per cent of the approximately 10 million new jobs created in the United States during the Obama era were temporary positions, either part-time or limited-term contracts.[11] For anthropologist Jan Breman and labour historian Marcel van der Linden, these trends have created a counterintuitive situation in which the employment structures of advanced industrial countries are increasingly moving towards those associated with developing countries. They note that, even in Germany – long held as the bastion of the Standard Employment Relationship – there has been a growing tendency towards part-time employment, mini-jobs, temporary work and limited-time contracts. Industrial relations scholar Guy Standing has referred to this trend as the rise of the 'precariat', a provocative combination of 'precarious' and 'proletariat'.[12]

These precarious labour markets typically have a strongly gendered component. In the United States, women now constitute just under half the total workforce as compared to less than a third in the 1950s. In contrast to the Fordist conception of the male breadwinner, shifts in labour markets and household incomes entail that a greater number of women must earn a wage. This raises a significant challenge for many women, who still find themselves locked into a gendered division of labour in which aspects of social reproduction such as childcare that was once undertaken or subsidized by the state have been increasingly transferred back to families who must purchase them as commodities. Feminist political economist Isabella Bakker refers to this process as the re-privatization of social reproduction.[13] It creates a double burden for many women who, in addition to shouldering most of the unpaid domestic labour, earn a wage in the formal economy. On the other hand, wealthier households might choose to hire a maid or a nanny, with the result that one woman's freedom from domestic chores is contracted out to another, often migrant, woman.

A novel part of the expansion of casual work has been the growth of what's called the 'sharing economy', which is becoming a key component of the contemporary service sector. Need a ride? There is an 'app' for that: Lyft, Sidecar, Uber or Wingz. Perhaps you do not have the time for grocery shopping this week. With Instacart someone will do it for you and deliver it. Even better: it's late, you're hungry and you don't feel like cooking or going out. With Caviar, DoorDash and Postmates, you can select what you want to eat from local restaurants and have it delivered. You can even track the status of your order by following the progress of the driver. From walking the dog (Wag!), waiting in line at the restaurant (Postmates), to picking up your dirty clothes and bringing them back clean (Washio), the so-called

Box 5.2 The changing workplace

One interesting transformation in contemporary work is the new fluidity between the public and private spheres, or the spaces of production and reproduction. Work during the Fordist era had typically been characterized by a relatively rigid separation between the two, encapsulated in the idea of a nine-to-five job. Work hours followed a relatively rigid schedule, and work itself was generally performed in a specific place that was distinguishable from the household. While this reality still exists for a great many workers, more and more work is performed outside the office, as mobile phone, wireless laptop and tablet computers reshape the spatiality of work. For companies, virtual workplaces are beneficial because it allows them to save money on office space, access a broader pool of talent, reduce office politics and colleague interruptions, and be more environmentally friendly. For workers, such flexibility is often perceived as positive, especially for those caring for children or the elderly. As Melissa Gregg argues, the freedom that communication technologies give us to work where and when we want means that our jobs, especially for professional employees, are at once more flexible and accessible than ever before, yet also potentially invasive of family and leisure time.[14]

sharing economy delivers convenience, flexibility and even eccentricity to consumers. What about the workers? Is the sharing economy as pleasant and fun for them?

Meet Andrew Callaway, a 25-year-old San Francisco native who decided to find out by working exclusively in sharing economy jobs for one month and producing a podcast – revealingly called 'Instaserfs' – about his experience.[15] One recurrent complaint made by Andrew was the lack of security that came from not knowing in advance how much he would make and therefore how long he would have to work. This might explain why he preferred working for Washio, a dry-cleaning and laundry delivery company, which assigned all his drop-offs at the beginning of the day. The company paid him $10.10 per stop, and he was able to complete 14 stops in five hours during his first day, earning about $28 per hour before expenses. Yet this was an exception, as Andrew rarely made much more than the minimum wage, and on some occasions less. During his first two weeks, close to $700 had been deposited in his bank account. Deducing work expenses such as gas mileage (he was, among others, a Lyft driver) and taxes, he cannot have made much more than $200 per week. Andrew saw nothing liberating in the sharing economy, which he described as 'apploitation' – a combination of application and exploitation – to highlight how cheaper and more convenient services for customers all too often rely on the exploitation of workers.

Andrew's experience raises important questions about power. On the one hand, customers benefit from the convenience, privacy and control given by technology as they can generate work whenever they want and monitor workers wherever they are. More importantly, however, it is their ability to rate workers that give them a remarkable power over workers, imposing a climate of fear and paranoia and producing a docile labour force. Uber drivers with a rating score below 4.6 or 4.7 out of five stars are very likely to be disconnected (i.e., fired) from the platform. Should we be surprised that a growing number of drivers offer free snacks and water to get high ratings and keep their jobs? Drivers do not hesitate to lie to their passengers when asked if they love their job, knowing full well that good ratings are based on their ability to uphold the illusion that the sharing economy is the tide that lifts all boats. On the other hand, firms retain the capacity to hold their workers in precarious, flexible forms of employment (see box 5.3). Take Deliveroo, for example, a British takeaway delivery firm operating in numerous countries.[16] In August 2016, the

Box 5.3   Uber drivers: employees or independent contractors?

Like many companies, such as Deliveroo, Lyft and Postmates, Uber insists on classifying its workers as 'partners' or independent contractors instead of employees, a legal provision by which the company does not have to pay for social security benefits, vacation time, payroll taxes and other fees such as workers' compensation insurance, gas mileage and vehicle repair. While drivers keep 80 per cent of their earnings and pay for their own insurance, gas and repairs, Uber takes 20 per cent of the fare, with the important difference that it decides the pricing. When Uber arrived in Los Angeles in 2013, drivers who worked full time could expect to earn a living wage. Thousands of drivers signed up, leasing and buying cars to take advantage of this opportunity. Within one year, however, Uber had slashed fares almost by half to compete against its rival Lyft. Drivers who used to make close to $20 per hour now work below the minimum wage on some days, as Uber transfers to its workers the costs of competition. Its business model is so dependent on flexible labour that it recently settled a class-action lawsuit to recognize drivers as employees and therefore entitled to reimbursement expenses, including gas and vehicle maintenance. Uber will pay up to $100 million to its drivers in California and Massachusetts to keep them as independent contractors.[17]

firm told its London-based workers that it would experiment with a new pay structure, switching from an hourly rate of £7 plus £1 per delivery to a fixed delivery rate of £3.75. As Michael Boyle, a cyclist who works in central London, said: 'The company is outsourcing risk to us.' On a quiet day, Boyle can take one order in four hours, which would amount to £29 under the old system and £3.75 under the new one. Following a week of protests, the firm finally accepted not to force its riders to accept new contracts.

The Uncertain Futures of 'Post-Formal' Work

The above sections have charted how technological change, the internationalization of production and the political erosion of the Fordist social compact with the rise of neoliberalism has led to a proportional decline of the Standard Employment Relationship in advanced industrial countries. This may herald an era of what we might call 'post-formal work' characterized by an increasing proportion of workers engaged in casualized, short-term employment that offers few securities. If this trend represents a return to an earlier epoch of insecure forms of employment, it is worth considering whether the Fordist era of formalized work represents an exceptional period rather than a new normal in labour standards.

There is certainly a growing sense that the nature of work is shifting rapidly with complex and unsettling consequences. Consider, for example, the experience of what sociologist Craig Lambert labels 'shadow work'. You are about to start university and have decided to paint and furnish your new apartment. You head to the hardware store to get paint and brushes, which you pay for at the self-checkout, before going to Ikea to buy furniture that you will assemble. On your way back home, you stop by the gas station where you pump your own gas, and then go to the grocery store where you scan and bag your own groceries. Upon returning home, you order from the Amazon website some of the books that you will need this semester. While enjoying the convenience offered by the modern retail experience, you have in fact been accomplishing unpaid tasks on behalf of businesses for which you never volunteered. From self-checkouts at cinemas and libraries to online banking and automated check-in and boarding process at airports, businesses and corporations are taking advantage of robotics and information technologies to download a growing number of tasks onto customers to increase profits by cutting on personnel costs.[18]

The rise of shadow work is simply one dimension of an intensifying automation of employment occurring across economic sectors. According to political economist Nick Dyer-Witheford, this trend encompasses the expansion of robots in production, the functional integration of world business operations through electronic networks, and the financialization of daily life through automated banking systems and credit card networks. The result of this logistical revolution is the creation of a planetary working class that is increasingly working itself out of a job. It contributes daily to the development of ever more complex and comprehensive digital networks and systems of robots that ultimately replace human labour. From drones delivering mail to autonomous public transport vehicles to bricklaying robots building houses to fully automated factories and farms, the army of programmers and engineers working at creating software and robots to automate existing tasks are contributing to both the displacement and the flexibilization of labour.[19] Some scientists suggest that robots could absorb as many as half of all jobs within a three-decade timescale.[20] In that scenario, we would need to address two key questions. How would the steady downward pressure on the availability of work impact labour markets, and who would be the losers and winners from such a dramatic transition? Would automatization accentuate current trends, turning formal work into an even smaller preserve and enforcing a profound informalization across Western economies? To that end, let us consider the question of informality in more detail, shifting focus primarily to developing world contexts in the next chapter.

Further reading

Kim Moody's classic book *Workers in a Lean World: Unions in the International Economy* (London: Verso, 1997) provides an excellent starting place for delving deeper into the transformation of formal work. A similar thematic is explored with a diverse cast of authors in the collection by Vivian Shalla and Wallace Clement, *Work in Tumultuous Times: Critical Perspectives* (Montreal: Queen's-McGill Press, 2007). Jamie Peck's *Workfare States* (London: Guilford Press, 2001) problematizes the institutional nature of labour markets and recent transformations in welfare policy. Susanne Soederberg has continued that analysis with a focus on credit and debt relations in *Debtfare States and the Poverty Industry: Money, Discipline and the Surplus Population* (London, Routledge, 2014).

Chapter 6
Labour in the Informal Economy

It may seem paradoxical, but at a global level an extremely large proportion of urban dwellers have jobs that – in official eyes – don't really exist. This is because they work in what is called the informal economy, a loose term that denotes a range of enterprises and livelihood activities that are not registered with or regulated by the state. Some people call it the 'underground economy', but most of the informal economy is neither underground nor hidden away. Rather, it is hiding in plain sight, perfectly visible on the streets of any city in Africa, Asia or Latin America. You don't need to look closely to find it in the marketplaces, the small workshops and the tiny family-run firms tucked into back streets; it is evident in the activities of street sellers, tradespeople walking door to door seeking odd jobs, casual labourers on construction sites and hired workers stacking shelves in stores or washing dishes in small street-side restaurants. Moreover, informality is far from just a developing world phenomenon. It is readily present in Europe and North America, where cash-in-hand work thrives in an off-the-books economy (see box 6.1).

In many urban zones in the global South the informal economy is how most people get by. Estimates suggest it provides a source of work and income for somewhere between one half to three-quarters of all non-agricultural employment in such countries.[1] Among the poorer sections of the population, informal activities are pivotal to household livelihood strategies as a source of income, whether through self-employment selling bulk goods on the street or by finding informal waged employment. At the same time, the goods and services produced informally are widely consumed, and not just by the urban poor. They provide a means by which urban consumers from all social classes get access to basic goods and services at affordable prices. From street-side food stalls to plumbers and construction workers, the informal economy is pivotal to how modern cities work. And while trying to count such informal activities is difficult owing to their off-the books nature, all measures indicate that informal employment continues to expand globally, with a majority of new jobs created each year attributed to the informal sector.[2]

Notwithstanding its undoubted importance, opinions on the informal economy are strongly divided. International organizations and governments often portray the informal economy as a reservoir of bad jobs that reproduces low productivity, poor wages and tax evasion. The ILO, for example, pledged in the summer of 2015 to mount an international campaign to end informality on the grounds that the lack of employment regulation presented a barrier to equitable socioeconomic development. For others, however, the informal economy stands as a beacon of entrepreneurship and ingenuity. It represents a vibrant marketplace that flourishes beyond the gaze of the state exactly because of the lack of constraining regulations. From this perspective, facilitating training and encouraging a better investment climate – rather than trying to regulate directly against informality – is the preferred way to encourage a transition to more formalized conditions.

How can such polarized perspectives exist side by side? In this chapter, we prise apart these debates on informality using our focus on power, networks, space and livelihoods to provide a way to understand the informal economy. As we progress, we'll see that extreme

---

Box 6.1   The shadow economy in Europe

Although the focus of this chapter is the informal economy in the global South, informality exists widely in industrial countries, although it is often hidden. In his 2013 report on the European 'shadow economy', Friedrich Schneider argues that informality takes two main forms: undeclared work, in which workers and businesses do not declare all wages in order to avoid taxes or documentation; and underreporting, in which businesses that rely heavily on cash transactions, such as cafés or small shops, report only part of their income to avoid taxes. Across Europe, this informality encompasses around 18.5 per cent of economic activity, ranging from 7 to 8 per cent in Switzerland to between 25 and 33 per cent of all economic activity in Eastern Europe. The construction sector is the largest area of informal work, although retailing, hotels and restaurants, and manufacturing all have sizeable shadow components.[3]

care needs to be taken not to overgeneralize our statements. There is a heterogeneity of activities within the informal economy, each of which needs to be assessed on its own terms. Different informal activities are structured by distinct relations of power and coordinated by different forms of networks, operate at different scales and offer varying livelihood options. We should therefore be extremely wary when analysts and policymakers refer to the informal economy as if it were a singular, homogenous realm with a shared set of characteristics and dynamics.

What is the Informal Economy?

The term informal economy was put forward in the early 1970s by British anthropologist Keith Hart in his work on the urban street markets of Accra in Ghana. While the informal economy tag was new, the activities Hart described were not. From household artisans and traders to beggars and scavengers, the small-scale economic activities that he analysed formed the bedrock of livelihoods in cities across the global South. By collecting these activities together under a catchall term, Hart was able to group together a diversity of urban economic activities that had a common characteristic of falling outside the regulation of the Ghanaian state. The drive to create this new category reflected Hart's desire to understand a pivotal question: did the informal economy represent a reservoir of poverty and exploitation bereft of any possibilities of dynamic development? Or could it provide a foundation for some form of sustained growth and income expansion – what we might term development?[4]

Hart's informal economy concept quickly spread among both policymakers and analysts alike. Its attractiveness stemmed from two factors. First, it appeared to put a finger on the pulse of a pressing development issue. As the cities of the postcolonial world expanded, so did the ranks of the unregulated economic activities and the number of households dependent upon them. At the same time, the informal economy concept seemed to provide a simple yet encompassing way to talk about these trends. Many policymakers began to talk about whether the informal economy was a good or bad thing as if it was a singular entity. Others – such as Hart himself – were uncomfortable with the level of generalization that this entailed.

This conundrum arises in part because the informal economy can only be defined by what it isn't, that is, as not formalized (see chapter 5). The ILO, for example, defines the informal economy as 'all economic activities by workers and economic units that are – in law or in practice – not covered or insufficiently covered by formal arrangements'.[5] In short, informality incorporates both firms and their workers that are unregistered with the state and therefore have no formal existence. The firms in question do not pay taxes – although they may pay bribes to state officials – and typically do not operate according to state regulations concerning health, safety, labour rights and other legally stipulated conditions for doing business. In this sense, they occupy a grey area in the law. The overwhelming majority of activities within the informal economy are not illegal in the sense that they don't produce or sell illicit goods such as drugs or contraband. On the contrary, they produce vital consumption goods and services that are relied upon by many people on a day-to-day basis. Yet they do so in a way that is not fully legal because of a lack of compliance with the regulatory prescriptions of the state.

To help cut through this complexity, it is useful to begin by clarifying three broad distinctions. First, the concept of informal labour refers to the status of workers who have no formalized contract, regardless of whether they work for an informal or formal sector firm. The emphasis is therefore on waged work that is neither recognized nor regulated by the state, even if it's done within a formal company that is fully registered and regulated. In downtown London, for example, workers cleaning the upmarket offices of corporate Britain are frequently without contracts. Aicha, a recent migrant to London from the Ivory Coast, begins vacuuming the floors at 5:00 a.m., but does not have a contract or any of the benefits in terms of the security that it would bring. Instead, a contractor pays her 'cash-in-hand' at very low rates on a weekly basis with no guarantee as to whether there will still be work the following Monday. The contractor is part of a formal firm, yet Aicha's employment is decisively informal, with low pay, no benefits and no security. For Aicha, the high price of living in London, the competition for jobs and the difficulty in getting her Ivorian skills and experience recognized in the UK job market compels her to take whatever work is available, even though she is aware of its precarious nature and her own exploitation.[6]

Second, the concept of the informal sector is normally used to refer specifically to the firms and enterprises that are not formally registered with the state. It is a term that draws attention to economic units with at least two workers that undertake productive activities and service provision, such as small firms and household businesses. For example, if you have ever walked through the backstreets of

Dharavi – one of the world's biggest slums located in Mumbai, India – you will have noticed how the narrow streets reveal an extraordinary range of informal enterprises crammed in amongst the housing: from bakers making flatbreads for roadside stalls, to a small family firm putting together bicycles from recycled parts, through to a larger company with ten employees making handbags and leather goods that are shipped out internationally. Together, these enterprises comprise an informal sector: firms of all shapes and sizes that share a common condition of not being formally registered and therefore falling outside direct state regulation. In the eyes of the state, they do not exist, yet they are everywhere and form the core of industry and employment in the slum.

Finally, the informal economy concept seeks to capture a broader scope of activities. It refers not just to the firms that make up the informal sector, but also to the informal labourers they may hire and the numerous self-employed workers who are not part of any enterprise yet engage in retail or other pursuits. This wider category is explicitly a catchall concept, and we need to be careful not to smother the marked differences between different activities and livelihoods within its scope. A dumpsite just outside central Lagos, Nigeria, featured in the BBC documentary *Welcome to Lagos* displays all facets of the informal economy: from individual scavengers who work independently to sort through the trash to find items of value; to the middlemen who buy materials from the individual scavengers, collecting specific materials in bulk; to the informal recycling companies that buy from the middlemen and then employ a range of informal workers to process the materials that the middlemen bring them. Here we see the informal economy in all its diverse facets: a mixture of own-account (i.e., self-employed) workers, informal enterprises and their informal hired workforces, all of which are operating in the same dumpsite that is run by the municipal government.[7]

Explaining Informality

Debates over the informal economy have moved on since the 1970s yet the key concern remains the one that animated Hart's original contribution some four decades ago: does the presence of a large informal economy represent a blockage to development, keeping workers trapped in low-productivity and low-wage jobs? Or is the informal economy characterized by vibrant entrepreneurship and dynamic competition that should be valued for providing an alternative means of earning a living? The literature on this subject has demonstrated wild swings from one pole to the other, often driven by political expedience. As a consequence, there has emerged an extremely divided literature on what causes and reproduces informality and what its consequences are. Here it is useful to highlight four contrasting perspectives.

1 The failure of development thesis

Within much development theory, there remains an assumption that the informal economy is an aberration destined to slowly but surely disappear. Based on the experience of Western industrialized countries, the very idea of development was often characterized as the spread of formalized enterprises and work relations.[8] From this perspective, the persistence of informality was seen as an unfortunate lag wherein urbanization had occurred under conditions of insufficient economic growth that left people trapped in traditional forms of employment. For the modernization theorists of the 1960s and 1970s, the perseverance of a large informal economy was widely expected to be temporary, with an expectation that it would ebb away over time as economic and technological development drew more and more people into formalized jobs. Solving the informal economy problem was therefore a question of correct growth promotion through appropriate macroeconomic policies, aided with suitable education policies to produce the right kind of modern workers.

Such expectations, however, have largely been frustrated. Despite economic growth, technological change and international economic integration, the informal economy in most countries in the global South has grown considerably over the past half century. For many countries in Latin America, Africa and parts of Asia, this trend was heightened during the 1980s and 1990s when the promotion of structural adjustment programmes involved the privatization of state-owned industries, thereby reducing a major provider of formal sector work. The subsequent decades have seen a consolidation of informal employment at extremely high levels (see Figure 6.1). Given its shadow status, getting accurate statistics on informal jobs is understandably hard and different estimates shift depending on the criteria used. Notwithstanding such issues, it is commonly accepted that more than half of non-agricultural employment is informal across the developing world. This incorporates around 82 per cent of non-agricultural employment in South Asia, 66 per cent in Sub-Saharan

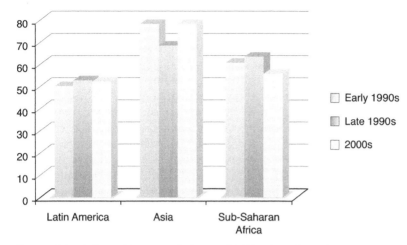

Figure 6.1 Informality around the world (% of total employment)
Source: data drawn from ILO and WTO (2009)

Africa, 65 per cent in East and Southeast Asia, and 51 per cent in Latin America. China represents a slightly different situation given the uniquely strong bureaucratic presence of the state. Even in such conditions, it is estimated that around a third of urban workers operate in informal conditions.[9]

For institutions such as the ILO, this trend represents a major problem because the failure of economic growth to translate into formal job creation leads to mal-development characterized by continuing inequality, poverty and vulnerability. In response to this deficit in decent work, the ILO has posited an integrated approach to secure a transition from informality to formality. This involves a combination of regional growth strategies designed to produce new and quality jobs allied to an expanded regulatory environment in which governments would actively enforce international labour standards. For the ILO, it is not feasible to wait for informality to fade away – rather, it must be stamped out of existence through stronger regulation and more inclusive growth. At their July 2015 annual meeting, the ILO made a recommendation that member countries actively seek to reverse the spread of the informal economy. Describing informality as a blockage to inclusive development and the rule of law, they argue that formalization is essential to achieve inclusive development and to realize decent work for all. Alongside regulatory efforts, the ILO recommends greater support for worker organizations and the expanded provision of training, finance and social protection to speed the transition to formalization.

2 The state inefficiency thesis

In contrast to the ILO, a perspective strongly associated with the IMF and World Bank argues that burdensome regulation is likely to be the problem, not the cure, to informality. Building from neoliberal thinking regarding the efficiency of the unregulated markets, these explanations attribute informality to the presence of excessive government regulations that make joining the formal sector either too costly or too difficult. As the Peruvian economist Hernando de Soto sought to establish in the mid-1980s, enterprises can face long delays and large costs in their attempt to formalize, including the time-consuming completion of a myriad of bureaucratic procedures and a frequent need for bribes to smooth the process along. Moreover, once formalized, firms need to submit tax returns and are expected to adhere to state regulations governing health, safety and employment legislation. As a result, many small and medium firms choose to operate informally as an entrepreneurial escape from the vice of the overburdening state.[10]

When these arguments first began to surface in the 1980s, the presence of a large informal sector was viewed as an expression of government failure in which excessive bureaucracy and poor law enforcement drives entrepreneurs into the informal sector. In the 1990s these concerns were used to consolidate the neoliberal agenda for state downsizing and bureaucratic retrenchment. Widespread economic liberalization was envisaged to remove market distortions and create a more flexible labour market in which firms and workers would no longer be ghettoed within the informal economy. The kinds of regulations that applied to many public sector workers – such as restrictions over the ease of hiring and firing, minimum wage levels, the mandatory provision of social benefits and the right to collective bargaining – were argued to be particularly burdensome on small businesses. In curtailing such regulations, institutions such as the IMF and World Bank were convinced that making the formal sector less formal would encourage firms to register and submit to less onerous regulation.

It should be noted, however, that in an era of general deregulation and government downsizing from the 1980s onwards, the informal sector did not fade away. On the contrary, it either persisted or expanded, with many technologically sophisticated small and medium firms continuing to concentrate in the informal sector. This led to a shift in the debate. If the informal economy continued to grow despite deregulation, neoliberals argued, then firms must prefer the flexibility of operating informally. Workers, it was added, might similarly choose informal employment for reasons of flexibility in household organization, working hours or pay systems.[11] From this perspective, to regulate informality would be counterproductive because it would stifle micro-entrepreneurialism and contribute to unemployment. Government policy should therefore not try to eliminate the informal sector but, rather, learn from it by understanding firm preferences and fine-tuning policies in a supportive manner. Instead of insisting on the immediate formalization of informal sector firms, governments should support the informal sector by providing better infrastructure, training and institutions. In time this will lead to a progressive upgrading in technology and size and, eventually, the voluntary transition of informal firms into the formal sector.

3 The exploitation thesis

While neoliberals cautiously celebrated the informal sector as a realm of entrepreneurial freedom, a more radical explanation sought to link the expansion of informality to power relations within capitalism. To do so, they rejected the idea of the informal economy as a separate and isolated economic realm. Instead, they stressed the close relationship between formal and informal sectors. In this view, the informal economy persists because it exists as a source of cheap labour, cheap inputs and cheap services for the formal sector. The development theorist Colin Leys elaborated on this perspective in particularly clear terms back at the beginning of the informal sector debates in the 1970s. What the informal sector does, he claimed, is to provide goods and services at very low prices that make possible the high profits of the formal sector.[12] For theorists like Leys, it was precisely this dependent relationship that explained why the informal sector refused to wither away. Exploiting the informal economy was essential for the profitability of the formal sector and local power holders saw little benefit in ending informality. If the informal economy didn't already exist, it would have to be invented.

There are two primary mechanisms that the exploitation thesis uses to explain this relationship. First, formal sector firms frequently cut costs by outsourcing parts of their production process to informal sector firms or to self-employed workers in the informal economy. Several advantages for formal firms stand out. Most evidently, subcontracting to informal sector firms enables formal firms to cheapen labour costs because informal firms and home workers are not governed by regulations over wage rates, contracts, social security and so forth. As Jan Breman sees it, informality is a means by which large numbers of marginal labourers can be drawn into the workforce under a precarious labour regime that leaves them prone to rampant exploitation.[13] At the same time, subcontracting also leads to a buttressing effect in which formal sector firms use their market power to drive down costs while also being able to easily shed contracts with informal firms in periods of slack demands. Put in the terms we proposed in chapter 4, formal sector firms create captive value chains with informal sector counterparts. Through these relationships, informal firms and workers end up taking on more of the risk for less of the reward.

Alongside this direct power relationship, there is a second facet to the functional relationship between formal and informal economies. As noted above, informal firms and workers often focus on providing basic consumption goods to households at rock bottom prices. As a result, the provision of cheap informal goods and services is recognized to lower the costs for the reproduction of labour in the formal sector. Informality therefore subsidizes formal sector labour costs, keeping wages low and profits high. For instance, workers in formal sector firms often will buy food and other essential consumption items at very low costs from informal vendors. Equally, middle-class households contract services ranging from maids and gardeners through to construction and security from the informal sector.

4 The marginalization thesis

If the exploitation thesis centres on a direct and hierarchical relationship between the formal and informal sectors, the marginalization thesis offers an alternative critical perspective which argues that most activity in the informal sector is undertaken as an isolated and marginalized realm of subsistence activities. The distinctiveness of this perspective is the insistence that marginalization is not an accident of history waiting to be remedied by favourable policies such as those propounded by the ILO. Rather, it is seen as an inherent feature of capitalism that no amount of economic growth will resolve. On the contrary, capitalist growth is argued to exacerbate the very problem it pretends to solve by creating an ever larger 'surplus' population that cannot be absorbed into formal employment and will survive only through recourse to informality.

Authors within this tradition typically build on a series of ideas put forward by Karl Marx, who argued that capitalism has an internal dynamic to separate people from the means of subsistence, making them dependent on selling their labour power in exchange for a wage. For Marx, not all this emergent proletarian would be absorbed within the industrial workforce. Rather, part of this working class would struggle to find employment and therefore exist as a floating population whose desperation to find jobs would depress wages across the economy as a whole. While Marx tended to envisage this surplus population as continually moving in and out of standard employment, others have argued that much of this surplus population remains almost permanently excluded from the mainstream capitalist economy. Argentine sociologist Jose Nun, for example, talked about a sizeable marginal mass in Latin American cities that was simply irrelevant to the formal sector.[14] Similarly, the Indian economist Kalyan Sanyal contends that capitalism in countries like India is defined by the way it produces a large segment of unwanted workers who are exiled to what he terms the 'wasteland' of capitalism. There they must subsist through a vast and varied range of informal activities in which the goal is not to generate profits but to provide the means for basic household subsistence.[15] Common to these accounts is the argument that this surplus of unskilled labour is getting bigger and operating under deteriorating conditions; and that state policies can – at best – only mediate the symptoms of exclusion rather than overcome the structural tendencies that produce marginalization (see box 6.2).

Box 6.2   Mike Davis and *Planet of Slums*

In his controversial 2006 book *Planet of Slums*, radical geographer Mike Davis used the reports of the United Nations Habitat organization about urban poverty to re-open arguments about surplus populations. He argued that the expanding urban cities of the postcolonial world have become a reservoir for a surplus population that is pushed off the land yet has no place in the modern industrial or service sectors. Articulating a worryingly dystopian future, he argues that the expanding urban slums remain the sole 'fully franchised solution to the problem of warehousing the twenty-first century's surplus humanity'.[16]

Breaking Down the Informal Economy

It may seem strange that four such distinct and seemingly opposed explanations for the persistence and impact of the informal economy can exist alongside each other. Part of the reason is that, while they all purport to explain the informal economy at a general level, they often focus on a specific segment of informal activities that they then generalize across the field. Notably, while Hart, the originator of the term, used it in a general sense to designate all unregulated economic activities, he felt immediately compelled to differentiate the informal economy into distinct subsectors, many of which had little relationship to one another. Although they might all be classified as part of the informal economy, there was scant connection between a street musician, a stall selling snack food and a household workshop making furniture. Each appeared to be characterized by very different livelihood dynamics, contrasting power relations and a distinct relationship to other sectors of the economy.

The tools of global labour studies can help us unpack how the informal economy itself is composed of distinct production networks and labour market segments. For example, those emphasizing the burdensome state as a cause of voluntary informality are generally referring to the impact of bureaucracy on medium size informal sector firms. Although such firms are an important part of the informal sector, they are not typical, but occupy a relatively privileged position. The marginalization thesis, in contrast, tends to focus on self-employed workers. While numerically significant, these workers do not encompass the entirety of the informal economy, but occupy an important facet within it. In short, these various explanatory rubrics are best understood not as explanations of the informal economy as a whole, but of specific groups, organizations and labouring relations within it.

So, how can we approach the informal economy in a way that retains an ability to explain why and how various types of informality exist without succumbing to broad overgeneralization? To start with, it is useful to examine the various types of actors and activities that are outside state regulation, with a keen eye to the forms of power and networks that structure their activities. For example, we can break down the informal sector into distinct groupings (see Figure 6.2). At the top end are autonomous, small-scale enterprises that employ workers and use varying degrees of technology. Below this is a second tier of small family-run informal enterprises that tend to employ primarily family labourers drawn through internal networks. Finally, there is the category of 'direct subsistence' which would include categories such as domestic workers and the self-employed in small-scale retail activities. The experience of different actors within the informal sector depends expressly on where and how they are integrated into this structure, and the varied assets – both physical and social – that they can use to shape their livelihood relationships.

Broadly speaking, the further we move down this typology, the fewer the assets and resources that households and individuals have.

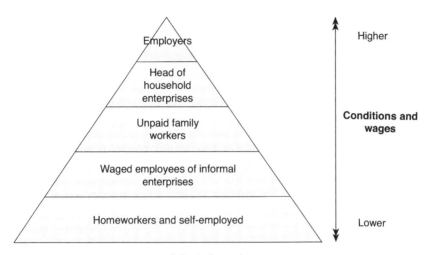

Figure 6.2 Main segments of the informal economy

As a result, they are relatively disempowered and often accept poor conditions of employment provided by others or struggle through self-employment in the most competitive and least rewarding sectors, such as refuse collection or petty street vending. New migrant arrivals from the countryside are often worst placed to negotiate the informal economy, given their often limited resources and tenuous networks by which to access employment within the urban setting (see chapters 7 and 8).

Notably, as we move towards these bottom segments of the informal pyramid, we also find an increasing prevalence of women and girls. This is because many of the most insecure and least rewarding jobs in the informal economy are heavily feminized.[17] For some mainstream economists, female overrepresentation in the informal economy is best seen as a voluntary choice and high rates of female participation reflect desirable characteristics of the sector, such as greater flexibility over hours and places of work. Given the fluctuating demands for labour in the sector, women are believed to more easily balance their roles as wage earners with their reproductive (homecare) labour when they are self-employed in the informal sector. In this sense, economists tend to see women as voluntarily choosing to forgo higher wages for the flexibility over time that informality affords them.[18]

Although voluntary flexibility may account for some experiences, this notion is sharply critiqued by others. For feminist political economists like Naila Kabeer, women find themselves overwhelmingly in the most exploited segments of informal economy because of power relations that strongly segment informal labour markets, pushing women into insecure areas with lower pay.[19] These segments include precarious self-employment tasks, such as itinerant vending and street garbage collection, labour within family-run workshops and street food production, and wage labour in subcontracted industries, such as garments and textiles that can sometimes be outsourced directly into the home itself. In the latter respect, Alessandra Mezzadri has provided a detailed analysis of the networks that link formal textile producers in Delhi with tiers of subcontracting that stretch deep into the households of semi-urban zones across North India. Positions within the network are strongly organized along gender lines, with household firms typically headed by men, while homeworkers are predominantly women. The different tiers of contractors seek to fix those below them into the production chain by advances of credit that tie households and individual producers into a relationship of dependency. In such relationships, those further up the chain have the greatest power to shape the distribution of risks and rewards. Women homeworkers at the bottom end frequently suffer from grave insecurity about the timing, duration and pay for orders. To the extent that they voluntarily choose such precarious employment, this is due to a paucity of options alongside the enduring dependencies that lock them into cycles of homework.[20]

This debate on gender highlights the strong segmentation of informal labour markets. For those at the top ends of the informal economy – small manufacturing and service sector firms employing informal workers – there can be notable market opportunities to exploit, particularly given the relative absence of regulation over practices, wages and working conditions. Operating in a regulatory vacuum, there may be little pressure to provide decent work conditions – hours of work, conditions and safety, minimum wages or security of contract. Power is, therefore, central to determining the quality of livelihoods available. As an informal worker, if an employer decides not to pay you for work already done, there may be little you can do. How can you challenge non-payment for a job that officially never existed in the first place?

While the absence of state regulation is a defining condition of informality, informal economy activities do not take place in an absence of rules or norms to regulate the activities of workers or enterprises. On the contrary, informal institutions frequently govern these activities and provide a structure of expected behaviour and conduct from different activities. They are informal because they are not codified and enforced by the state, but rest on shared expectations and actions among the group or network to self-regulate itself and enforce compliance. In this respect, by providing access to credit, markets,

Box 6.3   Children and youth in the informal economy

In the urban areas of the global South, child labour is disproportionately found within the informal economy, either within household enterprises or outside the family home. In their qualitative study of a young male working in Addis Ababa, the capital city of Ethiopia, Yisak Tafere and Alula Pankhurst note how the 12-year-old boy started washing cars for about thirty minutes after school. By the age of 13, he was washing cars for almost three hours in the evenings, a period that had extended to four hours by the time he was 16. For this child, it was possible to combine informal self-employment in the evenings with full school attendance. Other children were less able to juggle the contrasting needs of household livelihood strategies, missing days of school at a time to take jobs such as working in stores, running messages and working as a taxi or bus attendant. In contrast, girls were expected to focus more on domestic work chores within the household, only later moving into paid informal employment.[21]

training, information and political influence, informal networks can be pivotal tools for individuals and informal firms. At times, they can be supportive – with groups of similarly placed informal vendors of family firms sharing resources in times of need. Often, however, fractures within an expressly competitive environment can undermine solidarity. Kate Meagher, for instance, has shown that strong tensions in Lagos, Nigeria, exist between more established textile and cosmetic informal producers and a large number of tiny household workshops pursuing subsistence activities. These cleavages served to undermine the kinds of collective organizations that may have helped negotiate with state authorities for better support of the sector.[22]

In this respect, the presence of strong networks can consolidate power relations by effectively excluding outsiders and concentrating access to resources among a privileged few. In their study of onion traders in south-eastern Afghanistan, Adam Pain, Giulia Minoia and Wamiqullah Mumtaz showed how close networks between leading traders served to concentrate market power in a small set of hands. These tight networks had the effect of excluding other traders from market space, access to credit, contact with farmers and political influence with public authorities and customs officers. In order to avoid being shut out of the trade altogether, smaller informal traders were either forced to sell away from market centres or compelled to work for the dominant trading networks that closely controlled prices and strongly minimized their gains.[23]

The Politics of Informality

Labour, as we have consistently noted, always has a political dimension. Yet what kind of labour politics can operate in informal economies defined by high levels of disempowerment, segmentation and self-employment? At first glance, the kind of worker politics that is sometimes associated with formal employment such as unionization seems an uncomfortable fit with workers operating on a more individualized level of self-employment, small family workshops and so forth. For many observers, these hindrances to collective labour organization do not mean that the informal economy is without politics. Rather, it means that political action within the informal economy assumes different forms, some of which could be easily missed, such as the occupation and reorganization of urban spaces. For example, building on detailed studies in Cairo, Iranian sociologist Asef Bayat used the term 'quiet encroachment' to describe the silent yet pervasive advancement of the popular masses into the spaces of the formal, propertied and powerful in search of improved livelihoods. From Bayat's reading, the small, everyday movement of informal vendors and enterprises into spaces from which – officially – they should be excluded represents a political challenge that typically happens in a quiet and atomized manner. Through this encroachment, informality pervades urban space and challenges the idealized visions of order, property and modernity that are commonly shared by local elites. Interestingly, in Bayat's account, the quiet encroachment of the ordinary was a political precursor to a more open rebellion that occurred through parts of North Africa and the Middle East in 2011 known as the Arab Spring.[24]

This example has resonance in other geographic settings. The attempt of the Mexican state to formalize vendors in the historical centre of the capital in the early 1990s, for example, met the determined resistance of collective vendor organizations. After a decade of structural adjustment and austerity within Mexico, street vending had become a livelihood option for as many as 200,000 individuals who found few alternative employment opportunities. When the ruling party in Mexico City sought to 'modernize' the streets of the capital in the run-up to the implementation of NAFTA in 1994, it targeted informal vendors as a symbol of an old Mexico that needed to be abolished. A plan to move them off the streets into centralized market locations where they would be licensed and charged for rental space appeared to be a death knell for the more precarious sections of this workforce. A wide variety of informal vendor associations both bargained with and resisted the formalization attempts, seeking to frustrate plans if possible or, at least, bargain for better terms.[25] Not all aspects of such associational networks are beneficial, of course. Some vendor associations have become strongly associated with the power of cliques that operate in a quasi-criminal manner. Notwithstanding, these forms of informal worker organization have kept the ongoing state designs for clearing the streets of vendors in a relative stalemate that persists to the present.[26]

While there are many other examples of both individual and collective action in the informal sector, the purpose of the above examples is to show how power and contestation are very much part of the fabric of informality. Notably, as we examine in chapter 12, there have been some examples of progress in creating informal sector collective organizations, sometimes among the most disempowered sectors of the informal economy such as women refuse scavengers.

Further reading

The literature on the informal economy is vast, but a strong collection of recent writings with both analytical insights and case study material is provided by Supriya Routh and Vando Borghi, *Workers and the Global Informal Economy: Interdisciplinary Perspectives* (London: Routledge, 2016). Deborah Potts offers a very useful critical analysis of the ways in which informality is represented in the policy world in 'The urban informal sector in sub-Saharan Africa: from bad to good (and back again?)', *Development Southern Africa* 25(2), 2012, pp. 151–167. Finally, for a striking visual testimony to the vivid energies and trenchant difficulties facing workers in India's informal economy, see the photographic tour provided by Jan Breman, Arvind Das and Ravi Agarwal in *Down and Out: Labouring Under Global Capitalism* (Oxford: Oxford University Press, 2000).

Chapter 7
Agrarian Labour

¡Bienvenidos a la Republica Unida de la Soja!
Welcome to the United Republic of Soy!

Although it occupies a landmass larger than California, the United Republic of Soy is one Latin American country you may never have heard of. As you could guess from its name, it is famous for one thing: it produces the majority of the world's soybeans. Such a specialization might seem banal at first glance, but this would be to miss how soy has become one of the world's ultimate 'flex crops', with uses that stretch far beyond immediate human consumption. The oil derived from pressing soy, for instance, is widely used for both biodiesel and in the packaged food industry, while the primary purpose of the bean itself is animal feed. On this basis, the Republic of Soy exports heavily to the United States, Europe and China, where the crop is used to sustain the huge amounts of pigs necessary to satisfy our increasingly meat-centric diets. Without any sense of exaggeration, the multi-functionality of soy places the United Republic at the heart of the global economy.

The United Republic of Soy, of course, isn't a real country. It's the nickname used for an agricultural zone that extends across a vast swathe of South America's pampas. It cuts across the plains of southern Brazil, Paraguay and Bolivia, before rolling outwards through Uruguay and extending deep into Argentina. Here we find modern industrial agriculture at its height. Across massive farms that measure in hundreds of hectares, the fields are neatly standardized into seemingly endless rows of genetically modified soy plants. Giant farm machines roll through this landscape, spraying herbicides and undertaking both planting and harvesting functions that are fully mechanized. Most of these plants will never be touched by a human hand and, as a result, the United Republic of Soy is a landscape curiously devoid of people. Many smaller farmers have simply sold or rented their farms to the large soy producers, moving out of direct agriculture into paid employment in towns or cities.[1]

The contrast with the fields of south Asia and sub-Saharan Africa is marked. In the latter, agriculture tends to be heavily labour-intensive, largely undertaken by smallholder farmers who work the land exhaustively to grow crops for both subsistence and for sale. Fields the size of just two acres might be farmed by a family who may well supplement their agricultural activities with paid labour on other fields or in the local towns. In these cases, agriculture displays something of its original meaning of *agri + cultura*, the mix of farming and culture understood as a way of life and livelihood where humans work busily alongside nature to produce plants and animals.[2] At the same time, rural areas of Africa and South Asia are often designated as focal points of intense poverty, with 70 per cent of the world's extreme poor residing in such rural regions. Paradoxically, high rates of hunger and malnutrition are found among those working within the agricultural economy.

For some analysts, this extent of rural poverty indicates a failure of agricultural modernization. It implicates the absence of advanced technologies, efficient production techniques, improved varieties of crops and chemical inputs such as pesticides and fertilizers. This perspective would view the United Republic of Soy as a model for global agricultural development – a triumph of progress and productivity that mimics the trajectory of countries in Europe and North America where labour moved out of agriculture into the towns and cities. Others, in contrast, see the problem of rural poverty not so much as a lack of modernity, but as an expression of the adverse integration of agricultural workers into an international market order. They blame the subordination of agriculture to industry and the presence of deeply ingrained inequalities across rural areas for reproducing poverty and malnutrition deep within the belly of world food production. In this vein, international organizations such as the peasant movement La Via Campesina emphasize not integration with global production networks – often headed by powerful supermarket chains – but peasant self-sufficiency aided by a more equitable distribution of land, water and other critical resources.

How might we begin to make sense of these conflicting accounts of agricultural labour and livelihoods and the visions of progress and development that stand behind them? The tools provided by global labour studies provide a good entry point because they offer a way to analyse how agricultural labour takes shape differently across regions and scales. We can use our focus on power and networks to ask who has access to key productive assets within rural areas, including land, water, labourers, seeds, knowledge and so forth, which are critical components of successful livelihood strategies. This allows us to consider not only how and why agricultural intensification makes agriculture less labour-intensive, but also who benefits most from such transformations. To engage these questions, let us start our investigation not in the fields of the global South, but in the heartland of the world's largest agricultural producer by volume: the United States of America. Here we encounter a paradigmatic case of what's known as agricultural intensification.

Agricultural Modernization and the Intensification Imperative

If Thomas Jefferson were to look out over the agricultural panorama of the United States today, some two centuries after becoming the nation's third president, he would probably be rather disturbed. Jefferson had argued passionately that the foundation for a strong, democratic country lay in its agricultural economy, one that he saw most vitally founded in a robust class of family farmers rooted in the ownership of their own land. At present, however, the kind of family farm that Jefferson envisaged at the heart of American democracy is on life support. As the US Department of Agriculture reports, there has been a doubling of farm size across all the states over the past twenty-five years, with both land and production increasingly concentrated away from small and mid-size farms to larger, corporate entities.[3]

As a result, there is considerable polarization within US agriculture. At one end, the largest farms account for just 5.6 per cent of total farms but cultivate over half of all cropland. Although they may once have originated as family farms, these are now corporate firms that use economies of scale to produce bulk commodities for vast supply chains led primarily by supermarkets and large retailers. Given the competitive imperatives of such agricultural production networks, operating at a large scale using hired labour is a prerequisite for profitability. This has driven such farms to grow bigger in size. At the other end of the spectrum, the United States has recently seen a resurgence of very small micro-farms that are great in number yet occupy only 4 per cent of total cultivated cropland. These tiny farms typically focus on niche markets, such as the organic sector, and agriculture forms only a small or seasonal part of the income streams for families that pursue these livelihoods.

Between these two poles there is a widening gap precisely where we might expect to encounter Jefferson's social class of landholding family farms. Despite once forming the bedrock of American farming, the middle ground has been hollowed out. So why did this happen to Jefferson's agrarian ideal and why have the landscapes of agricultural labour changed so much? One place to start would be in the heart of the American Midwest in the century after Jefferson. By the mid-1800s the kind of small farmers that Jefferson valued had spread westwards, taking cattle and cereals with them out into the prairie grasslands. Many of these settlers were immigrants of European origin, often having been pushed out of agriculture in their home-lands and now seeking new lives in the Americas. Under this migra-tory movement, a frontier economy emerged that enclosed the rolling grasslands into parcels of private property, putting fences where once bison had roamed and using steel ploughs to cut through the thick native grasses to access the fertile soil below. The bison were all but exterminated from these lands and the original indigenous occupants suffered a brutal societal collapse as the military force of the state backed settler control over prairie land. Through this westward expansion of the agricultural frontier, both the social and geographic environment of the prairies was forever changed.

As vividly described by historian William Cronon, cities such as Chicago soon became hubs that facilitated the movement of large amounts of wheat, meat and corn eastwards to urban America and beyond.[4] Accelerated by the westward spread of the railways and coordinated by a large network of merchants and financiers, the American Midwest became tightly bound into agricultural markets that were increasingly global in scope. With telegraphs rapidly relay-ing the shifting prices of crops between distant markets, financial centres and local merchants, farmers soon began to dance to the rhythm of world grain prices. Price rises for wheat or beef offered the possibilities of increased profits, as when wars broke out in Europe. Collapses, in contrast, could spark destitution.

Although this integration proceeded apace, agriculture in the United States at the turn of the twentieth century was still undertaken primarily on small and medium farms. Change, however, was already being felt across the prairies. To safeguard themselves against price shifts, farms typically sought to increase their production volumes by investing in new technologies. In the early 1900s tractors became an increasingly common sight in the American Midwest, and by the

1920s threshers began to populate the landscape. This mechanization of agriculture had two pivotal effects. First, it tended to directly displace labour from agricultural production as one person using a tractor can do the work of several using hand or animal-drawn tools. Second, technological investments favoured larger farms, which could make efficient use of machines in large continuous fields that were devoted to a single crop – a practice known as monocropping.

As a result, competitive mechanization signalled the beginning of the end for many small farms. Unable to afford investments in new technology, small farms struggled to compete with larger farms which enjoyed economies of scale and had better linkages to markets. Intensification therefore had a double impact: it produced greater amounts of food, but also an increasing surplus of workers and small farmers ejected from agriculture. On the one hand, growing yields energized some parts of the rural economy and helped reduce food prices in urban areas. Simultaneously, former rural workers arriving in urban areas also provided a significant boost to industrialization (see chapter 5). On the other hand, the growth of agricultural productivity had a boomerang effect upon those growing the crops. A greater volume of output led to falling prices for agricultural produce, which immediately tightened the operating margins of farms and provided a brand-new impetus to intensify further. As if on a treadmill, farmers found themselves needing to run faster just to stand still.

Predictably, those with fewest assets and networks – such as smallholders in the American South who were the descendants of freed slaves – were often the first to lose out and the decades between the two world wars were characterized by a torrent of migration out of southern agriculture towards the industrial cities of the north and east.[5] At a national level, in the twenty years between 1939 and 1959, the number of farms fell by 40 per cent under a consolidation of land ownership in which the average farm size increased year over year. While small farms were the first to fold, over the subsequent decades it has been mid-size farms that have found it ever harder to compete on cost terms with the industrially organized large farms. 'Get big or get out', was a quote memorably uttered in 1973 by US Secretary of Agriculture Earl Butz, and this logic continues to prevail. Jefferson's dream of rural America was withering away at an increasingly rapid pace, hastened by a system of federal subsidies – some $20 billion a year – that are mostly directed to large-scale, rich farmers cultivating staple commodities such as corn and soya in the Midwest.[6]

The perverse structure of agricultural subsidies notwithstanding, one might logically ask here why anyone would question this trend of farm concentration if it leads to increased productivity and cheaper food? After all, contemporary US grain producers operate with yields of double the world average and some five times greater than producers in parts of southern Africa.[7] One immediate counterargument focuses on the premise of sustainability. Contemporary advocates of Jefferson's vision argue that smaller and diversified farms promote better stewardship of the land, which means that they are more ecologically sound than their industrial counterparts.[8] Smaller farms, they point out, tend to be relatively diverse, cultivating a range of crops and animals in an integrated approach. Today's large corporate farms, in contrast, tend to be highly specialized monocultures that use extensive mechanization and rely upon the heavy application of synthetic fertilizers to circumvent the kind of soil exhaustion that underscored the 1920s 'dust bowl' in the Midwest. At the same time, systematic monocropping has the uncanny effect of exacerbating pest problems by eliminating natural pest controls and biodiversity, requiring the concentrated use of chemical pesticides. Cumulatively, the intensification imperative has created a form of petro-farming, which sustains itself through the extensive use of diesel-powered machinery coupled to an array of synthetic inputs. These trends raise significant issues concerning (1) toxification through the leakage of fertilizers and pesticides into the wider environment; (2) soil erosion, in which vital topsoil washes off the land at a pace that is unsustainable; and (3) climate change, owing to the petroleum-based nature of modern farming in which an increasing amount of energy drawn from non-renewable oil-based inputs is used to produce mass quantities of food.[9]

A second counterargument raised against intensification focuses on labour. If intensification has largely displaced labour from the arable fields of the Midwest, other sectors of US agriculture retain significant labour-intensive elements for specific seasons and tasks. Within much vegetable and fruit production, for instance, manual planting, weeding and harvesting remain the norm. In these sectors, we encounter a mismatch between the seasonal rhythms of agricultural labour and the reluctance of corporate farming enterprises to commit to maintaining a permanent workforce outside these peak periods. Creating a labour regime composed of workforces that can be pulled into production as needed and discarded at other times has therefore proved pivotal to the profitability of industrial farming in these sectors. As a result, in the United States and Canada, the vegetable and fruit produce sector as a whole has become increasingly dependent on contract labour and, more specifically, on the use of temporary migrant labourers.

For farmers, the advantages of such a labour regime are many. Migrants from Mexico, Central America and the Caribbean often have excellent agricultural skills and their precarious situation frequently

Box 7.1   Industrial meat production and the 'ecological hoofprint'

If a suitably reanimated Thomas Jefferson were to tour the countryside of his home state of Virginia, he would probably be shocked to find it dominated by poultry and beef producers operating on a vast scale. This industrial model of meat production represents the pinnacle of intensification trends. First, there is massive concentration in the sector, with just 8,000 mega-farms responsible for 87 per cent of all pigs sold in the United States. Second, it produces volumes of meat on a staggering industrial scale. Across the United States, more chickens are currently killed in a single day than in an entire year in the 1920s. And third, it dominates other parts of the agricultural economy that are drawn into its production networks. Huge volumes of cereals and soy are now directed specifically for animal feed within factory farms.

The rise of industrial meat production reflects the increasing 'meatification' of our diets in the West, which raises major questions about both animal welfare and environmental sustainability. Industrial meat production is ruthlessly efficient at producing and killing animals to generate enormous quantities of cheap meat. At the same time, however, it also externalizes its major environmental costs. Not only is it extremely energy-inefficient to raise livestock as compared to growing crops for direct consumption, factory farms also produce massive amounts of local pollution, drain considerable water resources and contribute huge amounts of methane, which is a potent contributor to climate change. This phenomenon is not limited to the United States but is a global concern. The United Republic of Soy, as you'll remember, has created immense monocultures across Latin America's southern cone with a primary purpose of producing animal feed to sustain industrial meat production across Europe, China and North America. In the provocative term of geographer Tony Weis, this can be considered the 'ecological hoofprint' of mass meat production.[10]

puts strong pressure on them to comply with long hours, arduous work, low wages and poor conditions. The US government estimates that around half of America's two to three million crop workers are undocumented migrants, a figure that others suggest is woefully underestimated because it relies on data drawn from a self-reporting survey. What is certain is that the profitability of this sector relies explicitly on this low-cost labour force to fill jobs that are unattractive to US citizens because of low pay, limited benefits and difficult work conditions. Notably, such poor conditions exist in part because agricultural labourers have been historically excluded from federal regulations over the right to organize collectively and encounter

Box 7.2   Migrant labourers in Canadian agriculture

While the US agricultural sector relies heavily on undocumented migrants to cover labour intensive tasks, north of the border the Canadian government has promoted a more formalized system of agricultural migration called the Seasonal Agricultural Workers Programme (SAWP). The SAWP is often presented as a model programme for migrant agricultural labour, and there is no doubt that many Mexican agricultural labourers are expressly keen to secure a position on the programme. Applicants are overwhelmingly men between the ages of 19 and 40 who have agricultural experience, yet see little prospect of an agricultural livelihood in Mexico since liberalization opened the market up to large and subsidized American producers. The SAWP therefore appears as an opportunity to earn wages higher than are available in Mexican agriculture or the urban informal sector.

Despite its formalization, however, there remain enduring power relations running through the SAWP. Labourers are sent to a specific employer for the duration of their migration to Canada and have no ability to shift jobs. The employer scrutinizes their work performance, and a failure to live up to expected standards either in the fields or in personal comportment can lead to dismissal and deportation. Moreover, to be readmitted to the programme the following year, workers need to have their Canadian employer certify that they have been good and able labourers. This creates a major disciplinary effect in which the employer has the power to effectively preclude a worker at the tick of a box. There is little wonder, therefore, that employers frequently note the reliability and 'desire to please' of their migrant workers. As a number of case studies have shown, such a dependent workforce has little ability to exercise any contractual right to refuse dangerous work or overtime requests.[11]

deliberately lax regulation about pay rates in agricultural occupations, specifically regarding the imposition of overtime. Agricultural labour, therefore, has persistently remained only partially formalized, and the use of temporary migrants is the culmination of this long-standing trend (see box 7.2).

Exporting Intensification: The Green Revolution and Peasant Agriculture

So, if the direction of US agriculture has been to 'get big or get out', with a resulting dramatic decrease of agricultural employment, what has happened elsewhere? Has labour equally been pushed out of agriculture into other pursuits? The answer is complicated. Certainly, as the United Republic of Soy example demonstrates, there are cases in Latin America that resemble the US trajectory of increasing farm sizes, growing mechanization and the resulting destruction of smallholders as a social class. This is far from universal, however. Elsewhere in Latin America there is a strong and persistent backbone of smallholder farming that works its way up the continent through the Andes of Bolivia, Peru, Ecuador and Colombia, across Central America and into Mexico. Certainly, there are large farms in these regions, including a sizeable plantation sector. In Peru, for example, around 87 per cent of land is owned by just 5.5 per cent of the population, mostly large-scale industrial farmers cultivating commercial crops.[12] Yet smallholders persist, particularly in the highland regions, and make up the vast majority of farms despite their small size. At a global level, the figures are striking. There are estimated to be around 500 million smallholder farms worldwide, occupying around 60 per cent of arable land and providing livelihoods for more than 2 billion people. Smallholders are therefore the majority of the world's farmers, and estimates suggest they produce somewhere between two-thirds and four-fifths of the food consumed in the developing world.[13]

It is this preserve that helps account for why one-third of the global workforce still remains in agriculture. A pivotal question is whether these smallholders are simply a legacy of the old peasantries that will disappear over coming decades. Certainly, many international development organizations view them as a mass of workers that could be more efficiently deployed elsewhere once agricultural modernization takes sway. In this respect, the goal of agricultural intensification has indeed been heavily promoted throughout the global South. From the 1960s onwards, both the US government and international development institutions such as the World Bank sought to proactively diffuse what are commonly known as Green Revolution technologies across postcolonial regions. This approach to modernizing agriculture involved three chief components based on the US experience. First, it pivoted on the use of high-yield variety (HYV) seeds produced by scientists who interbred existing plant types to develop hybrids that would be stronger and more productive. Second, these HYV seeds were to be combined with the widespread use of synthetic fertilizers and pesticides to lock in their potential to deliver higher yields. Finally, a broader technological upgrading of agriculture was seen as a third pillar of the model wherein mechanization and more advanced irrigation could facilitate the economies of scale that would accentuate aggregate yields still further.

For proponents of agricultural modernization, this shedding of labour from agriculture provides a route towards decreased hunger and greater prosperity. The improved productivity of agriculture, it was argued, not only creates greater food supplies, but also energizes other sectors of the economy, creating a more rational division of labour that benefits the entire population through lower prices and new employment opportunities. In short, agricultural modernization was seen as a motor of development: transferring labour out of low-productivity agriculture into the cities where it might be more efficiently employed. At the same time – and in the context of massive rural unrest across Asia, Africa and Latin America – its backers held onto the idea that the technologically driven modernization of rural regions would undercut the threat of communist revolutions driven by a marginalized peasantry.

The impacts of the Green Revolution, however, remain hotly contested. In Pakistan, for example, strategies to boost agricultural productivity were widely coveted by the post-independence governments in the 1950s onwards and they enthusiastically embraced US aid in the 1960s that pivoted on Green Revolution technologies. The benefits of increased yields, it was expected, would energize the entire structure of the rural economy, providing trickle-down benefits to all social groups. As the Pakistani sociologist Akmal Hussain concluded, the Green Revolution was attractive to policymakers because it seemed to offer the possibility of accelerating agricultural growth without making deliberate changes to the rural power structure through land reforms or other redistributory policies.[14] Major yield increases in both wheat and rice harvests planted using HYV seeds appeared to confirm the virtues of the Green Revolution. Norman Borlaug, one of the principal protagonists of the new methods, wrote triumphantly from Lahore in 1968 stating that Pakistani farmers were discarding their traditional ways and accepting the new. Scarcity, he reasoned, had been displaced by abundance and enthusiasm was banishing despair.[15]

While the Green Revolution indeed delivered many of the productivity increases its advocates celebrated, both the positive and negative impacts were far from evenly spread. Within the labour-intensive agriculture that preceded the Green Revolution, small farms enjoyed a yield advantage over larger landholdings precisely because they could capitalize on their intensive labour. The new technology, however, shifted the balance in favour of economies of scale. In so doing, it created new forms of social polarization. Large landholders found themselves well placed to monopolize the benefits of technological change owing to their superior access to credit, land and, above all, their superior access to irrigation. As a result, the new technologies explicitly favoured what were termed 'elite farmers' with sufficient land, knowledge, power and networks to receive and apply the new technologies. For these farmers, a shift to HYV used in combination with chemical fertilizers and pesticides facilitated significant yield gains.

The impact on smallholders and rural labour, however, was far less certain. With land becoming profitable through the Green Revolution technologies, many landlords evicted their tenants from good-quality land in order to farm it themselves, resulting in a growing pool of landless or land-poor labourers seeking work precisely when mechanization was lowering demand for hired labour. Growing rural poverty therefore accompanied the introduction of Green Revolution techniques, and its advocates were caught by surprise when record yields were accompanied by an escalation of rural violence in which marginalized groups rallied against the impacts of rural social disloca-tion. Notably, the trend of growing poverty in Pakistan was only alle-viated in the late 1970s and 1980s through remittances from migrants to urban areas and the Gulf States alongside a modest attempt at land reform. Despite being a heartland of Green Revolution techniques, rural Pakistan also remains an epicentre of malnutrition, precisely because producing more food is not the same as providing equitable access to food.[16]

Rural Livelihoods and Global Integration

Notwithstanding its uneven impacts, the emphasis on agricultural intensification has remained a consistent focus of both international institutions and national states to the present. Promoting intensifi-cation is argued to be particularly relevant for many sub-Saharan African countries where the original Green Revolution was not heavily promoted. For organizations such as the World Bank, the key to generalizing the benefits is to better integrate smallholders into global agro-food production chains so as to deepen the com-mercialization of agriculture, facilitate better market opportunities for producers and allow them to access new investment and technolo-gies. It is specifically by linking smallholders into global production networks headed by Western companies and by generalizing the use of chemical fertilizers, pesticides and new varieties of seeds that the World Bank envisages smallholders harnessing the benefits of productivity increases that passed them by.[17] As you might expect, this process will inevitably see agriculture shed a large part of its workforce. For agencies such as the World Bank, this is a necessary and positive occurrence. The ensuing efficiency gains stemming from increased agricultural productivity are projected to facilitate a wider improvement of rural regions in which off-farm employment can expand to absorb workers released from unproductive smallholder farms. A new version of the US model of agricultural modernization, they expect, can be rolled out worldwide.[18]

Despite this projected win–win scenario, many smallholders are often reluctant to sever their ties to the land. Instead they frequently seek to pursue livelihood strategies that allow them to transfer funds from alternative employment back into agricultural production. In the World Bank's terms, such reluctance to move out of agriculture reflects a 'deep inertia in people's occupational transformation' that is ultimately a blockage to modernization.[19] In practice, however, things may be considerably more complex. Far from being irra-tionally attached to rural lifestyles, smallholders are acutely aware of the difficulties of exiting agriculture and the limited livelihood opportunities that may wait in urban informal sectors. As discussed in chapter 3, the ability to successfully enter a new labour regime is strongly shaped by the accumulated assets, networks and other sources of power that allow individuals or households to exercise a stronger control over their own circumstances. Those forced out of agriculture, however, generally leave on adverse terms and must often seek employment in unpredictable labour markets with limited assets, skills and networks. They are at risk of working in conditions that can reinforce vulnerability and poverty, including the possibility of forced labour (see chapter 9). In this respect, maintaining a foothold in agriculture while having varied household members seek income streams from other activities – often through regional or international migration – frequently seems a more risk-averse livelihood strategy.

Such outcomes tend to lead to a fragmentation of rural social structures, or what geographer Jonathan Rigg has termed a process of de-agrarianization, in which agriculture forms only one part of the livelihood strategy of rural households.[20] Take, for example, the kinds of rural households encountered in the semi-arid region of Telangana, southern India. Many households retain several acres of land with which they do a variety of things. They may set aside an acre or so for subsistence rice production, providing an essential foundation to household food security. Another part of the land might be used for producing vegetables, chillies, cotton or corn for regional markets, and a final part might be used to grow hybrid seeds under direct con-tract to a company in the local town. Some household members – and particularly women – will also perform waged labour for local land-owners at busy times of the planting or harvesting season. Some may travel to urban centres to work in the informal sector or household service, cleaning, cooking and so forth for the middle and upper classes. In short, these households diversify their income streams so as to ensure that some opportunities remain open even if others collapse. A drought that strongly affects local irrigation water, for example, might strongly decrease the returns to agriculture, so alternative means of pursuing livelihoods is of paramount importance.[21]

Dealing with such risks is not easy for smallholder households because it often places them in the condition of needing the support of other, more powerful social actors. In order to purchase the inputs necessary for agricultural production at the beginning of the season – seeds, fertilizers, pesticides and so forth – they often buy on credit from established merchants in local towns. The interest rates are high, but come with a proviso: smallholders can sell their crop directly to the merchants at the end of the season at a below market rate in order to receive a small discount on the loan interest. These kind of 'tied' relationships allow merchants who monopolize access to credit and inputs to profit from the smallholders' labour. In a similar way, labour contractors offer households payment up front at the beginning of the season in return for the labour of a household member for the duration of the season, whether it be in agricultural labour, mining, brick making or construction work. These lopsided agreements, in which smallholders become dependent upon more powerful social agents, approximate what in chapter 9 we describe as forced labour. Such are the realities of power and risk in small-holder agriculture, and it should be closely noted that women often bear the brunt of the hardest tasks and risks in both the home and the fields.[22]

The Contrasting Politics of Agrarian Change

Given the extremely uneven impacts of contemporary agrarian change, it is not surprising that it has given birth to a diverse range of local, national and international social movements that contest present trends.[23] One particularly noted example is the Brazilian Landless Workers Movement (*Movimento dos Trabalhadores Rurais Sem Terra*), or MST as it is typically known. Founded in 1984, the MST has sought consistently to challenge the heavy concentration of land ownership and the increasing mechanization of Brazilian agriculture, which displaced both workers and small peasants from the land. This brings us back full circle to the United Republic of Soy with which we started the chapter. For the MST, the expansion of the labour-displacing production techniques into areas formerly worked by labour-intensive smallholders represents an intractable political problem. Here, the clash between agricultural intensification could not be sharper. For the MST, soy-driven growth is a strategy that puts profits and productivity above rural livelihoods, promoting the growth of feed for animals in distant lands over food for Brazil's large food insecure population.

In terms of political tactics, the MST argues that the large inequities of land ownership in Brazil within and beyond the soy zone are best challenged by a combination of pressuring the formal political system alongside the direct occupation of land. Its strategy has been to find unused parts of plantations or large farms and support a process of occupation, settlement and cultivation. When government agencies get involved, the MST supports a process of negotiation aimed at securing land rights for the occupiers. Its first land seizure was in 1985, and, despite often brutal violence perpetrated against its members, this tactic of 'occupy, resist, produce' has enabled it to become one of the most dynamic and well-organized social movements in Brazilian history.

Notwithstanding its rapid growth, the MST is a complex organization with varied constituents, including landless labourers, marginal peasants and former plantation workers. As a consequence, various political ideologies circulate within the MST that coalesce sometimes uneasily around its central claim for land. In response, the MST seeks to maintain vibrant networks to tie local movements into its broader structure. Its activists travel widely between regional offices and local settlements to share information and discuss political strategies. These are then spread within the locality through informal networks operating across contexts as diverse as classrooms and soccer games.[24] At the same time, the movement has attempted to broaden its linkages beyond rural zones. To do this, the MST has portrayed the struggle over land as intimately connected to improving the lives of the lower classes living in cities by emphasizing that smallholder agriculture is better able to provide healthy food at affordable prices, while simultaneously slowing the pace of rural–urban migration.

If the example of the MST shows a struggle for land from below, there is a contrasting trend: the process of land accumulation by foreign investors – either purchased or leased – with the intention of producing food, animal feed, biofuels, timber or minerals for export. Such deals – termed 'land grabs' by critics – have been escalating since the early 2000s, with many estimates suggesting that at least 50 million hectares worldwide have changed hands.[25] The journalist John Vidal highlighted the tensions of this process in Ethiopia, focusing on 1,000 hectares leased by the government for ninety-nine years to a Saudi billionaire businessman. At the heart of this land is a twenty-hectare complex of giant greenhouses that produce market vegetables in computer-controlled conditions. Some 1,000 Ethiopian female agricultural labourers pick and pack a daily amount of fifty tonnes of tomatoes, peppers and other vegetables to be transported to destinations such as Dubai and other parts of the Gulf. As Vidal reports, this is simply the first leg of an estimated $2 billion plan to acquire and develop 500,000 hectares of land in Ethiopia primarily to produce food for the Saudi market.[26]

The paradox of growing food for export on fertile land in a food-insecure country is not lost on critics. They argue that while government officials receive kickbacks from these deals, local populations often forcibly lose access to land for cropping and grazing while water sources are similarly diverted for export agriculture. With insecure property rights and limited political power to challenge these processes, the potential for significant human rights abuses is high. The government, however, insists that these leases are of great benefit because investment will create jobs, increase labour productivity, transfer modern agricultural knowledge and techniques, and reduce both poverty and the country's chronic food insecurity. The transfer of land, it argues, presents merely a short cut to agricultural modernization that will benefit all Ethiopians, particularly as 40 per cent of the produced food is earmarked for sale within Ethiopia. The issue is far from settled, however, with The Oakland Institute, a California-based NGO, providing a detailed account of forcible displacements and the use of state violence in implementing these projects.[27]

The Futures of Agrarian Labour

Although working the land may be the original occupation for humans, it is one that currently seems profoundly uncertain, with a steadily declining percentage of the global workforce involved in agricultural work. Intensification – carried to its logical extreme – involves the global propagation of an increasingly mechanized, large-scale and input-intensive agriculture. Notably, agricultural technology corporations are currently envisaging entirely automated farms (see box 7.3). At the same time, one of the central tensions underlying this process is that the intensification of agriculture doesn't just produce an increasing amount of food; it also produces workers cast out of agriculture. Whether the projected gains in efficiency through agricultural modernization can provide employment opportunities for this population is an open question, particularly given the lack of assets and networks held by many rural households. This ties into the question of the expansion of urban informality (chapter 6) and various forms of migration, which we examine in the next chapter.

Such issues become more acute given the environmental contradictions of agriculture's present trajectory noted above. Despite an unshakeable faith in the virtues of agricultural intensification, institutions such as the World Bank and the Food and Agricultural Organization (FAO) have recently betrayed increasing concerns about the trajectory of the current food system. Given the projections of continued population growth, a declining rate of agricultural productivity growth and the escalating impacts of climate change, these organizations argue that humanity might well quite simply struggle to put enough food on the plates of a projected nine billion increasingly urbanized people by 2050.[28] Such fears have a visceral precedent. In 2007, spiralling food prices prompted protests among marginal classes in urban areas in many parts of the global South, including in Burkina Faso, Côte d'Ivoire, Haiti, Senegal and Yemen. Given the longstanding connections between sudden urban food insecurity and political violence, this trend rattled policymakers. UN General Secretary Ban Ki-moon pronounced that rising food prices 'could have grave implications for international security, economic growth and social progress', while the managing director of the World Bank, Robert Zoellick, talked of the world entering a 'danger zone'.[29]

International institutions are justified in their profound unease. With half the world's calorie intake derived from just three crops – rice, wheat and maize – commodity prices are like a finger on the pulse of global capitalism. Currently, the prices of key staples remain historically high and the implications of this rise are important given their fundamental role in the social reproduction of the urban working classes, particularly those who are most tenuous and often located in the informal economy. For international institutions, the solution is a movement towards 'sustainable intensification', a loosely formulated notion that seeks to combine productivity growth with a more benign set of environmental impacts.[30] For many transnational agrarian movements, the only solution is a pronounced transformation of agriculture that can revalidate more ecologically sound smallholders and ensure a more equitable distribution of the ample food that we currently produce. We return to this question in chapter 10. First,

Box 7.3 Automation and the future of farming?

It may not have made front-page headlines, but in February 2016 a Japanese vegetable company announced that it was opening the world's first fully automated farm near Kyoto, complete with industrial robots to carry out all but one of the tasks needed in the daily cultivation of tens of thousands of lettuces. Japan is characterized by a declining labour force and the government has largely blocked the entrance of migrant workers that would typically undertake this kind of agricultural labour in North America or Europe. Nonetheless, automation represents perhaps the ultimate culmination of the logics of intensification and mechanization that have been at work for several centuries. In the United States, major agricultural input companies such as Monsanto are betting heavily on the automation of cereal farming: producing drones to survey crops, satellites to drive tractors and remote sensing devices to guide the application of fertilizers and pesticides. Under such scenarios, remote computers could feasibly make all the pivotal decisions about planting, harvesting and so forth. For the companies involved, this is argued to be a necessary develop-ment for promoting a new wave of agricultural intensification. For critics, however, it marks an acute escalation of the tension between efficiency and employment, and may represent the final nail in the coffin of rural life.[31]

however, we delve deeper into the question of migration that is so central to both agrarian regions and changing urban labour regimes.

Further reading

In *Class Dynamics of Agrarian Change* (Halifax and Winnipeg: Fernwood Press, 2010), Henry Bernstein provides a succinct intro-duction to agrarian political economy. An excellent overview of agri-cultural labour and tensions in the contemporary global food system can be found in Haroon Akram-Lodhi's *Hungry for Change* (Halifax and Winnipeg: Fernwood Press, 2013). The question of 'land grabs' is dissected by a range of authors in the collection *Global Land Grabs: History, Theory and Method* (London: Routledge, 2014), edited by Marc Edelman, Carlos Oya and Saturnino Borras, Jr. Finally, a probing collection of essays on the United Republic of Soy can be found in the special issue of the *Journal of Agrarian Change*, 16(4), 2016.

Chapter 8
Migrant Labour

Labour moves! Both historically and in the present, large-scale movements of people have rewritten the human tapestry of the global economy, giving dynamism to new structures of production and consumption and reshaping livelihoods on a global scale. From economic migrants seeking a better life and greater economic opportunities to temporary migrant workers looking to contribute financially to their household through remittances, the relentless movement of people in search of work remains a defining feature of the contemporary age. In both sending and receiving countries, migratory flows transform labour market dynamics, economic structures and development trajectories. At times, the act of migration appears to open significant opportunities as migrants relocate to spaces where job opportunities may be more plentiful or better paid. Yet most migratory experiences are full of uncertainty and risks. While some workers migrate by choice in the deliberate pursuit of opportunity, many more are extremely reluctant to leave established homes, family and friends, all of which provide a degree of stability and security. As a result, the urge to migrate is often situated in the middle ground between a drive to take advantage of new opportunities and as a reaction to coercive socioeconomic constraints.

To understand this complexity, our focus on power, networks, space and livelihoods provides useful tools to help us unpack the forces that shape migrant trajectories. They provide ways to open up questions of why some migratory experiences offer opportunities, while others create new forms of precarious labour. Such unevenness, as we chart below, is driven in part by the complexity of how households plan their livelihood strategies by using social networks to provide much

Box 8.1   The symbolic power of migration

Browsing the BBC news website to get a morning fix of current affairs, two lead articles appeared strangely juxtaposed. On the left was the headline 'EU leaders to ratify migrant quotas' superimposed over a dramatic photo of a group of migrants landing a small boat on a beach. Directly next to this was an article with an alluring cityscape photographic background entitled 'The best places in the world to be an expat'. On clicking the latter link, we encountered an interactive map with clickable cities that showed the places where 'expats' had the highest average incomes and quality of life. There is an immediately striking contrast here. While both articles are referring to groups of people who move across borders to take up work, the language used to describe them is sharply divergent. Who counts as a migrant and who gets to be an expat? Only certain groups of people stemming from certain countries are able to claim the 'expat' tag, as the term symbolically marks out a difference between those migrating in conditions of relative affluence and power, and the rest.

needed resources, information and assistance to facilitate migratory patterns. Alongside this emphasis on migrant agency, however, we cannot ignore the bigger picture of strong structural constraints upon migrant trajectories. While labour moves, migration typically remains heavily controlled. States strongly limit the movement of people across borders and often have elaborate criteria for distinguishing between wanted and unwanted migrants based on skills, training, wealth and country of origin. Such migration controls, therefore, typically reinforce the creation of segmented labour markets and the production of specific migrant labour regimes in receiving regions. As we explain below, this means that different strata of migrants experience very different outcomes, and that migratory flows remain deeply rooted within the power relations constitutive of the global economy.

Understanding Labour Migration

A migrant worker, in the words of the United Nations, can be defined as 'a person who is to be engaged, is engaged or has been engaged in a remunerated activity in a state of which he or she is not a national'.[1] While providing a useful entry point, this definition is limited because much labour migration is not international in character but occurs within the borders of a given state. According to the 2015 World

Migration Report, there are some 740 million internal migrants in the world, outnumbering international migrants by around three to one.[2] Many of these internal migrants are agricultural workers or smallholders who are pushed out of agriculture and move temporarily or permanently to cities (see chapter 7). For some, internal migration is circular – a temporary yet frequent move into other urban or rural regions to take advantage of seasonal work opportunities. For others, it can become permanent, particularly if existing rural livelihoods have become unviable or if the opportunities for employment and availability of other services in cities make return impractical.

The distinction between internal and international migration can also be blurred in cases where there are porous and shifting borders. This is especially prominent in former colonial areas where political borders do not fit people's lived realities and sense of place and space. In southern Africa, for example, the movement of workers across permeable borders between Lesotho, Angola, Zimbabwe and Mozambique into South Africa is both longstanding and circular. Such workers form an important part of key labour market segments in South Africa, from mining to agricultural labour, and move seasonally between rural areas and cities on both sides of the border. This fluidity, however, can come with a price. Despite their porosity, crossing borders without official papers places migrants in a condition of vulnerability vis-à-vis both employers and officials. This typically relegates them to restricted labour market segments in which they have little power to shape their working conditions and are highly vulnerable to forms of exploitation including exposure to dirty, degrading or hazardous work.[3]

Given the intrinsic uncertainties involved in migration, any decision to migrate is never taken lightly. How, then, should we understand the forces driving migration that make it so central to the global economy? Geographer and cartographer Ernst Georg Ravenstein is usually considered the earliest migration theorist. Working from British censuses during the last quarter of the nineteenth century, Ravenstein identified a series of general propositions, or 'laws of migration', seeking to capture migration patterns. This approach was further developed in the 1960s by Everett Lee, whose so-called 'push–pull' model sought to understand migration decisions as a combination of four factors. First, one can identify a series of push factors in areas of origin such as war, political repression, unemployment, land shortage, gender oppression, famine and climate change. Second, pull factors in potential destinations may influence the decision to migrate; whether real or perceived, higher wages and standards of living, established networks of kin, perception of strong employment opportunities, potentially greater access to education and services, and greater political freedoms are common examples of pull factors. Third are the intervening obstacles between areas of origin and destination: distance and its associated costs, the presence of physical barriers (such as militarized frontiers, impassable mountains, threatening bodies of water), existing immigration laws and the presence of dependents. Finally, personal factors such as motivations, contacts and knowledge may facilitate or retard migration.[4]

This 'push–pull' theory of migration is a useful foundation for analysing the relative power a migrant possesses to shape the conditions under which they migrate. In this respect, it is helpful to make a distinction between forced or distress migration, on the one hand, and voluntary or accumulative migration on the other. The circumstances leading to forced migration are often heavily focused on push factors, in which movement is not voluntary but conditioned by forces beyond the individual or household's control, such as local shocks, military conflicts, environmental degradation and the search for a basic livelihood. Such circumstances create situations of unequal power in employment, given that migrants are coping with, rather than controlling, the terms of migration. Accumulative migration, in contrast, refers to a situation in which push factors are not as compelling and where the household has more time and resources to plan migration strategically. In this usage, accumulative migration occurs when a household plans migration for the purpose of increasing its assets or income streams.

Drawing from our understanding of livelihoods and networks respectively, two important considerations are noteworthy. First, it is typically households rather than individuals that are the main decision makers involved in these processes, and familial relationships – including differences of power between household members such as men and women – shape migration decisions and trajectories. From this perspective, labour migration can be understood as a household livelihood strategy in which some members migrate, or occasionally the entire family, to provide finances for reinvestment in economic activities in the home (see box 8.2). These might include investments in agriculture, small businesses or education by providing a basis on which to send children to school. Second, individuals and households are highly aware of the vulnerabilities involved in such livelihood strategies and tend to be risk-averse. This means that prospective migrants may decide not to migrate even if the expected income is higher at the destination. Alternatively, one member may migrate even if the financial returns are unclear so as to diversify income sources against unforeseen economic shocks such as crop failure, cattle disease, floods and drought. Finally, migration can occur as a response to relative deprivation rather than absolute poverty because less well-off households might send migrants to attain a higher socioeconomic status in relation to the community.[5]

Alongside livelihood strategies, networks also play a central role in migration strategies. Networks facilitate the flows of money, goods and knowledge that are pivotal to accumulative migration. For more affluent migrants, their networks might be based on professional contacts or organized through corporations or private agencies that can connect skilled labour to specific job vacancies. For less affluent households, a reliance on family, kin or community networks is typical. This often leads to the creation of transnational migration networks that link sending and receiving locations. Often referred to as 'chain migration', the formation of such transnational communities indicates how migration is a strongly path-dependent process rooted in social networks conducive to self-perpetuating cycles of migration. Those who have already migrated provide friends and relatives with information regarding administrative procedures, offer travel documentation and knowledge, and help connect them to housing and job opportunities. They also give advice about navigating new spaces and

Box 8.2   Remittances

Remittances are flows of money sent back home by migrants working abroad. It is estimated that international remittance flows exceeded $601 billion in 2015, $441 billion of which went to developing countries, a sum three times larger than official development aid. Rural areas receive between 30 and 40 per cent of remittance flows, and up to 90 per cent are spent on subsistence expenditures such as food, clothing, shelter, healthcare and education. Remittance flows are also indicative of the geography of economic power. While India ($72 billion), China ($64 billion), the Philippines ($30 billion), Mexico ($26 billion) and France ($25 billion) are the top recipients in absolute terms, as a share of GDP, countries such as Tajikistan (42 per cent), Kyrgyz Republic (30 per cent), Nepal (29 per cent), Tonga (28 per cent) and Moldova (26 per cent) are the top receiving countries. Top sending countries include the United States ($56 billion), Saudi Arabia ($37 billion), Russia ($33 billion), Switzerland ($25 billion) and Germany ($21 billion). With the average cost of sending remittances at about 8 per cent, and up to 20 per cent in sub-Saharan Africa and the Pacific Island countries, remittances have become a booming industry for banking and financial institutions.[6]

cultures and help them to find a job by contacting potential employers and fostering a sense of stability and community.

Those migrating in conditions of distress, however, are likely to be heavily reliant on labour contractors or human traffickers whom they will pay – often by going into debt – to facilitate migration. In the absence of close networks, these migrants are extremely vulnerable. Indeed, the possibility of dependence and entrapment can lead to forced labour, which is explored in depth in the following chapter. For such migrants, the structural vulnerability that impelled them to migrate is deepened through their dependence on complex and risky migration chains.

Consider, for example, the parallel histories of two men, Mthuthuzeli and Feng, who are migrant labourers in two very different continents. Mthuthuzeli, crossing the border from Lesotho, laboured as a gold miner for more than three decades in a large South African operation before being laid off in the early 2000s. Feng, from southern China, was employed by a Chinese company in the industrial city of Shenzhen in the late 1990s, where he spent long hours cutting and polishing stones such as amber, onyx, quartz and crystal for export to customers in North America and Europe. Besides being integral parts of a migrant labour regime for export-oriented industries, both men now suffer from silicosis, an incurable disease caused by the long-term inhalation of silica dust. In the absence of adequate ventilation or dust prevention, the workplaces in both sites had dangerous levels of silica to which all workers were exposed. Sadly, by destroying the lungs, the onset of silicosis leads to a chronic shortness of breath, rendering the sufferer unable to perform even basic activities. Unable to work productively, both men have been transformed from key wage earners into a significant livelihood burden upon their respective households.

Although these bodies were wrecked by silica inhalation in South Africa and China respectively, the processes that led to this human tragedy are clearly not a localized phenomenon. Despite the known risks of silica inhalation, both of their employers had neglected to implement appropriate safety mechanisms to prevent the creation and inhalation of dust. Similarly, in both cases, an absence of effective state regulation had compounded the issue. The global production networks that produced, respectively, the gold and ornamental goods largely for Western consumers displaced the risks of production down onto precarious workers. Notably, migrants like Mthuthuzeli and Feng were particularly vulnerable to dangerous working conditions because they had few assets, no power to influence conditions in the workplace, and limited employment opportunities within their home respective regions. In South Africa, predominantly male migrants move within the country to gold mining areas in search of work, whereas other labourers come from neighbouring countries such as Lesotho, Malawi and Swaziland. The latter are particularly sought after by the labour contractors who supply the mining industry because they have fewer alternatives and therefore are more likely to accept wages and working conditions that many South Africans would shun. Similarly, in China, many of those drawn into the gemstone industry were rural–urban migrants from interior regions who sought livelihoods in southern cities within a context of reduced civil rights owing to their lack of an urban citizenship. In both cases, owing to their marginality within labour markets, limited assets and networks, and an absence of effective political rights, these migrant workers had little power to avoid exposure to toxins that resulted in grievous bodily illness.[7]

Migration and the History of Uneven Development

If networks, livelihoods and their accordant power relations are central to understanding different migrant experiences, we also need to situate migration in relation to structural changes within the global political economy as a whole. The political economy theories that emerged in the 1970s, for instance, emphasized how migratory flows in both the past and the present were closely linked to processes of uneven development tied to the evolution of capitalism.[8] They stressed that labour migration can consolidate socioeconomic inequalities across countries by providing cheap labour to receiving areas and by contributing to the brain drain through the exodus of skilled migrant workers. As a result, the differentiated integration of immigrant workers into global production networks is pivotally linked to the reproduction of an uneven international division of labour. In particular, these theories question the idea of 'voluntary' migration. They argue that people move because their ability to live decently is undermined through uneven geographical development wherein the concentration of wealth in some regions is accompanied by – and directly related to – the underdevelopment of others. On the one hand, deprived areas often serve as sources of out-migration towards hubs of capital accumulation and development. On the other, migratory flows can exacerbate existing regional inequalities by providing a source of cheap labour to spur on accumulation.

This analytical position is closely related to historical experiences of mass international migration in the modern era. It is possible to identify six historical 'waves' of labour migration, starting with the Spanish colonization of America from the late fifteenth century to the early nineteenth century, which constituted the first act of an emerging global labour market and marks the beginning of the European conquests of Africa, Asia, America and Oceania.[9] Forced labour migration was pivotal to this process, as thousands were transported from the Bahamas to Hispaniola, and from Nicaragua to Panama and Peru. The process by which whole populations were displaced and exterminated – either through outright genocides or harsh labour conditions in the mines or diseases – gradually depleted the vast reservoir of labour contained in the Americas. This propelled the transatlantic slave trade as a new source of labour, with the number of African slaves in Spanish America increasing from about 31,000–40,000 in 1570 to 857,000 in 1650 and to 2,347,000 by the early nineteenth century.[10]

It is in this context that we must situate the slave trade as a second wave of labour migration. Portuguese Brazil was a frontrunner in the production of goods for export to Europe by introducing African slaves on sugar plantations. Yet it was the British Empire and its naval power that elevated the trade in human bodies to new heights as chattel slavery became central to commodity production in the plantations and mines of European colonial empires. From sugar to cotton, and from coffee to tobacco and gold, slavery became instrumental to a growing international economy. It is estimated that about 12 million slaves were taken to the Americas before 1850. Slave trafficking was abolished within the British Empire in 1807, but slavery itself was not abolished until 1834 in British colonies (slavery in the territories of the East India Company and the islands of Ceylon and Saint Helena was eliminated in 1843), 1863 in Dutch colonies and 1865 in the United States. Slavery became an institution as a result of European powers' need to secure a steady and reliable labour force. The emergence of global empires, the constitution of a world market and the rise of slavery were intimately interconnected.[11]

With the collapse of slavery in the nineteenth century, indentured labour became essential to the maintenance of European colonialism as Africans, Indians, Chinese, Japanese and Pacific Islanders were recruited through long-term labour contracts, which represents the third wave of labour migration. While some took the form of debt bondage, many entered formal contracts of indenture typically lasting five years, which transported them across the colonial empires for labour-intensive work, often on plantations, in mines or for infrastructure construction. Working conditions were harsh and legislation usually prevented them from changing employers or negotiating pay. With the abolition of slavery throughout the British Empire in 1834, the number of indentured labourers increased dramatically, ranging from 150,000 to 250,000 per decade from 1841 to 1910. It is estimated that about two million Indians worked in British colonies as indentured labourers, including on railway construction in Kenya, Natal and Uganda, and plantations in Ceylon, Fiji, Guyana and Mauritius (see box 8.3). Moreover, some 500,000 indentured workers were put to work in British colonies (Belize, Guyana, Jamaica, Malaysia, Trinidad and Tobago) and Dutch colonies (Dutch East Indies and Suriname), as well as in Cuba and Peru. In addition, up to one million indentured workers were recruited in Japan, mainly to work in Brazil, Hawaii, the United States and Peru.[12]

A fourth and radically different wave of labour migration came from European resettlement, which saw tens of millions of European emigrants and settlers transform the political geography of state formation and reshape the international division of labour. No fewer than 23 million individuals emigrated from the British Isles between 1815 and 1914. In many ways, the industrial development of the

Box 8.3 Networks and indentured labour in colonial Malaya

Between 1844 and 1910, some quarter of a million indentured labourers – often termed 'coolies' at the time – were imported into British Malaya from India alone. Here, different forms of indentured labour emerged according to the needs of the workplace and the forms of resistance and accommodation that indentured labourers pursued. Direct indentured labour involved plantations or mines hiring an intermediary who would be in charge of recruiting indentured labour. Prospective labourers would sign a five-year contract – notably, almost none would have been able to read the terms of the contract they were signing – and the costs of transportation and a fee for the recruiter would be deducted from the wages to be earned. In colonial Malaya, however, a slightly different recruiting mechanism became predominant called *kangani* labour. In this system, the plantation owner would send an already recruited indentured labourer to his home community to recruit new 'voluntary' labourers from amongst his social peers. This form of networked recruitment was seen as advantageous for two reasons. First, it was cheaper than using formal intermediaries. Second, it tended to reduce the absconding of indentured labourers because their own community members would be held responsible for their desertion. Here we see how the qualities of social networks – the informal links and ties within a social group – were put to use in a disciplinary fashion to secure and control a labour force.[13]

United States was based on its ability to offer land to displaced and impoverished European farmers, jobs to workers from stagnant economic regions such as southern Italy, asylum to the persecuted Jews from Eastern Europe, and economic opportunities to those escaping the Irish famine. Partly shaped by the uneven geographical development and pace of European industrialization, this labour force on the move tended to follow two general patterns of resettlement. First, colonial migration was especially strong within the British Empire as settler countries were seen as a solution to social problems in Britain. Impoverished and unemployed workers, destitute children, dissidents, convicts and orphaned children were encouraged, and sometimes forced, to resettle to Australia, Canada, New Zealand, Rhodesia, South Africa or the United States. Second, migration to noncolonial areas was more important in colonial powers such as Belgium, France, Spain and the Netherlands, especially after 1850. Although colonial migration remained significant in certain cases, such as the nearly two million French settlers living in Algeria, the number of migrants to noncolonial areas – especially the United States – tended to outnumber colonial migration.[14]

A fifth wave of labour migration took place between 1914 and 1945. Countries during the First World War relied extensively on forced labour (including prisoners of war) to replace drafted men. France imported some 200,000 colonial workers from Southeast Asia and Africa to address labour shortages, and recruited workers in Greece, Italy, Portugal and Spain to work in factories and agriculture. Similarly, Britain brought soldiers and workers from its colonies, and Germany prevented Polish workers from leaving while recruiting labour by force in the occupied areas of Belgium and Russia. Labour migration receded rapidly after the war as a result of economic stagnation and crises, rampant nationalism and xenophobic sentiments. The one exception was France, where nearly two million foreign workers from Algeria, Czechoslovakia, Italy and Poland worked in agriculture, construction and heavy industry between 1920 and 1930 to replace the high number of dead and permanently wounded soldiers. Labour migration reached new heights under Nazi Germany during the Second World War, as some 10 million men from occupied territories – mainly Poles and Russians, but also French and Italians – were forced to work in German factories to sustain the war effort. In addition, 2.5 million political prisoners, including communists, union leaders, labour movement activists and homosexuals, were sent to concentration camps where they were put to work. Moreover, at least 3.5 million Jews were sent to death camps where many were put to work before being killed.[15]

Finally, as wartime losses, nascent welfare states and rapid industrial development in Europe, North America and Australia exhausted indigenous supplies of labour, an important wave of guest workers arrived to address labour shortages as the industrial states of northwest Europe tapped into labour-rich countries in southern Europe, North Africa, South Asia and the Caribbean. During the 1950s, 1960s and 1970s, Belgium, France, the Netherlands and West Germany signed bilateral recruitment agreements with Italy, Spain, Greece, Turkey, Morocco, Portugal, Tunisia and Yugoslavia. Former colonial ties were also important, with France relying heavily on Algeria and the United Kingdom on Bangladesh, the Caribbean, India and Pakistan. In order to supply workers for their booming industries, Australia and New Zealand even created immigration schemes to prospective British subjects, with the Australian government subsidizing the passage of more than one million Britons. Most of the millions of guest workers moving to northwest Europe were low-skilled economic migrants from rural areas in search of a better life. Following the 1973 oil crisis and the ensuing recession, European governments started encouraging foreign migrant workers to return home. While some did, a great many stayed, with Turkish immigration to Germany and North African immigration to France continuing well into the 1980s as courts recognized their rights of residence and family reunification. As Swiss novelist Max Frisch put it at the time, European governments had 'asked for workers, but human beings came'.

States and Migration

By emphasizing how labour migration has been strategically mobilized within the formation of labour regimes, this historical account raises a critical point for our understanding of migratory dynamics. State regulation strongly shapes the flow of migrant workers and the conditions under which they migrate. By purposely directing migrant workers into specific labour market niches, different types of regulation shape segmentation. Skilled workers are often given preferential access to jobs. Governments in Australia, Canada, China, France, Germany, India, the Netherlands, New Zealand, the United Kingdom and the United States, for example, strategically seek to attract talent by facilitating the entry of skilled workers through increasing annual quotas, adapting current immigration programmes to business needs and designing new schemes modelled after targeted national and industrial priorities.

An emblematic example can be seen in how governments in the global North have encouraged the migration of doctors and nurses from developing countries to cover shortages of healthcare professionals and care workers. Similarly, states typically recognize the key importance of attracting skilled migrants for both education and research to maintain a competitive edge in the global economy. The trend manifests itself in the growing competition for foreign students, as states and leading universities have vested interests in attracting, forming and retaining tomorrow's skilled immigrants. Arguably, this will accentuate what is often termed the brain drain, as developing countries lose a pivotal segment of professionals, skilled technicians and highly trained individuals to the West. For instance, 93 per cent of highly skilled persons from Guyana lived outside the country in 2014; in Haiti the figure was 75.1 per cent, Trinidad and Tobago 68 per cent and Barbados 66 per cent. The impact of this demographic outflow of skilled labour on uneven development trajectories is marked.[16]

Projects such as free trade agreements and regional economic integration also have a significant impact on migration dynamics and there are a number of important political agreements to facilitate labour migration across borders. Consider the European Union, which guarantees the free movement of workers across the labour markets of member states. EU nationals taking up employment in another member state have the same labour rights, conditions of employment and legal protection as native workers. In addition to having access to the same social and tax benefits, EU nationals also enjoy the right of residence for themselves and their family members. The mobility of labour across national labour markets is therefore one of the most striking features of the European Union.

MERCOSUR provides another example. Established in 1991 by the Treaty of Asunción, it is a sub-regional free trade agreement on the movement of goods, services and people between Argentina, Brazil, Paraguay, Uruguay and Venezuela. Implemented in 2009, the 2002 MERCOSUR Residence Agreement extends to Bolivia, Chile, Columbia, Ecuador and Peru, and provides the right to reside in a host country for two years under a temporary permit, which can then be transformed into a permanent one provided that the person can prove that she has legitimate means to support herself and her family. The Agreement also recognizes the right to work and to equal treatment in working conditions, to access to education for children, and to family reunification. As an international treaty, however, the agreement does not have intraregional institutional mechanisms to ensure implementation and sanction violations. Moreover, fees for both temporary and residence permits often act as barriers to the movement of unskilled workers, thus effectively encouraging the legal migration of skilled workers and the irregular migration of low-skilled workers who represent the bulk of labour migration.[17] Once more, differential regulation over migration appears as a strong factor in creating labour market segmentation.

Notably, there is generally a strong structural demand for an unskilled, low-paid labour force in the lower rungs of the labour market. From the 1980s onwards, migrant workers became more important to the labour markets of advanced industrial countries as a result of declining birth rates, the democratization of higher education and rising demands for women's economic emancipation in the 1960s and 1970s. While women and teenagers continue to be recruited to fill some lower-paid jobs, migrant workers are increasingly mobilized for this segment of the market, as native workers tend to eschew low status, poorly remunerated jobs with little security. As a result, we can see the concentration of migrants within such sectors as agriculture, construction, cleaning, domestic services, care work and basic retailing.[18]

Migration therefore sits at a crossroads of power relations. Many countries desperately need migrant workers to fill gaps within their labour markets – particularly if they are cheaper than existing workforces. Simultaneously, they typically seek to control how migration occurs so as to create well-disciplined workforces. This can create strong tensions in migration policy. For instance, while many regional trade agreements, such as the ASEAN Economic Community (AEC) and the Common Market for Eastern and Southern Africa (COMESA), aim to implement unrestricted labour mobility across integrated markets, the reality is often far more complex (box 8.4). Free trade agreements typically go to great lengths to open borders to the movement of capital, goods and services by eliminating tariffs, facilitating trade liberalization and investment, protecting intellectual property rights and streamlining capital market regulatory frameworks. At the same time, however, they also tend to avoid incorporating provisions on labour mobility. Categories of migrant workers included in trade agreements are generally those essential for the free flow of capital, goods and services, including business visitors and salespersons, intracorporate transferees, independent professionals and contractual services supplies. While the EU and, to a lesser extent, MERCOSUR provide broader frameworks for intraregional labour migration, the overwhelming majority of bilateral and multilateral trade agreements cover only a tiny fraction of workers, thus greatly limiting the movement of labour across national spaces.

Box 8.4   The ASEAN Economic Community

The ASEAN Economic Community (AEC) was formally established in 2015 between ten member states in Southeast Asia with the goal of creating a single market and production base and facilitating the 'freer' flow of skilled labour in specific sectors through Mutual Recognition Agreements based on the recognition of shared professional qualifications. While supporting the free flow of goods and services, unrestricted labour mobility within the community is not on the agenda. The main professions covered by the AEC (e.g., engineering, healthcare) represent less than 1.5 per cent of the ASEAN workforce. While irregular migration remains an intractable problem, it is estimated that more than 87 per cent of intra-ASEAN migrants are low-skilled workers, employed in domestic, agricultural and construction positions or in food processing industries. The vast majority of migrant workers thus fall outside the scope of the AEC and are subject to restrictive labour immigration laws and regulations.[19]

Contemporary Trends in Labour Migration

Following the six waves of labour migration outlined above, a seventh, contemporary wave can be characterized by four main aspects. The first one concerns the rising proportion of female migrants. The vast majority of women entering Western Europe in the 1970s and 1980s did so in order to reunite families after men had migrated as guest workers in the 1950s, 1960s and early 1970s. More recently, however, the development of a feminized service industry within advanced capitalist countries has contributed to the expanded importance of female workers who are migrating independently in search of economic opportunities in domestic work, retailing, catering, hotels, assembly lines, healthcare and entertainment. Representative of this feminization of migration is what sociologist Rhacel Salazar Parreñas refers to as the international division of reproductive labour. Of the estimated 2.8 million female temporary migrant workers from the Philippines around the world, it is thought that at least half are employed as domestic workers and caregivers in countries such as Canada, Italy, Saudi Arabia and Singapore. Parreñas details, for example, how some 103,630 women left the Philippines to do domestic work in 2010 alone, compared to just 2,245 men. At the core of this trend is the absence of an egalitarian gendered division of domestic labour in both sending and receiving countries, which allows relatively privileged women to offload their reproductive labour and responsibilities onto low-wage, flexible migrant Filipina workers. While virtually all women workers migrate in order to contribute financially to their own households, many also leave to escape gendered oppression and the constraints placed on women at home. They actively seek to negotiate their position within an unequal chain of gender relations whereby constraints are transferred from privileged women to less privileged women.[20]

The second aspect of the contemporary migration wave relates to the shifting geography of migrant flows that has undermined the traditional distinction between countries of origin, transit and destination. In the 1950s and 1960s, for example, northern European countries mainly drew foreign workers from southern Europe. This changed in the 1980s and 1990s as a result of both lower economic incentives through the restructuring of core countries and growing economic development in countries of the periphery and semi-periphery. While traditional regions of emigration such as southern Europe are becoming regions of inward immigration, north African countries such as Algeria, Libya, Morocco and Tunisia, which used to be countries of origin to northern Europe, are reconfigured as transit and destination countries for migrants from sub-Saharan Africa. Today, many countries assume the simultaneous role of countries of origin, transit and destination, depending on the level of integration of their cities and regions in the global economy, the specificity of economic sectors and opportunities, and the presence of migrant communities which may facilitate migration.

Key to the shifting geography of migrant flows is the role of the state. As labour geographers Jane Wills and colleagues show in their study of London's new migrant division of labour, the British government's immigration regime has been reformed along neoliberal principles of economic competitiveness and labour flexibility to align it more closely with the demands of the United Kingdom's increasingly segmented labour market. The result is a differentiated points-based immigration regime that privileges highly skilled workers and entrepreneurs, benefits foreign-born unskilled and semi-skilled workers from the European Union and excludes unskilled workers from outside the European Union unless they enter the United Kingdom to reunite with family, as international students, as refugees or illegally. As the authors note, London's low-wage economy is directly tied to this immigration regime, with the outsourcing of services such as cleaning and catering highly dependent upon a low-paid, flexible and economically insecure migrant workforce. A net emigration country for most of the twentieth century, Britain has been a net immigration country since the early 1990s. By using immigration for economic advantage, the British government has not only transformed the country into a destination country; it has also put the immigration regime at the heart of a national economy based on a segmented labour market.[21]

Related to this is the increasingly temporary nature of migration, which forms a third fundamental aspect of contemporary dynamics. Contrary to previous waves of labour migration that were largely characterized by permanent resettlement, return migration is set to rise as many Western governments increasingly introduce temporary migration programmes and guest worker schemes. As we saw in chapter 2, the H2B visa system in the United States facilitates the inflow of skilled workers into specific professions such as IT for a closely defined period of time. While this provides significant opportunities for migrant workers in terms of wages and training, it does so in a way that makes workers dependent upon an employer for the duration of their migration. Similarly, the Seasonal Agricultural Workers Programme in Canada (see chapter 7) created a labour market segment of workers tied to specific farms and dependent on their employer to approve re-entry into the programme in future years. Here we see how migration and state regulation together form a labour regime, mobilizing workers into specific occupations, motivating them to work diligently, and simultaneously shaping the power relations operating within production by providing employers with an effective veto on their reapplication to the programme.

Such programmes are expressly designed to deliver a cheap, flexible and temporary labour force to prospective employers by enforcing strict legal controls on the mobility and rights of migrant workers within the labour market. Whereas countries such as Italy and the United States have implemented amnesty programmes to regularize irregular migrant workers in the past, others have used the same method to enforce temporary migration. For example, Spain brought some 700,000 illegal immigrants into the formal economy in 2005 by granting them working permits, which must be renewed and do not entitle them to legal permanent residence. Similarly, Malaysia's 2005 amnesty programme regularized 400,000 migrants out of an estimated 800,000 to 1.2 million migrants – mainly from Indonesia, Bangladesh, Myanmar and Nepal – into legal, temporary workers.[22] Immigration schemes are therefore increasingly modelled after a two-tier system. On the one hand, a welcoming attitude is given to high-end migration as skills and knowledge become key to global competition. On the other hand, low- and semi-skilled workers constitute a cheap and flexible labour force whose economic insecurity is directly connected with their precarious legal status on the labour market.

Finally, a fourth new trend relates to the changing geography of international labour migration: south–south migration now accounts for 38 per cent of total migration compared to 34 per cent for south–north migration.[23] For example, although there is a long history of south–north migration in Peru, primarily amongst the middle and upper classes, there has been a dramatic increase in new migration destinations since the late 1980s and early 1990s. In a period of high unemployment, political instability and entrenched social inequalities, emigration provided a potential escape whereby a more secure livelihood and upward social mobility might be achieved. While the United States, Spain, Italy and Japan represented important destination countries until the mid-1990s, employment opportunities in the global North have tended to dry up, either because of restrictive immigration policies or because of saturated guest worker programmes. In this context, Argentina, Bolivia, Chile and Ecuador have become important destination countries for Peruvians, especially for poor, unskilled urban workers. The relative proximity of these countries to one another, the comparatively low transportation costs, the capacity to enter the country legally, and a common cultural and linguistic heritage have acted as strong pull factors. Key to Peruvian migration is therefore its multiclass nature and the extent to which it defines emigration destinations. While the privileged classes continue to be the backbone of south–north migration, the rapid expansion of emigration since the economic crisis has given rise to a new host of destination countries, while reinforcing south–south patterns of migration, especially amongst poor urban working classes.[24]

The Peruvian case is just one example of the growing importance of south–south migration. At a political level, this trend is linked to tighter immigration controls in North America, western Europe and the Antipodes. From an economic perspective, however, economic activity has decisively shifted east since the 1990s, the result of which has been the constitution of important regional poles of economic development in East Asia and Southeast Asia, as well as greater economic integration in Latin America. While these transformations have reinforced uneven geographic development in the global economy, they have also shifted the geography of economic opportunities for prospective migrants through labour-intensive industrialization and rapidly growing service sectors, all of which are traversed by state-backed migrations regimes and vast informal networks of migration.[25]

Further reading

Robin Cohen's *The New Helots: Migrants in the International Division of Labour* (Aldershot: Gower Publishing, 1987) is a classic and helped launch global labour studies as a research paradigm. *Financial Times* journalist Toby Shelvy offered a powerful examination of migrant labour regimes in *Exploited: Migrant Labour in the New Global Economy* (London: Zed Books, 2007). For a comprehensive account of migration, gender and insecure work in contemporary Western cities, there are few better places to start than the collaborative book by Jane Wills et al., *Global Cities at Work: New Migrant Divisions of Labour* (London: Pluto Press, 2010).

Chapter 9
Forced Labour

Against a backdrop of coastal palm trees, four Thai workers discuss how they entered into a situation of forced labour. It began five years earlier when a labour contractor visited their village and offered to help the men into positions on a farm producing vegetables for major international food brands. Given the significantly higher wages than they were currently receiving, the men quickly calculated that after three years they would come out ahead despite the high registration fee that the contractor demanded. Borrowing the money to cover the fee and transport costs, the men set off for their new work only to find conditions were significantly different from those promised. On arrival, their passports were taken by their new employer, their accommodation and food provisions turned out to be very poor, and the wages they received were considerably lower than promised and whittled down further by a series of arbitrary charges and deductions. The workers quickly realized that they were labouring hard for poverty wages and would remain mired in debt from the initial transaction. Contesting their conditions, however, was impossible, since their employer simply threatened to return them in destitution to their village. They had become trapped in a work contract from which they could not escape, effectively stuck in a relentless struggle to try and minimize the loss over the three years. The most striking part of this story is where it took place. No, not in rural Thailand, but in the land of the free: on a large American farm in Hawaii that was part of a global production network for foodstuffs.[1]

As this distressing case illustrates, forced labour is alive and well in the heartlands of contemporary global capitalism. Forced labour is a world-scale phenomenon that appears in both rich and poor countries

Box 9.1   Qatar – Building the World Cup

The 2022 World Cup that will be held in Qatar deserves a red card. As a series of investigative reports have revealed, the roads, stadiums, hotels, ports and other major infrastructure projects supporting the world tournament are being built in part by a forced and captive workforce. Migrant workers drawn from across South Asia provide the primary workforce for these massive construction projects, yet do so with limited ability to leave their employers or contest the conditions they encounter. From the confiscation of passports and ID cards to the withholding of salaries, and long working days in the desert heat without food and water, as well as reports of physical assaults and labour abuses, migrant workers typically face dangerous working conditions and high levels of exploitation. As such, dozens have died while working in Qatar, which is, incidentally, by far the richest country per capita in the world. Disturbingly, billions of viewers will watch a game made available by the sweat, tears and blood of forced labour. Go see the short video![2]

and has proliferated precisely by linking spaces of accumulation with spaces of vulnerability (see box 9.1). From child labour in the cacao plantations in West Africa to forced labour in the UK food sector and construction industry, the unsettling reality is that most of us have unknowingly consumed goods and services made with labour that was coerced. Far from belonging to the distant past, the prevalence of forced labour within the global economy shows up in the production of a vast range of commodities such as shoes, clothes, cacao, fruit and vegetables, bricks, fish, cotton, rubber, iron and timber. All of these, of course, are regularly traded on world markets and integrated within the supply chains of major transnational corporations.

What is Forced Labour?

According to the ILO, forced labour 'refers to situations in which persons are coerced to work through the use of violence or intimidation, or by more subtle means such as accumulated debt, retention of identity papers or threats of denunciation to immigration authorities'. This can include practices such as slavery, human trafficking, forced sexual exploitation and debt bondage (see box 9.2), although certain exceptions are provided for, such as compulsory military laws, normal civic obligations, conviction in a court of law, cases

Box 9.2   Forms of Forced Labour

Slavery: 'The status or condition of a person over whom any or all of the powers attaching to the right of ownership are exercised.'
– Article 1(1) of the UN Slavery Convention

Debt-bondage: 'The status or condition arising from a pledge by a debtor of his personal services or those of a person under his control as security for a debt, if the value of those services as reasonably assessed is not applied towards the liquidation of the debt or the length and nature of those services are not respectively limited or defined.'
– Article 1(a) of the UN Supplementary Convention on the Abolition of Slavery, the Slave Trade and Institutions and Practices Similar to Slavery (1956)

Sexual exploitation: 'When an adult engages in a commercial sex act, such as prostitution, as the result of force, threats of force, fraud, coercion or any combination of such means, that person is a victim of trafficking. ... An adult's consent to participate in prostitution is not legally determinative: if one is thereafter held in service through psychological manipulation or physical force, he or she is a trafficking victim.'
– US Department of State, *Trafficking in Persons Report 2015*

Human trafficking: 'The recruitment, transportation, transfer, harbouring or receipt of persons, by means of the threat or use of force or other forms of coercion, of abduction, of fraud, of deception, of the abuse of power or of a position of vulnerability or of the giving or receiving of payments or benefits to achieve the consent of a person having control over another person, for the purpose of exploitation.'
– Article 3 of the Palermo Protocol

Child Labour: A situation 'in which the child appears to be in the custody of a non-family member who requires the child to perform work that financially benefits someone outside the child's family and does not offer the child the option of leaving.'
– US Department of State, *Trafficking in Persons Report 2015*

of emergency and minor communal services. For the ILO, to grasp forced labour is to counterpose it to its opposite, free labour, which it considers to be the ability to willingly enter and exit employment relationships without constraints, the threat or use of force, or other forms of coercion. Importantly, the ILO argues that low wages, poor working conditions, hazardous work or one's inability to leave a job because of a lack of alternative employment opportunities do not qualify as forced or unfree labour.

For global labour studies, the simple dichotomy between 'free' and 'forced' labour appears questionable. As we set out below, all employment relations involve relationships of power, and most forms of employment could be considered as taking place on a spectrum ranging from relatively more free to relatively more coerced labour relations (see Figure 9.2 below). A more critical approach to free labour can be found in the work of Marx, who argued that workers are free in a double sense. On the one hand, within capitalism workers are no longer tied to particular employers. Marx considered this to be an important emancipatory accomplishment. On the other hand, workers are also freed from ownership of the means of production necessary for independent subsistence. This means that their survival depends upon finding someone to hire them as a worker, creating a strong power imbalance. As a result, and contrary to the ILO, Marx would argue that the freedom of workers to enter or exit employment relationships is seriously undermined by their dependence on the market for survival. In the pithy words of economist Joan Robinson, 'the misery of being exploited by capitalists is nothing compared to the misery of not being exploited at all'.[3]

Notwithstanding these important analytical debates, the ILO's most recent estimates place at 20.9 million people – 11.4 million women and girls and 9.5 million men and boys – the number of victims of forced labour at any given time, a figure that corresponds to three out of every 1,000 people worldwide (see Figure 9.1).[4] Some

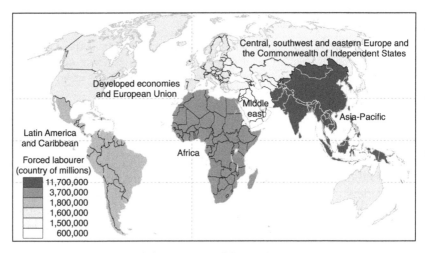

Figure 9.1   The regional distribution of forced labour
Source: Map prepared by Marc Girard from ILO (2012a)

have argued that the prevalence of forced labour is much greater than the ILO's estimates, which are said to vastly underestimate the importance of forced labour arrangements in today's global economy. For instance, Breman estimates that at least 10 per cent of the 395 million Indian workers toiling in the informal economy are bonded by debt to their employers.[5]

Given the widely accepted ILO definition of what constitutes forced labour amongst governments, NGOs and public authorities, we use the latter to make three general observations. First, it is crucial to remember that free labour is a geographically specific concept that emerged, as we saw in chapter 5, with the expansion of formalized work in many Western countries during the nineteenth and twentieth centuries. Contemporary understanding of free labour is the result of long and often bloody struggles for labour emancipation and the recognition of labour rights. From the eight-hour workday to the right to organize, from collective bargaining to the right to exit the employment relationship, key aspects of what we now see as the main features of free labour are the direct outcome of labour struggles, social movements and political parties enacting progressive labour codes. To this day, free labour remains an elusive category for most workers in the world. While a substantial segment of the hundreds of millions of workers who constitute the informal sector worldwide may not be expressly coerced to work, the fact that they have little to no access to legal protection, labour regulations and minimum working standards makes them vulnerable to forced labour.

Second, we need to recognize in what ways forced labour can become a rational choice for workers. In a global economy characterized by labour market insecurity and failures, situations where people find 'security' in forced labour arrangements are not at all uncommon. Consider the case of João Luís do Nascimento, who worked as a slave in Brazil for forty years. Throughout those years, Nascimento worked in the mines and on the farms and mills of the Amazon. Although he understood what was going on, his need to work, given his responsibility as the father and provider of a family of eight children, was always stronger than the dire nature of the conditions under which work was to be performed. Nascimento escaped from a sawmill in 2010, after enduring the worst conditions of exploitation he had experienced in decades. Forced to drink and bathe with the pigs, he worked for no pay and survived almost exclusively on rice. On certain days, he could not even stand because of his lack of nourishment, and his hands were cut to the bone because he was forced to work without gloves. As extraordinary as it sounds, Nascimento is a common story in Brazil. Officially abolished in 1888, slavery has in fact never really disappeared. It was only in 1995 that the government started confronting the problem. Yet, while more than 45,000 workers have been rescued since 2003, many have argued that they represent only a small fraction of cases, as workers are often too scared to speak. Moreover, this entrenched culture of exploitation has been happening for so long that government inspectors often confront situations in which the workers themselves claim to find nothing abnormal or outrageous. In Brazil, as elsewhere, poverty and the lack of economic opportunities continue to make some of the worst forms of labour exploitation attractive owing to the perverse security they provide.[6]

Third, a growing number of countries are implementing legal, state-backed systems of unfree labour. While the growth of prison work in the United States is indicative of this trend (see box 9.3), the country's criminal justice system has also become more and more harmful to workers. Federal, state and local governments in the United States increasingly threaten workers with jail as the criminal justice system makes it more and more difficult for them to resist employers' terms. Probationers and parolees, as well as people who are too poor to pay

Box 9.3   Prison labour in the United States

The Thirteenth Amendment to the US Constitution forbids slavery and involuntary servitude 'except as punishment for crime whereof the party shall have been duly convicted'. As a result, prison labour is legal in the United States. AT&T, Boeing, Dell, Honeywell, Microsoft, Target and Victoria's Secret are only a few of the corporations that moved part of their operations inside state prisons to cut labour costs and increase profits. Prison industries were generating an annual value of $2 billion in 2008, employing close to a million inmates on a full-time basis. Privately run penitentiaries pay their inmates as little as seventeen cents per hour. Not only are employers exempt from paying for unemployment insurance or vacations, they can count on a captive labour force that is never late, works full time and has no right to organize or strike. Punishments for refusing to work include being locked up in isolation cells and having family visits revoked.[7] Following a call for a nationwide prison labour strike that began on 9 September 2016, about 20,000 prisoners from at least twenty prisons in eleven states went on strike. After months of organizing using smuggled mobile phones, social media platforms and the support of allies on the outside, the largest prison work strike in US history called for an end to forced prison labour and slavery in America. As one of the exceptions mentioned above, however, the ILO does not consider the growing number of inmates convicted in a court of law and toiling for private and state corporations as constituting forced labour.[8]

criminal justice debts or child support, may be ordered to find a job or face incarceration, thus endowing employers with disproportionate power over workers who can neither refuse nor quit a job or challenge their employers. As Noah Zatz and colleagues note, this trend is posing a serious threat to workplace rights, challenging as it does the very foundations of free labour.[9]

Another preoccupying trend towards legal forms of servitude stems from the widespread adoption of 'guest worker' regimes, with more and more countries passing laws that reduce the rights of migrant workers. As work visas are redesigned to enforce strict restrictions on the mobility of migrant workers in the labour market, a growing number of these workers are caught in a system of labour control that oscillates between legal servitude and illegal freedom.[10] As Pei-Chia Lan explains in the case of Taiwan, underpinning workers' legal servitude is a dual logic that locks migrant workers in time – as they are prohibited from permanent settlement and family reunification – and space – as they are tied to one employer and do not have the right to switch jobs. Prohibitive placement fees ranging from the equivalent of five to fourteen months of wages further compound this power imbalance. Fuelled by the combination of relatively higher wages and the limited opportunities afforded by the government's system of quotas, placement agencies will pay employers to get contracts, while making their profits by charging higher fees to prospective migrant workers. In a system where employers get paid to hire and workers pay to work, most migrant workers will spend the first two years paying back placement fees and establishing financial stability, making money only during the third year of their contract. In this context, confrontation is rare, and many even voluntarily give up their days off to please their employers to have their contract renewed.

On the other hand, irregular migrants in Taiwan live in a state of illegal freedom. Enjoying the economic right of market mobility, they generally get better wages and can change employer if they choose to. While they lack legal protection, have no health insurance and are more vulnerable to certain forms of abuse such as having their wages withheld, they are generally less socially isolated, given that their illegal status reinforces their dependency on networks of nationals from their home countries to find a place to live and contact prospective employers. Similar policy frameworks exist in Canada, France, Italy, Spain, Sweden, the UK and the United States. As numerous studies have shown, the fear of losing their job and being deported leads many workers to endure unpaid work, abuses, sexual harassment and unsafe work conditions.

How Do People Fall Into Forced Labour Arrangements?

Rather than being a static condition, forced labour can be considered as a dynamic process located on a continuum of labour practices. Underpinning it are a multitude of factors whose interaction can produce vulnerabilities leading to unfree conditions of labour as workers' rights and freedom are gradually taken away. Poverty, low levels of education and literacy, trade liberalization and the lack of state support can all impact livelihoods in complex ways. Although the abduction of workers for exploitation remains one aspect of forced labour, more often than not people gradually fall into it. As Figure 9.2 suggests, in order to understand why people fall victim to forced labour, we must consider the social, cultural, economic and political determinants of vulnerability.

1 *What assets does a household hold?* This refers to the bundle of assets over which a household has control. Owning land and animals or having access to forest and water are key to the security of the estimated two billion people connected to smallholder agriculture worldwide. Similarly, a household member with specific knowledge and skills might be an important asset in a competitive labour market.

2 *What forms of social discrimination are present?* Social discrimination refers to the creation of hierarchies within society, notably by diminishing the humanity and value of certain individuals and social groups. For example, gender-based forms of inequalities are central to the systemic devaluation of both

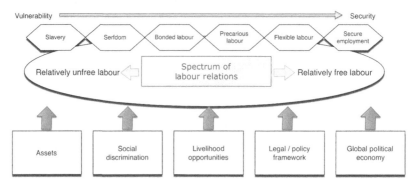

Figure 9.2   The spectrum of forced labour

skilled and unskilled female work and the creation of gendered labour markets characterized by inequalities in working conditions. In the same vein, racist ideologies and the uneven, adverse incorporation of migrant workers into national labour regimes constitute other examples of social hierarchies that place serious limits on workers' ability to escape harsh forms of labour exploitation.

3 *What are the livelihood opportunities within which households can use their assets?* This dimension refers to the ability of a household to use its assets in multiple ways. From the lack of employment opportunities to people's ability to access their means of subsistence, and from labour movements to the legal recognition and protection of labour rights, households can face adverse or enabling conditions. In other words, households exist within social and institutional contexts that can either valorize or diminish their assets.

4 *What is the legal and policy framework?* While states' legal capacity to prosecute employers is important to combat forced labour, other aspects remain essential. The presence of a social safety net for unemployed workers, government subsidies for small farmers and legal provisions for working conditions and labour rights all play an important role in determining people's vulnerability.

5 *What is the global political economy context?* Neoliberal policies based on import liberalization, cuts in government spending, financial liberalization, fiscal reforms, deregulation of capital and labour markets, privatization of state enterprises, land grabs and the commodification of everyday life have created opportunities for some and insecurities for many.

So far, we have seen examples of how these determinants create vulnerabilities that can lead to forced labour, including the global political economy of the World Cup in Qatar, the labour assets of migrant workers in Taiwan, the legal and policy framework enforcing prison labour in the United States and the livelihoods strategies of poor families in Brazil. Now consider caste discrimination, which affects some 260 million people worldwide. Most of them live in South Asia, with 201 million in India alone. Dalits, also known as 'scheduled castes' or 'untouchables', form the lowest group in a hierarchical system that divides people into unequal social groups. Those at the end of this social hierarchy are considered 'lesser human beings', 'impure' and 'polluting' for higher castes. Dalits are assigned some of the most dirty, degrading and difficult jobs. They suffer from social and economic exclusion and are often victims of violence. The vulnerability attached to caste discrimination and Dalits' systematic lack of power creates situations in which exploitation can proliferate. Caste-based forced labour across South Asia is particularly notable in the brickmaking industry and the sex industry and within agricultural labour. In each case, the weak economic position of Dalits and a lack of access to resources such as land increase their dependence on wage labour, while forcing them to accept loans. While some are pushed into bondage by a debt they can hardly repay, others are coerced into forced labour, often under threat of violence.[11]

In a 2014 report on caste-based discrimination, Human Rights Watch detailed the reality of manual scavengers in India. It was found that some 1.3 million people, 90 per cent of whom are Dalit women, were being assigned to remove human excreta.[12] While women were mostly employed to clean dry latrines, men were responsible for removing excrement from sewers and septic tanks. No one voluntarily chooses manual scavenging as a job. Even though they have the legal right to refuse to carry out these tasks, social pressure and threats of violence, eviction and being denied access to community land and resources often leave Dalits powerless. Denying or withholding wages are also common practice as a means of keeping Dalits tied to manual scavenging. Manual scavengers are paid less than the legally set minimum wage, and in rural areas women are often paid with leftover food, grain during harvest, and access to community land for grazing livestock and collecting firewood. While the employment of manual scavengers has been a criminal offence since 1993 in India, the practice remains widespread. State representatives, elected officials and village authorities not only fail to implement existing prohibitions on the practice, but they also participate in its perpetuation by refusing to intervene when Dalits who refuse to do this labour face threats of retaliation.

These different determinants can come together in detrimental ways to produce situations of extreme vulnerability, which in turn may lead to extreme forms of exploitation. While poverty, legal status, unemployment and social discrimination are powerful determinants that can help explain how people fall into forced labour arrangements, the inability for the vast majority of the world population to move across borders can also lead to situations of trafficking and forced labour. Indeed, the ability to move across countries to take advantage of work opportunities is the privilege of a minority. For the rest, irregular migration is typically their only option, leaving them vulnerable and often powerless as they pass through networks of brokers and traffickers who might deceive them during the recruitment stage about the wages they will be paid, their legal status in the country of destination and the type of work they are expected to provide. Their irregular status might force them further into adverse conditions as a result of accumulated debt, the confiscation of identity papers, the withholding of wages or the threat of denunciation to the authorities.

Why is Forced Labour Attractive to Some Employers?

The above section examined why individuals or households might be vulnerable to falling into forced labour situations. Now we should consider the other side of the equation: why is there a considerable demand for unfree labour? And why are employers willing to take such a risk in face of the legal constraints? The simple answer is that forced labour is big business. The ILO estimates that forced and compulsory labour generate annual profits of more than US$150 billion, and that 90 per cent of victims are exploited in the private economy. Why are employers resorting to such illegal practices to make a profit? Three main approaches try to explain why.

Legalist perspective

Legalist explanations focus on forced labour as primarily a problem of poor legislation – either in design or through implementation – that is solvable through governance mechanisms. Let us take two examples to illustrate this paradigm, one showing poor implementation in India, the other poor design in Cambodia. In the southern state of Tamil Nadu in India, the booming garment industry has come to rely heavily on Dalit girls.[13] In this highly competitive sector of activity, cheap and flexible labour is the norm. Temporary workers receive lower wages, have no benefits and are less likely to organize – for these reasons, they represent up to 80 per cent of the workforce. Employers have also shown a marked preference for female workers, whom they consider to be cheaper and more docile. Introduced around 2000 to guarantee manufacturers this labour force, the Sumangali Scheme is a recruitment system that promises to prospective workers a decent wage, comfortable accommodation, three nutritious meals a day and, most importantly, a considerable sum of money upon completion of their three-year contract, which is constituted by deducting money from wages. By 2011, some 120,000 workers were employed under the scheme, 60 per cent of whom were Dalits from the Arunthatiyar sub-caste, which is considered the 'Dalits of the Dalits'. Given that the garment industry in Tamil Nadu is heavily export-oriented, bonded Sumangali workers are part of the supply chain of major European and US clothing brands and retailers.

A typical working week is seventy-two hours – twelve hours per day, six days per week. Workers have four days off per month, but have to work on Sundays when required. Overtime is compulsory, yet rarely remunerated. Headaches, leg pain, stomach aches, irregular menstrual periods and heavy menstrual pains, tiredness, and weight lost are frequent complaints. Inadequate ventilation systems and excessive cotton dust have forced some workers to undergo surgery to remove balls of cotton fibre stuck in their bowels. When they are not working, Sumangali workers are confined to their living quarters. Employers often prohibit mobile phones and workers are kept under tight surveillance: guards from the mill accompany them when they go to the market once a fortnight. Up to 20 per cent of Sumangali workers are children under the age of 14. If we follow ILO Convention 182 on the worst forms of child labour and consider as child labour workers aged between 14 and 18 who perform work that is harmful to their 'health, safety or morals', then the scale of this form of exploitation under this scheme is substantially higher. The vast majority have no contracts. Moreover, workers are hired as apprentices and, as such, do not qualify for the minimum wage; they can conveniently be kept in that state for up to three years in Tamil Nadu. There have been numerous cases of workers who did not receive the lump sum that was promised when they were first taken on, and many of those who left before the end of their contract did not receive the portion of their wage that had been deducted.

Proponents of the legalist approach could make the argument that India is a classic case of how forced labour proliferates through poor implementation of legislation enacted to fight it. Indeed, apart from ILO Convention 182, which India has not ratified, the country already has the legal framework to combat forced labour: the work week of seventy-two hours and the hazardous working environment are breaches of the country's Factories Act; caste discrimination is illegal under India's constitution; the employment of children under the age of 14 is a violation of India's Child Labour (Regulation and Prohibition) Act; and holding back part of the workers' wage under the Sumangali Scheme violates the Indian Bonded Labour System (Abolition) Act. It is the government's failure to implement an already comprehensive legal framework that explains the persistence and pro-liferation of forced labour in India.

Anthropologist Larissa Sandy's research on sex work and anti-trafficking measures in Cambodia provides us with another example of the legalist approach.[14] At the core of the issue is the following question: is sex work free labour or forced labour? According to many public health officials and governments, all sex work is forced labour, and should be criminalized accordingly. In this paradigm, sex workers are viewed as victims of sexual violence and exploitation and they must be rescued. This is the approach that the Royal Government of Cambodia adopted with the promulgation of the 2008 Law on the Suppression of Human Trafficking and Sexual Exploitation. The law criminalizes sex work by equating it with human trafficking, thereby rendering sex work a form of unfree labour and sex workers victims of forced labour. In so doing, the law provides for a whole new domain of state intervention such as brothel raids and rescue inter-ventions, tighter border controls and restrictions on migration.

For the global sex workers' rights movement, however, the view that all sex work is by nature forced is problematic, since it crimi-nalizes all sex work regardless of context. The movement proposes instead the 'sex as work' paradigm, which distinguishes between free and forced monetized exchanges. According to this analysis, while some workers are forced into the sex industry, others find it an income-generating activity that expands their livelihood strategies. The movement argues that recognizing sex workers as workers with labour rights is essential to providing them with safer working envi-ronments. Indeed, many argue that the criminalization of sex work has reinforced the marginalization and oppression of sex workers in Cambodia and reduced their safety and well-being by forcing them to travel and work under hazardous conditions. Since 2008, the violation of sex workers' rights and liberties has increased, including arbitrary arrest and detention without due process. In contrast, if one accepts the premise set forth by the Cambodian authorities that all sex work is forced, then one could argue that the resilience of forced labour betrays the need to update the 2008 law, provided that its implementation will be carried out to the full extent of the law.

While recognizing the importance of regulatory changes, critics would point out that the legalist approach does not really concern itself with why Dalit girls ended up in a situation of bondage in India, or how Cambodian women are put in a position of vulnerability in which sex work becomes a livelihood strategy. Critics might therefore suggest that the legalist approach tackles the symptoms – rather than the causes – of forced labour.

Developmentalist perspective

In contrast to legalist explanations, developmentalist approaches maintain that forced labour is not so much an issue of governance as a social phenomenon associated with a lack of economic development in a given country. Forms of economic and political modernization are likely to root out most instances of forced labour because, from this perspective, they have no place in a modern economy. Eighteenth century political economist Adam Smith was the first to condemn slavery on economic grounds. Free workers were deemed economically more efficient: not only were they cheaper than slaves and worked harder and better because it was in their interest, they were also crucial as consumers to the constitution of a national market in goods and services.[15] In contrast, slaves were seen as inhibiting productivity growth and technological development, and pose adaptability problems in a dynamic, competitive market environment. Smith's economic argument against forced labour has influenced thinkers such as Thomas Robert Malthus, John Stuart Mill and Max Weber. His view that economic growth is as likely to cure forced labour as regulatory measures has been central to liberal, neoclassical and some streams of Marxist economics.

Cocoa production in West Africa provides us with an example of how the lack of economic growth can lead to child slavery.[16] For the $75 billion chocolate and cocoa-based products market, West Africa is a key region, with Côte d'Ivoire and Ghana contributing over 50 per cent of the world supply. Since its independence in 1960, Côte d'Ivoire has used its national marketing board as a financial instrument for development projects, buying from the producers at a fixed price and selling at higher prices on international markets. Plummeting international prices in the 1980s destroyed the previous two decades of rapid economic growth. After the government defaulted on its debt in 1987, structural adjustment forced it to balance its books on the back of coffee and cocoa farmers by cutting their payments by half, thereby causing widespread economic hardship. Under pressure from the World Bank, the government abolished the Cocoa Board in 1999, only to create five new bodies to regulate the cocoa trade in the following years. Between 1999 and 2003, levies on exports increased ninefold and cocoa taxes almost tripled. Exporters downloaded these extra costs onto smallholders, who were no longer protected by a guaranteed minimum price. Amidst widespread poverty, producers became increasingly dependent on family labour, including child labour, and instances of child slavery and trafficked children on cocoa plantations have surfaced. About 820,000 children in Côte d'Ivoire were working on cocoa-related activities in the early 2000s, 40 per cent of whom did not attend school. In this respect, developmentalists would argue that economic growth is a much better way to under-mine child labour and promote education than regulations, as poor families depend much more on family labour than those with higher standards of living.

Breman's comparative study of agrarian bondage in India and Pakistan constitutes another example of the impact of modern eco-nomic forces in the countryside.[17] Defining bondage as a relationship of servitude and patronage through which the landless are bonded to large landowners, Breman traces the different developmental path taken by both countries. In India, agrarian relations have been trans-formed in important ways through the progressive commercializa-tion of agriculture launched by land reform initiatives that followed the country's independence. The introduction and dissemination of capitalist social relations in the countryside has in turn set in motion a process of modernization and economic growth that proved central to the diversification of the rural economy and the dissolution of bonded relationships. With farmers and landowners moving away from labour-intensive crops, daily wage labourers gradually came to replace the permanent workforce of farm servants. Meanwhile, the monetization of consumption further undermined the patronage relationship that had characterized landlordism. At the same time, the establishment of a democratic political system has tended to erode traditional relationships of servitude and submission, making it more difficult for the state to ignore the grievances of the rural elec-torate and deny the rights of its citizens.

In contrast, the lack of land reform in Pakistan has preserved land-lordism as an oppressive system, delayed the diversification of the rural economy and kept agrarian production in a semi-feudal state. The situation of the lower classes was made even worse in the 1970s, as Pakistani landowners started switching to crops that are less labour intensive and require labour on a cyclical rather than permanent basis. While the precarization of employment relationships in the agrarian economy is further compounded by the lack of adequate work in the main towns, the state has failed to intervene on behalf of the land-poor and landless masses. As Breman argues, whereas the traditional form of bondage has virtually disappeared in India, the tillers of the land in the province of Punjab in Pakistan continue to be trapped in a state of subjugation with little to no freedom of action.

While socioeconomic change in many parts of the world has indeed broken down older forms of bondage in rural areas, it has also pro-duced new forms of forced labour, even among the most dynamic economic sectors. Critics would stress that economic growth and development are linked to contemporary forms of forced labour. They might also suggest that the uneven distribution of power within the global economy has in fact undermined labour rights and people's ability to resist forced labour.

Critical perspectives

Critical perspectives have argued that capitalism produces both free and unfree labour unevenly across space. Two causes are generally highlighted – the cost of labour and the need for labour. According to Jean Allain and colleagues, direct producers and intermediaries do not use forced labour because they are intrinsically bad people, but because it makes business sense to do so.[18] Businesses, including both producers and intermediaries, use forced labour either to lower costs or to generate additional revenues. Consider market concentration in the food retail sector, which is driving forced labour conditions within food supply chains as retailers' unprecedented power allows them to command low prices, quick turnaround and high quality from farmers and suppliers. In 2011 in the European Union, the largest five retailers in every country had a combined market share of more than 60 per cent in thirteen member states (Austria, Belgium, Denmark, Estonia, Finland, France, Germany, Ireland, Luxembourg, the Netherlands, Portugal, Sweden and the United Kingdom), with market concentration exceeding 80 per cent in Denmark and Estonia. In most countries, market concentration among two or three major retailers is the norm. Two supermarket chains — Coles and Woolworths — control over 70 per cent of Australia's food retailing sector, while Wal-Mart and Kroger had 43.2 per cent of grocery store sales in the United States in 2013. In Canada, three retailers held 55.5 per cent of the grocery and food retail sector in 2011. Similar consolidation can be observed in South Korea, Brazil and elsewhere.[19]

The net result is an hourglass-shaped global food system. Masses of farmers and small producers compete to supply a smaller number of processors, manufacturers and wholesalers. These supply the handful of large retailers at the choke point, which sell directly to the global population of consumers. Food retailers' unprecedented power as buyers within national and global markets gives them the ability to set the terms under which the food supply chain operates. Their ability to impose contracts and prices with tough deadlines is key to understanding the growing demand for sub-minimum wages and working standards in the food industry. In order to meet their obligations, stay afloat financially and weather the efforts of retailers and processors to lower costs, producers and suppliers often subcontract labour and other low value-adding business activities. These agencies may in turn outsource their activities to a third party, either because they are unable to meet their obligations or because they want to take advantage of a lower-cost provider. Labour supply chains operating through multiple intermediaries and stages of subcontracting are particularly vulnerable to forced labour. Retailers' hold over global food production and their ability to command low prices places strong downward pressures upon direct producers, creating the conditions of insecurity under which forced labour can flourish.

A six-month investigation by journalists in 2014, for example, revealed the relationship between retail business models and the structural need to lower the cost of labour by linking the seafood in major supermarkets in the United States and the United Kingdom with slavery in the Thai fishing industry. With an annual turnover of $33 billion (£20 billion), the Thailand-based Charoen Pokphand (CP) Foods is the world's largest prawn farmer. To feed its farmed prawns, CP Foods buys fishmeal from suppliers that own, operate or buy from fishing boats manned with slaves. Most of them are Burmese and Cambodian migrant workers who pay brokers to help them find a job in Thailand, but who are instead trafficked into slavery and sold to boat captains. Many work for years without being paid. They are held against their own will, endure torture and regular beatings, work 20-hour shifts, kept in chains, suffer hunger and malnourishment, and often witness fellow slaves being killed in front of them. CP Foods supplies international supermarkets, including Aldi, Carrefour, Costco, Iceland, Morrisons, Tesco, the Co-op and Walmart. As Bob Miller, CP Foods' UK managing director, admitted: 'We'd like to solve the problem of Thailand because there's no doubt commercial interests have created much of this problem.' Consider watching the 'Supermarket Slave Trail' video produced by investigative journalists Kate Hodal, Chris Kelly and Felicity Lawrence.[20]

As Tom Brass has argued, however, unfree labour is not always about the cost of labour, but also about the need to secure labour by keeping workers captive and therefore less likely to leave or strike.[21] One of Brass's most useful points is related to his argument that forced labour is a form of labour control that precludes the possibility of exit for the worker. This creates a power relationship of strong dependency that can be used to lock labour into intensive work under poor conditions. One important example of this can be found in the agricultural sector, where farmers and other producers, who rarely have the labour capacity to harvest time-sensitive crops, will require a fixed labour force. Consider the case of Uzbekistan.[22] Every autumn since 1991, the Uzbek government has forced farmers to deliver annual production quotas and citizens to weed cotton fields and harvest cotton. During the 2015 harvest, more than one million citizens were forced to pick cotton, including students, teachers and doctors. Failure to fulfil production and field work quotas can lead to the loss of land and jobs, to fines, confiscation of property and verbal and physical abuse. Students refusing to work also face disciplinary measures and retaliation, including poor grades and difficulty finding employment. Wages are substantially lower than market wages, and workers have to pay for accommodation, food, transportation and other expenses. Workers are also fined if they do not meet their quotas, in some cases leaving them indebted. Citizens have been arrested, attacked, beaten and intimidated by police for resisting forced labour. Government repression and human rights violations are widespread, and citizens have little to no trust in the impartiality of the courts. Yet, the government's forced labour system is allowed to continue in part because of the World Bank, which has indentured the country through agricultural loans to the government or through private loans to textile companies sourcing Uzbek cotton. While the Cotton Campaign has led more than 250 companies to take the Cotton Pledge, under which they 'commit to not knowingly source Uzbek cotton for the manufacturing of our products', the reality is that most Uzbek cotton is exported to Bangladesh and China where it enters global apparel companies' dense and opaque supply chains.

Proponents of the critical perspective would point out that unfree labour is not an anomaly under capitalism, but very much part of its history and development. They might argue that while the legalist approach fails to question the causes of forced labour, developmentalists are unable to account for the fact that forced labour under global capitalism is tightly integrated within the supply chains of major transnational corporations. Given the inequality of power between capital and labour in the global economy, this perspective would suggest that forced labour is likely to increase in the future.

Further reading

While Kevin Bales' text *Disposable People: New Slavery in the Global* Economy (Berkeley, CA: University of California Press, 2012) provides a legalist account of forced labour, the collection edited by

Jan Breman, Isabelle Guérin and Aseem Prakash focuses on India to provide a variety of developmentalist and critical perspectives: *India's Unfree Workforce: Of Bondage Old and New* (New Delhi: Oxford University Press, 2009). In *Labour Regime Change in the Twenty-First Century: Unfreedom, Capitalism and Primitive Accumulation* (Leiden: Brill, 2011), Tom Brass offers a comprehensive Marxist approach to unfree labour. Finally, openDemocracy has produced a collection of short, easy-to-read contributions on contemporary issues of trafficking and slavery: https://www.opendemocracy.net/info/bts-short-course.

Chapter 10
Environment and Labour

The first thing that hits you is the smell. When the wind isn't up, acrid smoke from workshops simply hangs listlessly in the air, giving it a vile odour that assaults your sinuses. This is Guiyu in southern China, reputedly the world's biggest recycling site for global e-waste. It is hard to picture it now, but not too long ago this town of 150,000 people was set in a rustic agricultural region nestled close to the coast. Nowadays, if people know that rice comes from fields adjacent to Guiyu they won't eat it. Their caution is for a good reason. The town's agrarian origins were permanently erased in the mid-1990s when Guiyu was transformed into an industrial landscape for the mass recycling of electronic goods. Piled high and wide in the city streets, mountains of digital discards are dumped by the truckload and set upon by an army of salvage workers who drag them into small workshops for processing. You'll find all sorts here: motherboards and circuitry, broken monitors, old keyboards, toner cartridges, cabling of all types and innumerable cellphones. Many of these goods were originally assembled not far away in the factories of southern China before being shipped halfway around the world to Western consumers. A steadily growing portion of items come from within China itself, where the scale of digital consumption increases exponentially year on year.[1]

Within the town itself, no one much cares about the provenance of the goods. The 5,000 informal waste recycling companies, many of which are little more than informal household workshops, simply process whatever comes. Their labourers are mostly migrants drawn from interior China who circulate between workshops depending on where employment can be found. Picking through the fallen consumer icons of years past, these modern scavengers often use fire to burn off plastic coverings to uncover scraps of copper buried inside, or acid baths to strip components from motherboards. To an extent, the profligacy of consumer society is to their gain. The industry provides a source of livelihood for thousands of households. Wages for recycling, however, remain low and many are aware that the job puts their health at great risk. The fumes, the chemicals and the smoke all take a depressing toll on the labour force and fill the local environment with hard metals and toxic residues. News agencies such as the BBC have reported that Guiyu has the highest level of cancer-causing dioxins in the world, and scientific studies reveal that children in the town have abnormal levels of lead in their blood.[2] Notably, women workers are often on the frontline of this toxicity because they are commonly given the task of removing the smallest components from circuit boards using harsh chemicals.

The case of Guiyu opens up a series of questions about how labour is connected to the transformation of nature. At one level, that labour involves transforming nature may seem relatively self-evident. After all, the basic point of production is to change one set of materials into another more complex or useful set, whether it is mining ore for iron, growing a field of wheat or building an airliner. Things get more complex, however, when we consider how labour transforms nature at different scales and with different consequences for different sets of people. In the Guiyu example, the recycling of discarded electronic components simultaneously transformed workers' bodies and the local landscape. What was once an agricultural region rapidly became an industrial town composed of factory workshops and whose streets are filled with post-consumption waste and whose soils are troublingly toxic. At a wider scale, the growing piles of discarded items in Guiyu bear testament to a worrying trend. As labour becomes more productive and directed towards creating the enormous quantity of commodities that humankind consumes on a day-to-day basis, its ability to transform nature intensifies, raising pressing questions about global environmental change.

Using its combined focus on the spatial scales at which environmental transformations occur and the networks that facilitate them, global labour studies is uniquely well placed to examine how labour transforms nature. Most importantly, it allows us to consider the power relations between who benefits from these transformations and who carries the risks. As geographers Piers Blaikie and Harold Brookfield once tersely argued, we cannot overlook how one person's accumulation can be rooted in another's degradation.[3] To this end, the following sections consider the unequal and contested dimensions of labour's transformation of nature across scales, starting with some fundamental theoretical questions about the reciprocal ways in which societies produce nature and nature produces societies.

Producing Nature

Most of us tend to make a distinction between society and nature as two separate realms in which nature is something out there rather than in here. This often means conceiving of nature as some sort of pristine space untouched by human activities, or at least as something we might see when taking a walk in the park. Such conceptualizations are problematic, however. Where does nature end and society begin when, for example, you turn on a kitchen tap and water flows from it? Throughout our day-to-day lives, we encounter social and natural processes bundled up in complex ways. Marx was one of the first thinkers to reject the nature–society dichotomy when he argued for an approach that could recognize their intimate connection.[4] For Marx, the key to the relationship is labour through which humans appropriate and transform the materials of nature according to their needs. As a result, what unites social organizations as diverse as hunter-gatherer groups to advanced capitalist societies is that they all work with and through nature in order to secure their existence. For this to happen, societies produce new natures – from fields of genetically modified soybeans to dense urban sprawl.

Building on this point, geographer Neil Smith has explored more specifically the relationship between capitalist development and the production of nature.[5] In contrast to previous economic systems, capitalism is unique in that it organizes the relationship between society and nature at a global level. At the core of this process is the production of nature for profits. Consider, for example, the rise of the biotechnology industry for global agriculture. As sociologist Jack Kloppenburg Jr. has showed, the dramatic growth of private companies in plant breeding is linked to their ability to circumvent biological and institutional obstacles. First, private breeders have sought to free themselves from biology by creating hybrid seeds that give greater yields. The catch is that these seeds are sterile, which makes farmers dependent on commercial markets year after year. Second, private breeders have also been able to extend property rights and patents within plant breeding and therein centralize control over seeds among a limited number of private hands. Once an activity located in the public domain, the improvement of the genetic stock of plants is now firmly in the hands of just a few companies which seek to further commodify seeds as a means to accumulate profit. The result is an unprecedented concentration of political, economic and scientific power in a global biotech oligarchy.[6]

If society produces nature, the reverse is also true. Far from being a passive and inert realm, nature's biological and geophysical processes and properties actively shape society. The need for societies to work through nature imprints itself upon a host of social institutions and processes, including technological developments, legal frameworks, labour relations and investment strategies. Critical resource geographers have been particularly attentive to the ways in which nonhuman nature challenges commodification. Gavin Bridge, for example, has showed how the biophysical properties of natural gas shape society in important ways.[7] The risks associated with the physical and chemical properties of gas – flammability, fluidity, changing volume and unpredictability – mean that its distribution through pipelines is limited to a continental level. At the same time, producing natural gas as a commodity requires the application of specialized labour to control its natural variability. Indeed, to rescale natural gas transportation from continental to global markets necessitates a process by which gas is cryogenically cooled to minus 162°C that transforms it into a liquid occupying 1/600th of its initial volume. Liquefied natural gas can then be loaded onto tankers that will ship it to terminals where gasification (liquid to gas technology) can occur before being distributed throughout the network. As this example demonstrates, nonhuman natures leave their firm imprint upon society and its spatial forms.

One key aspect of this discussion on the symbiotic relationship between society and nature is the recognition that environmental problems are not something external to society with which it has to cope or adapt to, but manufactured by societies through their labouring activities. The following section looks at these ideas through the example of oil production in Nigeria in which the benefits and costs of producing new natures fall unevenly upon different social groups.

Oil and Labour in the Niger Delta

As you fly across the southernmost tip of Nigeria where the African mainland juts out into the Gulf of Guinea, you see the great Niger river fan out across shallow coastal flats to form one of the three largest wetlands in the world. It is an area of immense biodiversity, home to more than twenty different ethnic groups, and a bountiful region for agriculture and fishing. The Niger delta, however, also happens to sit upon sizeable reserves of oil and gas. Since the 1970s, the rapid exploitation of these resources has propelled Nigeria into being one of the top ten oil producing countries worldwide. This boom in extraction is the cumulative result of decades of labour that have transformed the delta into a major oil production hub. Mangroves and forests have been cleared, waterways canalized and dredged, networks of roads built, ports and refineries constructed and miles upon miles of pipelines have been laid to form a network through which oil can flow. This ongoing labour of environmental transformation is typical of resource frontiers, and the resulting transformation has been immense in both scope and scale. Pipelines criss-cross the delta; gas flares illuminate its skies; major refineries, storage facilities and loading ports crowd upstream riverbanks and the coast; and large tracts of land have been spoiled by the dumping – both deliberate and inadvertent – of waste. Labour has quite simply reworked the physical landscape, leaving a new nature in its wake.

For the delta's population, the results of this transformation have been profoundly uneven. The Nigerian government has long maintained that oil and gas extraction is pivotal to national development and wealth creation. This is true to an extent, for it is readily apparent that the oil industry is a potential source of immense wealth. Nigeria now exports some two billion barrels of sweet crude oil per year – primarily to Europe – and this accounts for over 90 per cent of the country's export revenues. Most of the oil companies working in Nigeria are major international corporations, although the state-owned conglomerate still performs a significant degree of extraction, processing and distribution in the nation. Given the massive rents available to both foreign and national oil companies, the scale of corruption is colossal. Nigeria's auditor general revealed that $16 billion of oil revenue went missing in 2014 alone.[8] Such systematic graft speaks to the close links between Nigeria's ruling elite and the oil industry, an incestuous relationship that has developed over decades.

Further down the chain, however, the issue of wealth transfer is far murkier. While the industry generates jobs for both skilled and unskilled workers, the heavy segmentation of labour markets means that the benefits of employment are unevenly distributed. On a gendered level, both frontline and managerial jobs are comprehensively masculinized, with around 70 per cent of total jobs going to men, a figure that rises to 99 per cent for executive managerial positions.[9] At a second level of segmentation, there are also clear divisions between Nigerian workers performing the technical processes of surveying, drilling and extracting and contracted foreign workers who work alongside them. Notably, such 'expatriate' workers often have superior contracts even when performing the same tasks as their Nigerian counterparts.[10] Third, there are strong distinctions between core workers – those in skilled jobs with relatively long-term contracts and benefits – and a large and growing peripheral segment of less-skilled workers who suffer from limited job security, poor pay and few contractual benefits.

By Nigerian standards, core workers in the oil industry have often been considered something of a privileged sector. This relative advantage in terms of formalized contracts, pay and benefits stems in part from their essential role in controlling the flow of oil. Working at a key nexus point of the country's wealth generation affords them a degree of political power within the broader political economy of Nigeria. Such workers benefit from active unions, and industrial actions such as strikes pose a considerable threat to oil companies and the state. As a result, oil worker unions have often been persecuted by military regimes seeking to either control or simply destroy them. More recently, a new corporate strategy has emerged to reduce workers' influence and to lower costs. By replacing formalized jobs with short-term contracted workers, oil companies have sought to reduce the number, status and political power of core workers.[11] Many unions in Nigeria have fought a rearguard action against this flexibilization, arguing powerfully that such processes concentrate wealth further and create a greater expanse of insecure workers. Such arguments, however, must be made in a context in which the government is closely allied with the interests of the oil companies, given their overwhelming contribution to foreign earnings, to government revenues and to the lining of the pockets of compliant officials.

Outside the immediate work of oil extraction, the transformation of the Niger Delta has had troubling implications for local communities. On the one hand, minority ethnic groups that inhabit the delta region do not typically staff the core jobs within the oil sector. To the extent that they find oil-related jobs outside basic service tasks, it is in the arduous labour of expanding and maintaining infrastructure. This is work that is poorly paid and can involve direct exposure to toxins. At the same time, the development of oil has driven an expansive and extremely detrimental transformation of the local environment as oil spills and chemical contamination undermine agriculture, fishing and other resource-orientated livelihoods. Even the industry's own

Box 10.1 New natures in Indonesia

For a visual account of the transformation of colonial Indonesia into an extractive economy see the short film produced by the Goodyear Tire Company in 1920 (http://www.youtube.com/watch?v=8PgQDW9kbUQ). It shows clearly how the production of rubber for Western consumption involved a process of massive environmental transformation in which building roads and levelling the forest were explicitly portrayed as an act of civilizing a 'primeval jungle'. Through its commentary and visuals, the film reveals the complex relationships between taming the forests and transforming local peoples and indentured labourers under a projected vision of progress and development. This captures how the work of environmental transformation at resource frontiers is typically dressed up in the language of progress and development, despite the inherent manifold tensions and contradictions.

statistics note that there is, on average, one oil leak a day and the true figures are likely to be at least double that toll.[12] Women often bear the brunt of this environmental transformation, as they are part of a gendered division of labour that overwhelmingly assigns them the livelihood tasks of subsistence agriculture, gathering food and other materials from the forests where the negative effects of environmental transformation are most severe. This means that they experience first-hand through their own labour how the expansion of the oil frontier despoils the local environment.

Planetary Transformations: Work and the Anthropocene

The scramble to extract oil from the Niger Delta and the resulting conflicts over environmental transformation might seem a world away from the factories of coastal China or the densely packed aisles of a Walmart store in central Chicago. The three are, however, closely linked. Global production networks and the immense productive powers of labour in the modern era are entirely dependent upon the extraction and utilization of carbon-based energy forms. This reliance includes the immediate energy to power factories and also the fuel that facilitates global supply and distribution networks, as well as the provision of inputs such as plastics that are extensively used in most types of production. In short, the global scale of production and the globalized networks that facilitate it are heavily dependent on the particular qualities of oil, natural gas, coal and other energy forms. The labours of extraction in the Niger Delta, mass production in southern China and mass consumption in northern cities are, in this respect, closely related.

Oil in particular provides a highly concentrated package of hydrocarbons that is uniquely able to power the productive systems that facilitate what we term modern society. As political scientist Timothy Mitchell notes, current forms of political and economic life would not exist without the energy derived from oil. From the food we eat to the houses we inhabit, the vast majority of goods and services we consume on a day-to-day level is powered by oil and other fossil fuels, particularly in the centres of consumption located in the affluent West.[13] As a result, while we often celebrate the astonishing increases in the productivity of labour that stands behind our ability to produce ever greater numbers of consumption items, it is the combination of labour with the energy latent within carbon-based energy forms that has powered these trends. This inevitably leads to pivotal questions about the future of labour in a world of limited quantities of oil and other resources and the potentially crippling effects of climatic change and other forms of global environmental change.

For global labour studies, a key question centres on how to best conceptualize these powers of humans to produce nature on a global scale. One currently fashionable way to do so is to use the idea of the Anthropocene. The Anthropocene thesis argues that, through our labouring activities, humans presently exercise a commanding influence over the earth's geology and ecosystems to the extent that it warrants designating an entirely new geological era.[14] According to scientist Naomi Oreskes, there are now so many of us cutting down trees and burning billions of tons of fossil fuels that humans have become geological agents who have changed the chemistry of the atmosphere, caused sea levels to rise and the climate to change.[15] Oreskes might also have added that we have simultaneously become biological agents of mass destruction, creating the conditions in which animal species are being wiped out at a pace that parallels only the most severe mass-extinction events in earth's history.[16]

For scientists such as Paul Crutzen and Will Steffen, this transition represents a historical moment of profound anxiety. In geophysical terms, the immediate future will be less biologically diverse, less forested, much warmer and marked by extreme weather events tied to climatic change. All this is closely connected to the way we produce, distribute and consume goods, putting labour at the heart of the

Table 10.1 Planetary boundaries

Presently within safe zone	Presently within zone of uncertainty	Presently within danger zone	No established criteria
Stratospheric ozone depletion	Climate change Land system change	Biospheric genetic diversity	Atmospheric aerosol loading
Ocean acidification		Biogeochemical flows (phosphorous and nitrogen)	Novel entities
Freshwater use			Biospheric functional diversity

Source: from the Stockholm Resilience Centre[17]

Anthropocene. The deep apprehension expressed by Crutzen and Steffen is closely tied to the idea of planetary boundaries. The latter are a set of key ecosystem processes that represent tipping points: if humans impede or shift these processes too far, then they will undermine the ecological foundations necessary for our societies to flourish. In churning the earth in the pursuit of mass production for consumption, these analysts argue, humans are already trespassing far outside a number of critical thresholds for a sustainable future (see table 10.1).

The anthropocene thesis is a bold statement that focuses our attention on the profound global impacts inherent in the way that humans produce themselves and nature on a day-to-day, year-to-year basis. There are, however, some questions that need addressing. First, analysts disagree markedly on the start date for the new era. While Crutzen and Steffen emphasize the industrial revolution – specifically the role of fossil fuel consumption for mass production – others have backdated the era to the conquest of the Americas and the rise of colonial capitalism, in which landscapes were systematically transformed on a continental scale.[18] The issue is important because it raises the question of whether the Anthropocene emerged from technological changes – i.e., the rise of combustion engines that could harness fossil fuel usage – or if it is rooted more deeply in the emergence of capitalism and its inbuilt drive to intensify production and expand outwards. In short, the seemingly simple question of putting a date on the Anthropocene drives to the heart of whether the issues identified can be resolved through technical change – i.e., a transition to clean energy – or requires a more fundamental reconfiguration of social order (box 10.2).

Box 10.2   Societies beyond oil?

In the stimulating and provocative book *Societies Beyond Oil*, sociologist John Urry provides four visions of a future of depleted oil and climatic change. Paying close attention to how oil shapes the ways we work, live, communicate and organize our collective affairs, Urry's future scenarios range from the wildly optimistic – a magic bullet solution in which technological change facilitates the relatively smooth replacement of oil with hydrogen-based power sources – to the dystopian – an 'oil dregs' future in which tightening supplies of oil cause a collapse in productive systems, incredible social disruption and endemic conflict. For Urry, the only scenario that is both realistic and desirable is a managed powering down of societies based on a profound localization of economies. The resulting societies are materially less well off because labour productivity is undercut by the end of easy oil. Yet they can still meet a broad range of social needs. Ultimately, however, Urry's warning is stark: the material bonanza experienced within Western societies over the twentieth century was akin to a free lunch, and one that is proving increasingly indigestible. Using the last dregs of oil to implement far-reaching changes to how we produce, distribute and consume goods, he argues, is a matter of urgency.[19]

The second contention is that the Anthropocene concept appears to contain some uncomfortable generalizations. While it emphasizes the role of humanity in profoundly reshaping the earth system, the global population is not a unified actor. Put bluntly, there is no 'we' in Anthropocene. As the British economist Nicholas Stern noted in his signature report on global warming, a disproportionate share of the climate change burden falls on poor regions of the world that are precisely those areas that have done least to contribute to the problem in the first place.[20] We should therefore be extremely cautious of the emphasis on humanity in general within the Anthropocene thesis. Those who accord the greatest benefits from the labours associated with global environmental change are often very different groups of people from those who reap the worst consequences. The accelerated erosion of coastal lands in southern Bangladesh by rising seas and more extreme cyclones, for example, hits the poorest of the poor hardest. These include smallholder farmers, landless labourers and particularly women and children whose contribution to global warming is miniscule. At the same time, they have the least resources in terms of assets and networks to deal with the changing nature of the environment in which they live. It is perhaps not surprising that analysts are concerned about an upsurge in migration away from areas worst affected by climatic change. Growing numbers of 'climate refugees' have the potential to create new groups of precarious labourers heading towards the informal sectors of expanding urban centres worldwide.

Labouring through the Anthropocene

So what does this mean for the future of labour within our globally produced new nature? Is there a way forward that can reconcile advances in labour productivity with potentially catastrophic environmental change and resource depletion? The answer, of course, depends on who you ask. In the dominant paradigm of ecomodernism, the solution is to develop new labour processes that are ever more efficient in order to minimize the environmental impacts of existing and future production. According to ecomodernists, to have a 'good Anthropocene' requires that humans use their growing social, economic and technological powers to simultaneously improve living standards, stabilize the climate and protect the natural world.[21] Rather than draw back from capitalist modernity's tendency to produce more and more, the way forward is to better harness technological innovation to increase efficiency in all areas of production and consumption, therein minimizing or severing the link between production and environmental degradation. This is the only way, ecomodernists claim, to reconcile ending global poverty with the constraints posed by environmental change.

To this end, ecomodernists promote the idea of 'decoupling' to refer to the simultaneous process of increasing productivity while decreasing the intensity of resource and energy use. The United Nations Environment Program (UNEP), for example, has argued fervently that decoupling is not only possible but also essential for future prosperity in a planet of limited resources. It is important to note that there are two uses of decoupling. The first is relative decoupling, which refers to a decrease in the rate of extra materials used for each additional unit of growth. Under this scenario, the production of each additional refrigerator or car would require fewer inputs than before, in terms either of raw materials or of energy required. As a consequence, there would be a gradual but sustained decrease in the environmental impact for each extra commodity produced. While such efficiency should rightly be valued, the trouble with relative decoupling is that the positive impacts can easily be washed away if overall levels of production and consumption increase. This trend is known as the Jevons paradox, named after nineteenth-century

English economist William Jevons, who noted how increased efficiencies in the coal industry led not to the decreased resource use he expected but to an expanding scale of production and consumption.

In response to this quandary, the idea of absolute decoupling represents a situation in which increases in the scale of production proceed alongside a reduction in total material resources used. By producing 'more with less', absolute decoupling is the ecomodernist's holy grail. It would allow economic growth to continue while environmental pressures decrease. In practical terms, absolute decoupling is seen to stem from technological and organizational changes that combine increasingly efficient production methods powered by clean energy with streamlined logistics and final products made of more durable materials that can be easily recycled at the end of their lifespan. On the one hand, new production methods and technologies need to be created, placing a heavy onus on technology as the solution to environmental woes. On the other hand, the state-of-the-art production methods that currently exist need to be generalized on a global scale, weeding out inefficient forms of production. The latter would potentially have important ramifications in the realm of work because it implies technologically advanced production methods displacing labour-intensive ones with potentially troubling implications for employment.

While many have questioned whether it is feasible to achieve absolute decoupling, ecomodernists point to a few key instances. The European Environment Agency, for example, notes that eleven out of twenty-eight economic sectors experienced an absolute decoupling of greenhouse gas emissions from the growth in economic output in 2000–7.[22] Unfortunately, part of this decoupling may be merely a paper accomplishment because the environmentally intensive aspects of production have largely been shifted away from core countries through global production networks. In its shift to becoming the 'workshop of the world', China has also been transformed into the 'chimney of the world', to use Andreas Malm's provocative phrase. As Malm notes in his study of fossil fuel usage, China alone accounted for close to two-thirds of the expansion of global greenhouse gas emissions between 2000 and 2007, the exact period of apparent decoupling in Europe.[23] Has Europe been able to absolutely decouple some of its production from greenhouse gasses simply by importing 'dirty' goods produced elsewhere? This process, in which the environmental costs of global production are displaced from advanced countries towards those in the global South, is sometimes called environmental cost shifting. By adopting a global focus, this concept presents a more complex picture of labour, production and

environmental transformation, in which costs and benefits are unevenly shared between and within countries.

As an example of this kind of analysis, consider how, on the UN's
World Environment Day in 2013, the Mongolian president Tsakhia
Elbegdorj announced plans to turn Mongolia into a wind power
hub for Asia.[24] This initiative seemed like an expressly welcome
development that could play a key role in moving towards absolute
decoupling. After all, Mongolia's wide grassy plains are sparsely
populated and enjoy fairly consistent winds that can power an expansive array of turbines. The development of clean energy, therefore,
seems to be a win–win situation and, despite the bulk of technology
and expertise being sourced from foreign firms, the sector potentially offers new employment opportunities for skilled segments of
the Mongolian labour market. There is, however, a major sting in the
tail of this clean energy initiative. Much of the funding for the wind
farms comes from state taxation of mineral extraction, including the
development of coalmines across the steppe. Mongolia, it turns out, is
sitting on enough coal to fuel every power plant in China for the next
half-century and is seeking to rapidly develop these resources with
aid from both private investors and international institutions such
as the World Bank. Mongolian coal extraction therefore stands as
the energy base for a pyramid of global production networks linking
Chinese production to consumption on a world scale.

Two tensions are particularly notable. First, as the scale of
Mongolia's state-supported mineral extraction and its accompanying
infrastructure expands, the fragile local ecosystem is degraded and
water resources are diverted. Similar to the Niger Delta case above,
this transformation of nature has a major impact on local livelihoods.
In particular, the labour of nomadic herding that has been a traditional and sustainable occupation for at least a third of the population is disrupted by the growth of mining operations. The burning of
Mongolian coal in China creates localized air pollution while, at the
same time, directly contributing to global climate change. The latter
affects Mongolian herders through its tendency to increase both
summer droughts and intense winter storms on the grasslands. When
the two occur in the same year, livestock mortality is very high and
many herders are forced to relocate to the outskirts of Mongolia's
capital, Ulaanbaatar, where they struggle to construct new livelihoods in the informal sector.

The tensions of energy use, extraction and environmental transformations are aptly captured in this brief example from Mongolia.
Ecomodernists, of course, would indeed commend the heightened
extraction of coal as long as it powers a shift of Mongolia towards

Box 10.3   The behemoth of coal in Inner Mongolia

For a penetrating cinematic exploration of the labours of environmental transformation in an open pit coal mine, watch the Chinese documentary film *Behemoth* by Zhao Liang (2015). The visually astonishing trailer is here: http://youtu.be/kxmgCakyGH4.

a green energy future. Like the Mongolian government, they would view pastoral herding as a quaint yet anachronistic occupation that only offers a very basic form of livelihood. Far better is to embrace a future of modernization and – ultimately – green growth, even if it means initially contributing to the climate change problem by accelerating extractivism. Paradoxically, selling coal to power an international division of labour and consumption is the best route towards a sustainable future for Mongolia. Herders – the victims of this transformation – would be better off moving to the cities where rents from resource extraction can, in theory, be recycled to build hi-tech service and industrial sectors that will provide new employment opportunities. For most herders, however, such a transition means selling their animals to embark on a risky migration with few assets, skills or networks to face a labour market in which they are very much located in the bottom segments. Such are the inequities of global environmental change.[25]

Beyond Decoupling?

It is these kinds of contradictions that have made some authors extremely suspicious of the decoupling thesis on the basis that it naturalizes existing power imbalances in the production and consumption of goods and places an unwarranted faith in technological solutions. In response, a more radical political strategy has been put forward under the label of degrowth. This provocative thesis suggests that Western countries need to radically shift their values away from pursuing unbounded consumption so as to voluntarily and deliberately shrink their economies and curtail their environmental footprints. In short, to move towards sustainability on a global scale, countries in the West need to slow down fast through wide-scale social transformations that do not rely on the uncertainties of potential technological breakthroughs to maintain mass consumption.

Degrowth isn't simply about societies remaining essentially the same but consuming less. Rather, it is about deep-rooted social change as a means to develop shared prosperity without economic growth. Pointedly, degrowth requires going beyond capitalism because pressures to constantly expand the scale of production and consumption are hardwired into the latter's *modus operandi*. In its place, degrowth seeks to create new imaginaries tied to localism – i.e., creating networks of production that are scaled to the local rather than the global – and egalitarianism, wherein a redistributive principle would predominate over competitive accumulation and consumption. In this vision, the practice of work must become something new at both individual and collective levels because, under a planned shrinking of production and consumption, overall employment would certainly fall.[26]

While the degrowth movement is largely concentrated in the advanced industrial countries of the West, its basic arguments have long historical precedents in both Western and non-Western thought. Mahatma Gandhi, for example, famously argued that the pursuit of 'Western civilization' would bring ruin to India and put forward an alternative path based on locally networked rural economies in which work had a spiritual, not simply a material, purpose. This was an argument that Gandhi emphatically lost in the post-independence period as India aggressively pursued industrialization in an attempt to modernize and develop. Nonetheless, his ideas of a society of modest consumption, appropriate technology and social solidarity continue to resonate among some communities, particularly those wracked by the insecurities of a globalized economy. Present-day Indian activist scholar Vandana Shiva, for example, has reworked some of Gandhi's ideas, noting that it is specifically women who feel the burden of environmental change under extractive regimes such as forestry or industrial agriculture. She has explicitly sought to re-energize Gandhi's propositions about the self-determination of local communities in which a more harmonious and sustainable form of living can be founded as a counter to a destructive and exploitative globalized economy.[27]

In a parallel fashion, a number of Latin American activist scholars have put forward similar arguments under the title of *buen vivir*. Building on indigenous ideas of community and nature, Uruguyan sociologist Eduardo Gudynas places *buen vivir* as an alternative to development. At a point in which many Latin American countries have been expanding resource extraction as a way to support development goals, *buen vivir* rejects this reliance on fossil fuels. Instead, it focuses on ideas of community well-being and the intractable connection between society and nature that is lost through what Gudynas terms the commodification of almost everything.[28] While *buen vivir* represents a counter-reaction to the domination of utilitarian values in contemporary Latin America, its protagonists have been reluctant to put forward an encompassing framework of alternative goals, objectives or policies. Given that *buen vivir* can only take expression through deliberation at a community level, they argue, there can be no singular masterplan. Instead, like degrowth, there is a need to fashion ways of living that are ecologically sound and organized according to localized principles reflecting distinct cultural criteria and a hybridity of knowledge. Some of the ideas present in *buen vivir* were drawn into the recently redrafted constitutions in Bolivia and Ecuador – including the formalization of the 'Rights of Mother Earth' in the Bolivian case. The interpretation and enforcement of such 'rights of nature', however, remains closely contested (see box 10.4).

Box 10.4   The Rights of Mother Earth

Debates over the rights of nature touch upon a raw political fault line in contemporary Latin America. In countries such as Ecuador and Bolivia, the exploitation of oil and gas resources has been represented by many progressive governments as the only way to foster both modernization and more socially equitable societies. Indeed, ambitious social welfare reforms, including the roll-out of poverty reduction strategies and key health and education initiatives, have been funded largely through the rents provided by exploiting hydrocarbon resources. At the same time, however, the detrimental impacts of extractivism upon both local environments and the global climate have led to concerted resistance – often headed by indigenous movements – that is often mobilized around the concept of *buen vivir*. As Rickard Lalander has noted, the idea of *buen vivir* (or *sumak kawsay* in Quechua) challenges the dominant understandings of welfare, common good and development that animate conventional politics in Latin America. This has created a significant conceptual and practical challenge for progressive parties because *buen vivir* rejects the telos of expanding production and consumption as a means to progress. In contrast, it argues forcefully that real progress should be measured first and foremost in terms of a harmonious coexistence with the environment and other human beings. In 2007, Ecuadorian president Rafael Correa raised these tensions to a global scale when he offered to halt oil extraction in the Ecuadorian Amazon provided the international community compensated the country for doing so at half the dollar value of the oil that lay under the forests ($3.6 billion). His proposal was met by pledges of just $200 million by 2013, and as a consequence local conflicts over extractivism have continued apace in the Ecuadorian Amazon.[29]

Thinking Forward

In many respects, ecomodernists and degrowth perspectives mark out two opposite poles of thinking about the relationship between labour, production and nature. If the Anthropocene thesis holds true, however, humanity may be confronted by a shrinking middle ground between these perspectives. In this respect, the tools of global labour studies prove exceptionally useful for digging into the uneven impacts of how we produce nature in concrete case study situations. As our exploratory examinations of Guiyu, the Niger Delta and Mongolia highlighted, the environmental change produced within the international division of labour systematically produces unequal distributions of wealth and risk. As a consequence, it inevitably generates conflict and contestation and it is incumbent upon us as analysts to recognize and understand the roots of such struggles. Chapters 11 and 12 move our study towards the politics of global labour, starting with one of the principal *zeitgeists* of the past decade: the idea of corporate social responsibility.

Further reading

Perhaps the most comprehensive account of mainstream sustainable development through decoupling is provided in the UNEP's report *Labour and the Environment: A Natural Synergy* (Geneva: UNEP, 2007). This work sets out an agenda for 'greening' production. An equally extensive, yet far more critical account of the interrelationships between capitalism, labour and the transformation of nature is offered in Jason Moore's challenging work *Capitalism in the Web of Life* (London: Verso, 2015).

Chapter 11
Corporate Social Responsibility

In December 2014 the British Broadcasting Corporation (BBC) aired an investigative documentary provocatively called *Apple's Broken Promises*. Based on undercover reporting, the documentary alleged to show poor labour standards in various parts of Apple's supply chain. As one of the world's most iconic brands, Apple has long promised to ensure decent conditions for all workers involved in the manufacture of its products. The documentary, however, appeared to show a number of troubling practices, such as exhausted workers falling asleep during their 12-hour shifts on assembly lines making the iPhone 6 outside Shanghai, and child labourers mining tin in Indonesia that would end up in Apple's computers. These incidences seemed to clash dramatically with Apple's much heralded position as a leading advocate of corporate social responsibility (CSR) and to throw considerable uncertainty over whether CSR can adequately safeguard labour standards across long and complex supply chains. While Apple did not deny the existence of the practices captured on film by the BBC, its senior executives angrily rejected the implicit suggestion in the documentary that the company didn't care about those workers in its supply chains. They pointedly argued that Apple is an industry leader in its efforts to transparently discover, investigate and fix problems in the operations of their suppliers. For Apple, the BBC had focused on a remaining few problems rather than acknowledging the virtue of Apple as a socially responsible company across most of its global production network. Other analysts suggested that the problems are more widespread than Apple dares admit.[1]

At one level, there is little reason to disbelieve Apple's assertion that they are especially active in designing and implementing CSR

Box 11.1   The BBC's report on Apple

You can read about and view a shortened version of the BBC's investigation, including footage of workers in both China and Indonesia, at: http://
www.bbc.com/news/business-30532463.

measures. By the standards of the global electronics industry, Apple
is unquestionably ahead of the game. It has an extensive monitoring
programme and exercises a transparency in its CSR operations that,
while far from perfect, stretch considerably beyond the efforts of
competitor firms. This, however, raises a deeply troubling question.
If one of the most well-resourced companies explicitly committed to
CSR suffers from ongoing violations of core labour standards across
its supply chains, what does this say about the structural factors
that impede the effectiveness of CSR as a whole? In particular, what
happens in other, less visible parts of the supply chain? Part of the
reason that Apple is so active in defending its brand from accusations
of malpractice is that it knows that a variety of consumer and media
eyes are upon it. What then occurs in firms that are less in the spot-
light yet still pledge allegiance to the idea of CSR?

The purpose of this chapter is to explore these questions by using
the concepts developed previously to help explain why CSR initiatives prove to be so uneven in their effectiveness. To do so, we need to
prise open CSR across global production networks to see the varied
and often contrasting purposes it serves and the complex relationships between consumers, firms, subcontractors and workers that it
impacts. As the chapter demonstrates, it is only by understanding the
complexity of these relationships that we can better appreciate both
the possibilities and the limits to CSR as a means of promoting decent
labour standards.

What are Labour Codes of Conduct?

At a general level, CSR refers to a voluntary set of practices by which
corporations establish criteria and goals beyond their primary aim of
making a profit when planning and enacting their business strategies.
Sometimes termed 'the triple bottom line', CSR criteria might include
environmental goals, the promotion of human rights or – as is our
present focus – ensuring that workers across the supply chain enjoy

a core set of rights and employment standards. This concern with labour standards represents a reaction to criticism that corporate outsourcing strategies led to a 'race to the bottom' in which jobs moved from relatively well-regulated employers in advanced industrial countries to regions where sweatshop conditions prevail. Given this informalization of labour relations through outsourcing, implementing CSR is sometimes held to be a race back up from the bottom, in which the quest for profit can be tempered by ethical considerations about worker rights.

The primary tool used for these purposes is called a labour code of conduct. This amounts to a series of standards that a lead firm agrees to uphold across all parts of its production network, irrespective of local laws and standards in the country in which subcontractors are located. These codes can include provisions for maximum hours of work during a week, the conditions of work (e.g., health and safety), regulations regarding minimum pay and benefits (such as maternity leave), and employee rights to representation (such as the right to form a union or collective worker organization). In effect, labour codes of conduct provide a degree of formalization of the labour contract that otherwise might not exist (see chapter 5). Their distinctive feature is that they are established and upheld not by the state, but on a voluntary basis by the lead firm in the production network. There are no formal enforcement mechanisms, such as externally imposed sanctions if violations are found. As a result, lead firms have taken on a role in coordinating not only the technical side of their production networks, but also in regulating its social dimensions. Given that many firms have outsourced to suppliers located in regions where there is little governmental oversight of labour relations, this is a significant responsibility and has raised questions as to whether such firms are able to adequately self-regulate.

As we saw in chapter 4, global production networks in industries such as electronics and clothing are often very complex, involving tiers of subcontracted companies that produce the various components or parts that make their way into a final product. In the case of Apple, for example, its labour code of conduct is meant to apply to all workers across this network, whether a small supplier that produces just one simple microchip or a larger company that assembles the final product. In pursuing these regulatory goals, many corporations design their own individualized codes of conduct specific to their supply chains, while others sign up to general ones that have been set at an industry-wide level. The Social Accountability Index (SA-8000), for instance, was created in 1987 by a consortium of industry representatives, nongovernmental organizations and labour unions

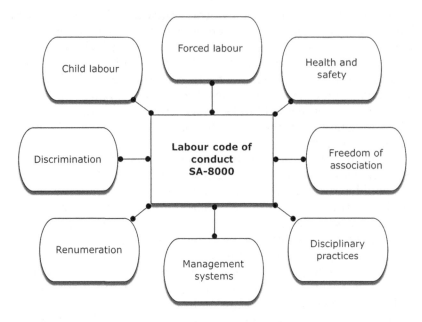

Figure 11.1   The SA-8000 labour code of conduct
Source: SA International: http://www.sa-intl.org/

in order to try to provide a standardized code across sectors. Based around core labour standards established by the ILO, it sets out provisions against the use of child or forced labour; non-discrimination in hiring and an absence of employee harassment within the workplace; the need to provide a safe and healthy workplace; freedom of association and the right to collective bargaining for employees; limitations on overall working hours (forty-eight hours per week) and overtime (twelve hours maximum per week); and the need to provide a living wage (see Figure 11.1).

While generalized codes like SA-8000 attempt to provide consistency across industries, individual corporate codes of conduct still show divergence in terms of the rights they attempt to guarantee and, in particular, how implementation can be enforced and monitored. Given that labour codes of conduct can act as a type of indirect power that conditions the actions of companies across supply chains, lead corporations often look for a degree of wiggle room by implementing their own codes. In particular, small yet important differences often show up between the relatively strong language on freedom of association and payment of adequate wages of the SA-8000 and that of lead brands. For example, while the Walt Disney Company's code of conduct is similar to SA-8000 in many respects, its provisions for the collective organization of workers are less exacting and it does not require manufacturers to pay a living wage sufficient to meet basic needs and provide discretionary income. Instead, it requires them to follow local laws on wage rates that may be entirely insufficient.[2]

Getting the regulations right is evidently a critical aspect of codes of conduct. That said, enforcement is the key to ensuring that CSR initiatives do not simply remain appealing statements on corporate websites without substantive purchase on the ground. Many analysts worry that there can be a significant gap between the criteria and goals set out in codes of conduct and actual practices on the ground. At present, the primary mechanism for implementing codes of conduct within labour intensive industries is that of the audit. Through this process, lead firms periodically arrange to have their suppliers examined at the factory level in order to judge whether they are indeed living up to the standards set by the code of conduct. While some firms undertake their own auditing processes, most are now performed by specialized companies that are hired by the lead firm and work in tandem with them to conduct factory visits across the supply chain to observe conditions and degrees of compliance. The SA-8000 system, for example, offers independent certification bodies that are accredited and overseen by Social Accountability Accreditation Services (SAAS).

Audits typically involve factory site visits – sometimes unannounced – in which auditors visually inspect working and safety conditions and then conduct interviews with both management and a representative selection of workers. Factory documentation, such as the employment register, payment records and worker time cards, will typically be inspected to judge issues such as work hours and overtime pay. Auditors are not investigators; they have no rights to information or observation beyond what is presented to them by the company, yet factories are expected by lead firms to work with the auditing process. Based on an examination of the official records and interview data, alongside onsite observations, auditors seek to judge the extent of compliance with core social responsibility metrics and to provide advice to lead companies on what needs to be improved and what methods should be used to do so. Quite how many times a factory might be audited depends heavily on how large and how well integrated into the supply chain it is. A large supplier such as Foxconn or Yue Yuen might expect a yearly audit. Others, however, might expect an audit every several years, while smaller firms that take occasional contracts could escape the system entirely.[3]

Advocates of CSR suggest that such an auditing process should help raise labour standards across industries. There exists considerable evidence, however, that auditing is not as efficient as corporations make out. You may recall the disturbing tragedy at the Rana Plaza factory complex in Bangladesh in 2013, which was noted in chapter 4. In this industrial disaster, an eight-storey building full of garment workshops collapsed, killing 1,300 workers and injuring at least 2,500 more. On the day prior to the tragedy, large cracks had been seen in the walls of the building leading to the closure of small retail stores on the bottom levels. The factory operators nonetheless insisted that their workers return to work as normal. In the world of fast fashion, meeting the delivery dates of lead firms is paramount. Regrettably, the building was structurally unsound, in part because it had never been designed to accommodate the sheer number of clothing factories packed inside, and tragedy struck.

In the immediate wake of the collapse, some leading clothing brands, such as Benetton, denied that they had goods produced in the building and argued that their CSR practices would prohibit subcontracting to unsafe factories. Photos of United Colours of Benetton garments among the rubble of the factory, however, suggested otherwise. As a result, many brands had to confess that, given the complexity of their subcontracting networks, they could not always monitor where goods were being produced. Other brands simply expressed dismay. The executive chairman of Canadian brand Joe Fresh stated that he was deeply troubled that his company could be part of such an unspeakable tragedy despite what he insisted was a clear commitment to the highest standards of ethical sourcing.[4] Joe Fresh was not alone in working with factories located in the complex. Walmart, Carrefour, J. C. Penny, Matalan, Mango and many others sourced from companies in the building, all of which had active codes of conduct concerning worker safety. Indeed, two of the factories operating within Rana Plaza were registered with the Business Social Compliance Initiative. Both had been audited and approved prior to the collapse.

In this respect, the Rana Plaza disaster shines a light on an open secret within the industry: auditing is an incredibly convoluted process whose results are uneven at best. Questions were immediately raised about whether codes of conduct are well designed and whether implementation through auditing is an effective means of enforcing codes in practice. There is no simple answer to this. While labour codes of conduct might seem a relatively straightforward technical tool, in practice they comprise a highly political process because they straddle a number of crucial tensions across global production networks. At a most basic level, labour codes of conduct appear to clash with labour regimes designed to produce workforces shorn of basic rights that can be compelled to work intensely over an extended working week for low wages. It is no surprise, therefore, that the imposition of codes of conduct – which seek to retroactively raise standards across these supply chains – is an inherently contradictory process with uneven outcomes.

To understand this complexity, let us break down the various purposes that codes of conduct serve and the kinds of power relations they influence. It is useful to think of the way that codes shape four overlapping relationships (see Figure 11.2). First, they impact on the relationship between lead firms and their primarily Western consumers concerning the issue of ethical consumption. Second, they impact on the competitive relationship between various lead firms for which

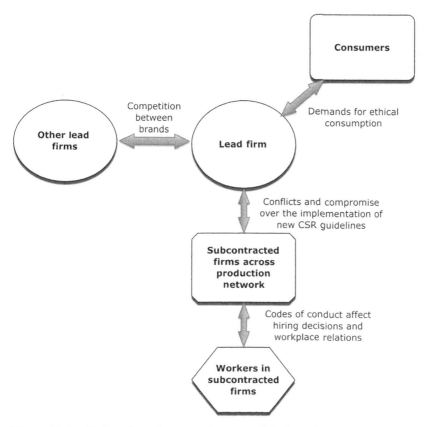

Figure 11.2   Codes of conduct stretch across global production networks

their brand – including their CSR commitments – plays an active role in safeguarding market share. Third, we must consider the relationship between lead firms and their subcontractors over who pays for the improved workplace conditions that CSR implies. And, fourth, we must consider the changed relations between producer firms and their workforces, which frequently conflict over working conditions and labour rights. As you can see, this represents a very complex set of relationships that encompass both the politics of consumption, located primarily in the affluent North, and the politics of production, with labour intensive manufacturing now occurring primarily in the global South. We sequentially examine these two sides of codes of conduct in the following sections before looking more closely at their uneven impacts.

Codes of Conduct and the Politics of Consumption

To understand why codes of conduct emerged, we need to grasp a key aspect of corporate strategy: branding. Whenever you watch a commercial, you will have experienced at first hand how high-profile firms earnestly seek to associate their products with esoteric ideals of freedom, liberation and accomplishment. 'Just do it!' proclaims Nike, intimating that the purchase of their shoes and other athletic clothing is correlated to individual achievement and a new freedom from personal and social constraints. From car companies to fashion lines, building allegiance to a specific product is sought not through a functional description of the product at hand, but by enshrining that product as representative of specific lifestyle ideals and emblematic of desirable values. Building a brand, of course, is not new. It did, however, become a dramatically more widespread business strategy in the 1980s and beyond, implemented with a new kind of intensity and sophistication.[5]

There is an Achilles heel to this kind of branding campaign. Having production networks operating at a global scale, lead firms for numerous consumer icons are deeply entangled in subcontracting to low-cost factories that frequently rely upon labouring conditions and wages that consumers might find unpalatable. As a result, many of the products that are being marketed have unseemly histories of production that clash starkly with the narratives of freedom and liberty that are used to sell them. A 2004 study of the production of University of Connecticut branded sweatshirts on sale at the campus store, for example, showed that Mexican factory workers received a unit share of just $0.18 for creating hooded sweatshirts that retailed at $37.99.[6] A contradiction therefore emerged between the brand idea of consumption as a means of personal empowerment and the disempowerment and exploitation of workers within the supply chain.

In the 1990s, consumer-activist groups dramatically seized on this contradiction in a brazen attempt to name and shame multinationals and publicize the poor labour conditions found across supply chains. There had, of course, been a wide range of anti-sweatshop and consumer activist movements in existence since the advent of industrial capitalism. However, these took on a distinct form in the 1990s, coalescing around the issue of the globalization of production becoming a race to the bottom in labour and environmental standards. Such movements often acted in solidarity with workers' movements in producer countries, specifically where local movements had been thwarted in their attempts to form collective organizations and press for greater rights.[7] As a result of the vocal attempts to name and shame branded corporations for labour standards in subcontracted factories, the latter suddenly found their elaborate branding exercise to be a source of vulnerability. Their attempts to cloak core consumption items from sports shoes to laptops in idealist rhetoric seemed threatened by consumer activists who linked these brands to exploitation, poverty-level wages and environmental destruction. As the American sociologists Edna Bonacich and Richard Appelbaum argued, while outsourcing enabled lead firms to shift production sites to avoid organized workers, they are unable to easily avoid militant consumers.[8]

This tactic caused no shortage of concern within corporate boardrooms and created a new category of corporate analysis: brand risk. No company wanted their heavily leveraged brand to be associated with, for example, child labour or environmental destruction. Under repeated accusations that corporations were putting profits before people, the idea of CSR arose as a rear-guard action, a mechanism for deflecting criticism and disarming threats to the brand. This movement was strongest in companies that carried a very visible brand, whose marketing opened them to consumer activism. With sales predicated on a successful brand, corporations became acutely aware that negative associations could lead to their losing ground to competitors. Creating and propagating codes of conduct therefore emerged as an important aspect of competition between lead firms. As an example, whereas Nike was repeatedly affected by 'name and shame' campaigns about sweatshop labour during the 1990s, Reebok claimed the ethical high ground by promulgating its labour code of conduct. Ethical corporate conduct entered as a new factor alongside product price, style and quality in affecting the competition between these leading brands. While Reebok's code of conduct had unclear impacts upon work conditions in supplier factories, it nonetheless pre-emptively deflected unwelcome consumer group attention away from their supply chains and onto rival companies.[9]

With these dynamics in play, codes of conduct have emerged since the 1990s as a new social standard in the marketing of commodities for branded corporations that felt themselves to be most susceptible to consumer activism. Rather than passively reacting to activist movements, corporations now proactively declare their commitment to social responsibility as a positive and enduring reason for consumers to select their product vis-à-vis competitors. This shift towards corporations becoming a driving force in elaborating and implementing codes has elicited a parallel shift in the activities of consumer activist groups. While the anti-sweatshop movement had coalesced around the tactics of naming and shaming corporate malpractices, the introduction of elaborate codes of conduct changed the landscape. Many NGOs now seek to work with the corporate sector in an attempt to force them to generate more comprehensive codes of conduct or to find better means of implementing codes across production networks. In short, they have moved from naming and shaming to an attempt to force corporations to live up to the requirements of their codes of conduct.

Box 11.2   H&M's conscious consumption campaign

Swedish clothes retailer H&M is a leading proponent of ethical consumption as part of its brand image. It claims that looking good should 'do good' too. Offering seven commitments to worker rights and environmental stewardship, H&M suggests that Western consumers can rest assured in their ability to enjoy cheap yet ethically sound clothes. That said, words are not necessarily the same as actions. Despite H&M's pledge to introduce a fair living wage to 850,000 workers across its supply chain by 2018, observers have suggested that the road to achieving this claim is not at all clear. The Clean Clothes Campaign – a leading NGO focused on worker rights in the apparel industry – critiques the lack of transparent reporting on progress towards securing this aim. The campaign argues that, while the company loudly proclaims its conscious brand as a means to sell clothes, it provides inadequate data or benchmarks by which to back up its claims. In particular, the campaign suggests that the use of closely controlled model factories by H&M to test its worker rights provisions is unlikely to be generalizable across the supply chain because of the uniqueness of those trial sites.[10]

Codes of Conduct and the Politics of Production

As a form of self-regulation, codes of conduct are emphatically a top-down mechanism. They are created or adopted by lead firms that insist on their implementation within subcontractors throughout the production network. This has resulted in a shift in the mechanisms of power and control that operate between lead firms and suppliers. At one end of the supply chain, lead firms are driving the codes and their auditing procedures as part of a display of 'good corporate citizenship', as a key marketing device. At the other end, however, suppliers face increasingly exacting standards that potentially bite into their ability to turn a profit under heavily competitive conditions. In industries such as textiles and shoe production, the full implementation of codes of conduct could threaten to interrupt the intensive labouring conditions that are necessary to react to the demands of flexible production to meet fluctuating demands such as the ability to impose obligatory overtime upon workers.[11]

In this respect, codes of conduct become a source of tension and conflict between networked firms struggling over the distribution of profits within a global production network. This significantly complicates the picture of codes as a simple technical device for ensuring worker rights. As one Guangdong factory owner quoted by the *Financial Times* made very clear, codes of conduct have added to the pressures felt by labour-intensive manufacturers at the bottom end of global production networks. The owner stated that factory operators were under enormous stress because 'customers place late orders, they change their orders part way through manufacturing and they pay their bills late. At the same time they ask us to provide better training for our staff, better health and safety and better accommodation. We just cannot do it all.'[12]

This imbalance highlights a further key tension within codes of conduct. Under pressure from some consumers, lead firms promise to implement ethical production. Simultaneously, however, they promise to maintain low prices and seek quick turnarounds on orders to meet shifting consumption deadlines. They are often unwilling to raise prices to accommodate the added regulations. On the contrary, keeping high-street prices low is seen as a necessity imposed by competition. As a result, the costs are often displaced downwards, with lead firms using their direct power over contractors to try and enforce compliance with the threat of losing the contract for noncompliance. At the other end, factory owners are typically bemused by the emphasis on installing worker standards and rights that seem to violate the cheap production imperative. If implemented fully, a new form of labour regime would be created, and one that is less conducive to lead firms' demands in terms of flexible production. So, in a situation in which suppliers feel they cannot 'do it all', it is important to consider closely the various strategies that they pursue under the crosscutting pressures to reduce costs while implementing CSR measures. Again, there is no single answer to this because suppliers react in distinct ways to the imposition of codes of conduct.

The Uneven Outcomes of Labour Codes of Conduct

So how do companies within the supply chain seek to square the circle and deal with the ever present demands towards cost-effectiveness, while managing the criteria put forward by codes of conduct? There are four main reactions. First, some suppliers promise rigorous adherence to codes, making a virtue out of strong compliance and seeking to ensure that lead firms trust them as suppliers with no brand risk. Second, other firms may pursue technological upgrading, substituting more expensive workers with technology. Third, some firms pursue selective implementation of codes, complying with some aspects while subverting others. Finally, some suppliers undertake clear-cut duplicity and fraud, hiding their lack of implementation. To be clear, many suppliers implement some combination of these strategies, adding to the complexity of outcomes. Let us examine each in turn.

Rigorous adherence

For some firms, explicitly making adherence to codes of conduct a central aspect of their contracting strategies can pay dividends. This in part reflects the issue of trust noted as a key part of production networks. Specifically, in cases where a lead company feels it is exposed to a high degree of brand risk, subcontracting to a firm that promises meticulous adherence to CSR standards might be worth an extra premium on the unit cost of goods. For example, consider Yue Yuen - the giant Taiwanese shoemaker we discussed in chapter 4. Despite a long history of poor labour standards within its Chinese factories, in the run up to the 2008 Beijing Olympics the company assured lead firms that it would spotlessly adhere to codes of conduct going far beyond local norms in terms of wages and working conditions. To do so, it showcased a number of model factories for these purposes and was successful in sealing large contracts with Adidas and other major brands, with the latter willing to pay something of a premium to ensure not only perfectly coordinated delivery of products, but also that no embarrassing revelations of poor work conditions would scar the brand in the lead-up to a major commercial opportunity.

Perhaps more audaciously, in an attempt to secure contracts some countries have declared themselves to be model production zones in their entirety. Cambodia is an important example here, with the Cambodian state and garment producers agreeing to an industry-wide set of standards modelled on SA-8000. The small mountain kingdom of Lesotho in southern Africa is another example. As sociologist Gay Seidman recounts, in 2007 the Lesotho government surprised everyone by declaring the country to be sweatshop-free, and therefore a suitable location for ethically minded garment firms to source from. In both cases the countries were seeking to exploit a niche that would make them attractive to lead companies. For Cambodia, the expectation was that the very low price of labour prevailing in the country would compensate for upholding labour standards across the industry. A 2015 Human Rights Watch report, however, suggests that the results have been mixed, with patchy implementation of regulations and violent suppression of workers seeking a rise in the minimum wage.[13] In Lesotho, the role of the ILO's 'Better Factories' programme helped the country market itself as an ethical production site and improved factory conditions. The small nature of Lesotho's garment sector, however, caused Seidman to caution whether it could stand as a generalizable model for the industry as a whole.[14]

Technological upgrading

If adherence to labour codes of conduct will raise labour costs, then what about pursuing technological upgrading – i.e., substituting workers with technology? In many respects, this strategy sits comfortably alongside the intentions of many firms to raise their position within global production networks by becoming more technologically sophisticated and, therein, capable of performing a wider range of more complex functions. At the same time, governments are often keen to promote upgrading as a way of regional development, believing that more sophisticated firms offer better salaries and strong horizontal linkages to other firms in the area.

Yet, as we noted in chapter 3, technological upgrading is not an easy task, nor is it necessarily beneficial for workers. On the one hand, less labour-intensive firms are indeed more likely to comply with codes of conduct because profitability should arise through productivity increases rather than an intensive labour regime. That said, as Florian Butollo notes in his study of electronics and garment producers in southern China, technological upgrading does not automatically entail a raise in labour standards. On the contrary, global production networks in both industries can involve the combination of cutting-edge technologies with the ongoing exploitation of cheap migrant labour. In short, without improving regulations and the legal standing of workers to negotiate their conditions, hi-tech production can exist hand-in-hand with low labour standards.[15]

Selective implementation

Many suppliers tend to selectively engage with some criteria but not others. Specifically, they seek to accomplish the easiest, cheapest and most visible aspects set out in codes of conduct, while stalling or undermining others. Consider the survey of 192 textile, apparel, foot-wear and electronics factories in Indonesia, conducted by Tim Bartley and Niklas Egels-Zandén. In their exhaustive account, the authors highlight precisely the vast unevenness of codes of conduct on the ground in Indonesia owing to very selective implementation of codes. Workers in factories covered by codes of conduct were certainly the recipients of better health and safety measures and also less likely to suffer from having delayed wages. Permanent workers at such factories were also more likely to receive written contracts. That said, the study failed to show any relationship between codes of conduct and the payment of minimum wages, the proportion of non-permanent labour contracts, and legal infractions regarding use of casual labour. In particular, there was no relationship between codes of conduct and the presence of collective worker organizations – or what are often termed 'process rights' – that codes supposedly facilitated. To the extent that it existed, worker organization tended to be limited to representation on committees to ensure compliance with health and safety and other technical matters.[16]

What this study highlights is that, because codes are often implemented selectively, they are strongest in helping ensure basic health and safety procedures and ruling out some of the worst forms of worker abuse, including the withholding of wages. At the same time, implementation is typically weakest where it comes to empowering workers themselves. Codes of conduct are applied in ways that tend not to fundamentally challenge the politics of production by allowing workers to exercise greater voice and agency within the factory setting and, as such, to potentially protect their own rights. In short, codes are applied selectively to ensure that no shift in the labour regime as a whole occurs, with employers seeking a form of implementation that maintains the prevailing top-down and managerial approach that accords well with strongly disciplined factory settings.

Duplicity

The selective imposition of codes highlights the issue of duplicity and fraud. Given the pressures upon them, many firms seek not only to selectively implement codes, but also to find ways to entirely circumvent them. These forms of duplicity are an unethical yet entirely logical response of many small labour-intensive firms to deal with CSR pressures in conditions of rampant competition between suppliers. The resulting fraud often occurs with a degree of sophistication beyond that of the auditing schemes that are meant to regulate them. Much as the business schools in the Western world have been busy creating courses on CSR principles and implementation, local labour NGOs in China report the existence of anti-CSR courses that offer guidance on how to circumvent those very methods.[17]

Small and medium-sized factories often operate parallel systems of time cards, contracts and salary details for employees, with one set for the auditors and another marking the real state of affairs. Given that most auditing visits are pre-announced, suppliers can hide away underage workers by either moving them to other factories or giving them time off. Notably, the auditing procedure can be very brief, with a small team visiting a 1,000-employee factory over a day with a long checklist to review, including all types of manufacturing issues from wages and working hours to child labour and health and safety concerns. Interviews with workers that occur within the workplace are a notoriously problematic means of uncovering issues because there is a strong power relationship between employers and employees. The latter fear for their jobs – particularly if employers have sequestered personal documents or withheld wages, which gives them direct power over the worker – and there are multiple accounts of employees being coached on the 'right answers' to give to auditors.

A further form of fraud is the use of model factories for auditing purposes. A 2013 *New York Times* investigation, for example, showed in detail how suppliers deliberately fooled Walmart auditors by shifting goods between factories to imply that all goods had been produced at a state-of-the-art factory with ideal conditions, rather than in their actual places of production.[18] This system of having one 'model factory' for auditing purposes alongside a number of 'shadow' production sites is magnified through the practice of further subcontracting, in which factories pass on parts of orders to smaller companies outside the sphere of audits. The use of child labour within Gap's supply chain, for instance, was discovered by an undercover reporter in 2007 who traced a web of subcontracting practices deep into the informal sector of India's textile industry. Even if it wanted to, Gap could not audit the practices of firms it did not know were part of its supply chain.[19] This takes us back to the starting point of our analysis, with the BBC exposé of supplier practices in Apple's production network. Notwithstanding the most sophisticated auditing system available, the BBC report suggests that duplicity was very much a part of day-to-day operations amongst Apple suppliers – including its second major assembly subcontractor Pegatron – which assumed that managing the auditing process was simply part of the culture of global production networks.

Here we encounter a final yet extremely important point about codes of conduct. One of the strongest structural constraints on the effectiveness of codes of conduct as a means of enforcing labour standards is that none of the parties involved in designing and implementing regulation has an interest in seeing labour abuses coming to light. Put simply, there is a set of explicit power relationships involved in the auditing procedure that reinforces rather than challenges the status quo. Neither the lead firm nor the subcontractor has any interest in labour abuses being revealed. The lead firm seeks to avoid any reputational damage, while the supplier does not want to be blacklisted from future contracts. At the same time, the workers themselves tend to be understandably hesitant to speak out against their employers for fear of losing their jobs or costing the firm a contract. Moreover, auditing firms themselves are only partially independent from multinational corporations upon which they depend for further contracts. Auditors know that they can be easily replaced by an alternative auditing company. Given that there are many auditing firms for lead companies to choose from, an auditor that earned a reputation for doing too good a job in uncovering abuses might well find itself ignored for future contracts. In this respect, auditors find a need to work closely with lead firms and their impartiality can be compromised. Indeed, most auditors sign stringent confidentiality agreements with the lead firms they work for, therein ensuring that they cannot release or discuss the findings of their audits beyond the firm itself.

Beyond Codes of Conduct?

Having examined how codes of conduct are stretched across complex relationships between consumers, lead firms, suppliers and their workers, we can better appreciate why their outcomes are typically uneven. On the one hand, in some conditions, clearly defined codes accompanied by increased monitoring can indeed lead to some improvements in work conditions, particularly in terms of the most visible infractions such as health and safety, minimum wages and limiting forced overtime. On the other hand, we can also see how the nature of power relations that stratify global production networks provides a significant impediment to the realization of labour standards as envisaged in codes of conduct such as the SA-8000. Organizations such as the anti-sweatshop movement Clean Clothes Campaign, for example, contend that for codes of conduct to be genuinely effective they would have to be less top-down and instead encourage the self-organization of workers within the workplace. In short, empowerment would need to be a key aspect of any substantive mechanism to improve work conditions across industries. These aspects of codes of conduct, including freedom of association and collective bargaining, are often the least well articulated and implemented. Yet, where worker movements have already gained traction, they have in some circumstances been able to draw on corporate codes of conduct and the potential support of international consumer activist groups as resources to aid their campaigns. It is precisely these aspects, therefore, that we address in the following chapter.

Box 11.3 John Oliver slams the fashion industry

British comedian John Oliver is well known for his scathing critiques of hypocrisy among both politicians and the corporate world. In this YouTube video (https://www.youtube.com/watch?v=VdLf4fihP78), we can see the fashion industry being pilloried by Oliver for pushing cost pressures downwards onto suppliers who respond by exploiting labour forces. If Oliver is correct, where does the burden of responsibility lie between consumers, branded companies, suppliers, governments and workers themselves?

Further reading

Although an older text, the general introduction to the subject by Ruth Pearson, Gill Seyfang and Rhys Jenkins (eds) *Corporate Responsibility and Labour Rights: Codes of Conduct in the Global Economy* (London: Earthscan, 2002) provides a strong foundation. For illustrative yet contending perspectives on the efficiency of auditing as the principal means of enforcing CSR, the following two approachable articles provide a usefully sharp contrast: Stephen Goldberg, Ashley Gist and Stanton Lindquist, 'Auditor's Guide to Corporate Social Responsibility', *Journal of Corporate Accounting & Finance* 22(4) 2011, pp. 51–59; and Genevieve LeBaron and Jane Lister, 'Benchmarking global supply chains: the power of the 'ethical audit' regime'. *Review of International Studies* 41(5) 2015, pp. 905–924.

Chapter 12
Organizing Global Labour

One of the biggest recorded strikes in world history happened on 2 September 2016, when Indian workers staged a one-day work stoppage to protest Prime Minister Narendra Modi's programme of labour market flexibilization. In the name of promoting economic growth, the proposed legislative changes would increase permitted working hours and make it easier for employers to lay off employees without severance. While formal sector employees challenged the impacts of this reform on working conditions, they also emphasized the need to extend formalization outwards towards millions of domestic servants, bricklayers, pushcart drivers and other informal workers. Almost 90 per cent of India's 500 million workers toil in the informal economy, with no social security benefits or pensions, poor working conditions, poverty-level wages and few to no labour rights (see chapter 6). It is in this context that a united platform of ten trade unions called for a general strike and issued a twelve-point charter of demands, including price controls, social security and pensions for all, a rise of the minimum wage, the enforcement of existing labour laws and an end to contractual labour.[1] Rather than allowing the Modi government to informalize the formal, they argued, it was imperative instead to find new ways to formalize the informal.

Beyond its vast size, what is significant about this mobilization is the way it forces us to think about how labour organizes politically beyond the narrow terms of collective bargaining and legal regulations. Labour organization takes many forms – from workplace unions, to mutual insurance funds and self-help groups, through to national or international worker confederations – and new forms are constantly emerging in the present digital age. Many trade union movements are becoming acutely aware that they must build their activities and social roles in innovative ways far beyond the formal sector workplace. This raises pivotal questions for global labour studies. How should we understand the metamorphosis of labour organizations within the context of rising global social and economic inequalities and the challenges of an increasingly globalized capitalism? And what new forms of networked labour organization might be needed to address the myriad needs of workers across national borders, crossing both formal and informal domains? Answering these questions requires that we first familiarize ourselves with the organizational forms of the labour movement and the power relations inherent to their operations, before examining historical forms of internationalism and the new constraints that confront labour organization in the twenty-first century. On this basis, we can examine both the possibilities and challenges facing new forms of labour organization.

What is Labour Organization?

When we think about labour organization, it is often labour unions – the collective organization of workers within a specific firm – that spring to mind. This is understandable, given the historical importance of unions as perhaps the foremost expression of labour organization. However, while recognizing the importance of unions, it is important to note that the idea of labour organization incorporates a broader range of organizational forms, including diverse types of associations, unions, organizations, political parties or works councils. These have the common characteristic of operating as a means for workers to promote their collective interests either at the level of a firm or more widely across society, or even globally.

Although they may serve various roles and functions, all forms of labour organization typically pivot on a fundamental issue: power. Put simply, labour organization emerges as a counterbalance to the power discrepancies between individual workers and employers. The employment relationship, as we have examined in earlier chapters, is a lopsided one. Sometimes workers have significant assets or networks by which to negotiate strong contracts and working conditions. More often, however, the compelling need to find employment means that many workers accept terms offered to them from above with limited ability to shape the characteristics of the labour regime into which they are inserted.

This is where labour organization comes in. Through collective organization and solidarity, workers seek to influence their terms of contract and conditions of labour by bargaining in a way that is impossible on an individual level. The foundation of this power is the ability to interrupt the labour process within a given firm, either by refusing to accomplish work according to given schedules, or, more dramatically, through bringing work to a complete halt by a strike. While often a last resort, it is the power of a strike that is the ultimate sanction that workers hold to influence employers. As labour historian Marcel van der Linden notes, it is precisely the ability to threaten a strike that ultimately defines what a labour union is.[2] That said, in addition to intervening directly in the politics of production, labour organizations often seek to offer other benefits to their members through forms of mutualism including provisions for sickness insurance, affordable savings and loan provisions, and support for the raising of children. These collective services represent an important role for labour organization in the sphere of social reproduction, particularly if there is an absence of state provision. Notably, in the context of informal sector organization – where there is a heavy prevalence of self-employment, familial firms and shifting employment relations – it is often these functions that can predominate.

One of the tensions in this process, however, is that the formation of unions can lead to their bureaucratization. In seeking to narrowly protect the interests of members, overly insular and administrative unions can become closed off and lose sight of the wider social contexts and issues that affect labour more generally. This form of business unionism is sometimes critiqued for defensively preserving the rights and benefits of a specific group or strata of employees, therein consolidating labour market segmentation. At times, this has given rise to the idea of a labour aristocracy as a relatively privileged group of unionized workers whose collective organization serves their own narrow interests, particularly when unions are incorporated as part of the state apparatus (see chapter 5).[3] While such forms of relative privilege do exist, most union movements are increasingly aware of the need to build horizontal linkages in support of wider social goals. As the India example above accentuates, this includes the goal of supporting the extension of formalization to new categories of workers. There is also an international dimension to this strategy. In a world of capital mobility where investment and outsourcing can pit workers across borders against each other, forms of labour internationalism also predominate. The struggle to find ways to express commonalities of interests between workers across national borders, however, is difficult. Within the context of trade liberalization and the formation of global production networks, the global division of labour can be extremely divisive. To understand these issues better, it is necessary to delve deeper into the question of power within labour organization.

Labour Organization and Power Relations

The labour movement as we commonly understand it emerged and developed in the repressive and violent context of early industrial employment relations. From the late eighteenth century to the early twentieth century, unions and labour associations in Western countries and their colonial empires were typically treated as criminal organizations prohibited by law. Acute struggles surrounding the politics of production and the ensuing fear of working-class radicalization led to an increasing acquiescence of states and employers towards unions in an attempt to maintain industrial peace. While this led to the staggered decriminalization of labour unions in the late nineteenth and early twentieth centuries, the creation of legal frameworks that formalized the rights and obligations of both employers and employees remained a drawn out and uneven process. As we saw in chapter 5, this transformation reached its furthest expression in the post-war class compromise that formalized a role for labour organizations in managing industrial relations. The institutions and expectations of the Fordist period, however, have since been systematically restructured through the advent of neoliberal policymaking. With its emphasis on the flexibilization of labour markets and the informalization of employment relations, this ongoing trend raises new questions about labour organizing in the context of changing power relations on a global scale.

In the context of labour organization, direct power is the power that workers can yield based on their location in the economic system. On the one hand, workers' marketplace bargaining power is greater if labour markets are tight owing to a scarcity of specific skills, low levels of unemployment, or institutions that give workers a high level of autonomy to choose when and how they engage in wage labour. If those conditions exist, worker organizations may enjoy significant leverage in their negotiations with employers. On the other hand, workers' workplace bargaining power is shaped by the strategic location occupied by specific groups of workers in the economy. For some, their privileged position within time-sensitive, integrated production processes gives them scalar capabilities and power far beyond the workplace. As we saw in chapter 10, for example, the centrality of Nigerian oil sector workers within the national economy gave them substantial political clout and scalar capabilities that stretched far beyond the workplace of oil rigs and fuel refineries. Similarly, when a company invests significant sums of money to acquire land, build plants, buy equipment and hire workers, it is necessarily committing itself both financially and geographically to a particular location. It therefore may find difficult to relocate in the event of a labour conflict, forcing it to compromise with labour organizations. It is on this basis that many corporations prefer to invest when political restrictions limit the ability of labour organization, such as in many export promotion zones located in developing world contexts.[4]

In contrast to direct power, indirect power refers to an actor's ability to influence the institutional, regulatory or normative context and therein set the rules that actors play by. One expression of this power is the relative ability of labour organizations to engage the political process and participate in statecraft through party–union alliances, potentially exerting an influence over the formation of key regulatory laws. There is a long history of labour-backed parties in Western industrialized countries – including Australia, Britain, France, Germany and Sweden – pushing for democratic reforms and progressive labour laws. Unionized workers do not always have political parties of their own, however. As with the Revolutionary Nationalist Movement in Bolivia, the Brazilian Labour Party (dismantled by a coup in 1964) and the Socialist Party of Chile, workers and trade unionists may instead use broader political coalitions to advance their interests, fight for democracy and promote social justice. This reflects what community organizer Steve Jenkins calls advocacy power.[5] When workers are not strong enough to force changes in a specific employer or industry, they can try to achieve their goals by persuading elite institutions and decision makers to take action on their behalf. Advocacy activities such as trade unions lobbying government officials for better labour regulations are commonplace but frequently tenuous because labour organizations typically do not have the resources or organizational strength to influence the political process to the same degree as corporations.

Notwithstanding these constraints, the complexity of global supply chains also creates new opportunities as corporations potentially become more vulnerable to symbolic power such as international campaigns that name and shame their overseas activities. As we examined in the previous chapter, a growing number of consumer activist groups and labour organizations strategically raise public awareness about working conditions in the manufacturing sectors around the world. In so doing, they seek to mobilize consumers to press companies to ensure that their supply chains are free from forced labour and that their suppliers and subcontractors respect minimum labour rights and standards. Through international campaigns and groups such as the Clean Clothes Campaign, United Students Against Sweatshops and the Committee for Asian Women, labour conflicts are migrating into the public domain of citizenship and consumption. Public awareness about companies' sourcing practices has prompted many of them to adopt a more proactive approach to controlling symbolic power, notably through the establishment of corporate social responsibility principles as a management strategy seeking to diminish the potential of being shamed publicly. This creates opportunities for collaboration between labour organizations and nongovernmental organizations.[6]

Workers North: The Decline of Organized Labour in the West

Changes in the political economy of work have created significant shifts in the relative power that workers might accrue in different geographical locations. If we consider the traditional realm of union membership and collective bargaining in the West, the period since the 1980s represents a period of significant decline in the power of organized labour. Table 12.1 gives us a sense of the decline of trade union density, with the percentage of workers represented by unions cut by half between 1980 and 2010 in OECD countries. This decline has had major ramifications for how power operates in both labour markets and the workplace. First, the ability of workers to bargain over contracts has been undermined by trade liberalization, labour flexibilization and the constitution of a global labour market of readily available workers, especially in the manufacturing sector. As a result of the logistics revolution and the digitalization of the economy, companies are less and less dependent upon geographically delimited networks of suppliers and service providers, giving them greater power to shift production locations to take advantage of different labour regimes. Put simply, the formation of global production networks tends to loosen corporate ties to what were previously considered strategic locations, thereby reducing workplace bargaining power for fear of relocation.

This mobility of capital versus the relative fixity of labour recalibrates the power of organized labour, creating what political scientist James Piazza calls 'globalising quiescence'.[7] Compared to the more militant decades of the Fordist era, there has been a dramatic decline in the number of days lost due to strikes since 1980. There is little doubt that the offshoring and outsourcing of productive activities

Table 12.1 Trade union density (selected countries)

Country	1960	1970	1980	1990	2000	2010
Australia	50.2	44.2	48.5	39.6	25.7	18.4
Belgium	39.3	39.9	51.3	51.1	56.2	53.8
Canada	29.2	31.0	34.0	34.0	28.2	27.2
Denmark	56.9	60.3	78.6	74.6	73.9	67.0
Finland	31.9	51.3	69.4	72.5	75.0	68.6
France	19.6	21.7	18.3	9.8	8.0	7.7
Germany	34.7	32.0	34.9	31.2	24.6	18.6
Ireland	45.3	53.2	57.1	51.1	38.0	32.7
Italy	24.7	37.0	49.6	38.8	34.8	36.0
Japan	32.3	35.1	31.1	25.4	21.5	18.4
Portugal	–	–	54.8	28.0	21.6	19.8
Turkey	–	29.0	39.5	35.2	28.2	8.9
United Kingdom	40.4	44.8	51.7	39.7	30.2	26.6
United States	30.9	27.4	22.1	15.5	12.8	11.4
OECD countries	34.7	34.7	34.1	26.6	20.4	17.7

Source: OECD.http://stats.oecd.org/Index.aspx?DataSetCode=UN_DEN#

to countries where labour is cheap have undermined workers' bargaining power in Western countries. Similarly, the increased automation and streamlining of productive processes have profoundly transformed the industrial and manufacturing sectors where unionization had historically been dominant. Through a comparative study of Mexico, Spain and Venezuela, Katrina Burgess demonstrates how this has placed considerable challenges for party-affiliated unions by creating a 'loyalty dilemma': either trade union leaders remain loyal to a party implementing reforms that are harmful to workers, or they stay loyal to the workers at the risk of being sidelined from the legislative process. From Britain and Poland to South Africa, many labour-backed parties have adopted economic reforms that threaten the livelihoods of their traditional sources of political support. Even social democratic parties in Austria, Germany and Sweden, as well as socialist parties in France and Spain, have implemented labour market flexibilization reforms that appear to contradict the interests of their political bases.[8] Presently, this accounts for a sense of deep crisis in the identities and strategies of European labour movements and their allied political parties.

Within this changing political context, governments have proved to be increasingly willing to enact labour laws that restrict the right to strike, particularly in the public sector. In Italy, Portugal and Spain, for example, strikes are not permitted to interfere with certain services, including transport and hospitals, energy supply, water provision, solid waste collection, education, and the post. Another type of government intervention is when governments force workers back to work through special laws. Between 1982 and 2016, federal and provincial governments in Canada enacted ninety pieces of back-to-work legislation, fifty of which imposed in whole or in part the content of the resulting collective agreement.[9] This trend is accentuated further by workfare policies and cuts in social services that increased workers' dependency on wage labour for survival (see chapter 5), as well as temporary worker programmes designed to introduce new precarious workers into labour markets (see chapter 8).

With the numerical decline of organized labour in Western countries, retaining advocacy power has become central to many union strategies. Judging that they do not possess the power to oppose reforms that are harmful to workers, many union leaders will choose to remain loyal to their traditional parties in the hope that they can attenuate the scale and scope of the reforms at a later date. This strategy is often aided by a shift in tactics. As Jeremy Tanguy has showed for France, while the number of strikes lasting than two days has decreased, other forms of protests, such as one-day walkouts, demonstrations, collective petitions, work-to-rule and the refusal to work overtime, are on the rise at the collective level.[10] In particular, more individualized forms of labour conflict have tended to emerge, as expressed through individual acts of protest and conflict within workplaces, such as absenteeism, indiscipline, tardiness, high turnover, negligence, grievance arbitrations and confrontational attitudes.[11] While collective actions with work stoppage have greatly decreased since 1980, an appreciation for this new repertoire of contention at both the individual and collective levels helps to nuance the labour quiescence thesis. It highlights the limits of a conception of labour conflicts based solely on strikes and grievances, and shows the multifaceted nature of labour conflicts over the last decades (see Table 12.2).

As one part of this shift, labour organizations have increasingly relied upon digital technologies as platforms for building labour activism across dispersed networks, a phenomenon referred to by Bruce Robinson as 'cybersolidarity'.[12] Trade unionists have used the Internet to launch email and boycott campaigns as diverse as the 2005 campaign in support of illegally imprisoned trade unionists in Eritrea to the 2016 campaign to demand the release of the Alexandria shipyard workers arrested for organizing a peaceful protest. While most campaigns are about supporting striking workers or reminding governments and companies that violations of workers' rights

Table 12.2 Individual and collective labour conflicts

Individual	*Collective*	
	With work stoppage	*Without work stoppage*
Refusal to work overtime	Strike	Petition
	Sabotage	Marches,
Personal conflicts and tension in the workplace	Occupation of factory	manifestations, rallies and demonstrations
	Sickout	Refusal to work
Absenteeism	Picketing	overtime
Judiciarization		Work-to-rule
Arbitration		Lobbying
Courts		Boycotts

to organize and strike go against international law, including ILO conventions, others have explored the potential that information and communication technologies create for transnational solidarity.

Consider the 2007 labour dispute between IBM Italy and its 9,000 workers after the former rejected a pay rise, cancelled performance bonuses and refused to meet with workers' representatives. Second Life is a virtual world comprising buildings, cities, green spaces and avatars, which are generally virtual humans controlled by real ones. IBM has spent considerable sums of money to acquire land and buildings in this virtual world, with public areas destined as sales and marketing tools, and private areas that only IBM employees can access. After careful coordination and preparation, about 1,850 avatars from thirty different countries converged on IBM's virtual campus for a twelve-hour 'virtual strike'. Placards and banners were visible and passers-by were encouraged to sign an online petition. With the number of virtual protesters rising and news of the protest going viral all over Second Life and the web, IBM Italy finally agreed to resume negotiations and reinstate performance bonuses.

Workers South: New Working Classes and Labour Movements

The above section examined changing power relations and focused predominantly on the advanced industrial countries. We should be careful, however, not to overgeneralize the experience of advanced capitalist economies because the changing geography of labour also creates new spaces of worker organization. As the case of the Indian general strike that opened this chapter indicates, the labour movement is both active and innovative in many parts of the world. In part, this relates to the production of new working classes through the globalization of production. The so-called newly industrialized countries (NICs) that emerged in the 1970s and 1980s, for example, witnessed rapid economic expansion and industrial development accompanied by the growth of large industrial working classes and powerful new labour movements, especially in Brazil, South Africa and South Korea. As capital moved to China, India, Malaysia, Mexico and Thailand in the late 1990s, similar upsurges in labour militancy became noticeable. While the intensity, frequency and severity of labour protests varies greatly from one country to another according to its social, political, economic and institutional history, global economic restructuring has effectively been 'manufacturing militance'.[13]

To understand the frontlines of this global shift in labour organization, we can pause to consider labour relations in contemporary China, the so-called 'workshop of the world'. Predicated on the historically large inflow of migrant rural workers into the urban sphere, Chinese industrialization relies on heavily segmented labour markets that sharply differentiate the conditions experienced by migrant workers, urban workers and those trapped in declining former state-owned industries. Within this context, the official All China Federation of Trade Unions (ACFTU) has occupied an uncomfortable position. Although it nominally exists to protect worker rights, the ACFTU remains a bureaucratic arm of the state aimed at ensuring industrial calm under which export-orientated production can be scaled up. This has led to strong tensions within Chinese workplaces, as industrial workers increasingly moved outside the formal dispute resolution mechanisms to take their grievances to the streets.[14] As industrial relations scholar Eli Friedman notes, this upsurge of activism has strengthened the hand of the labour movement within China in pushing for pro-labour legislation, increases in minimum wages and sectoral-level collective bargaining. By threatening social stability, Chinese labour militancy has been pivotal in securing a degree of formalization that previously only existed on paper, not in practice. That said, independent labour movements remain only quasi-legal, and shop-floor bargaining is compromised by the ambiguous and anti-democratic position of the ACFTU as the country's 'official' union. This creates an incredibly complex and regionally uneven tapestry of labour organization across contemporary China. It nonetheless challenges the notion of the twenty-first century as an era of uniform retreat for union movements and labour rights.[15]

If the Chinese case represents a reassertion of more traditional workplace politics, an important part of retooling labour organizations elsewhere has been the attempt to transcend the workplace and its focus on the immediate politics of production. While traditional unionism has been rooted in the idea of a union that defends collective rights in a given workplace, the strategy of social movement unionism seeks to bridge the divide between workplace and community or – put more analytically – between the sphere of production and the sphere of social reproduction. Anchored in labour organizations of the global South, social movement unionism has typically sought to build coalitions for social justice by overcoming the fragmentation of specific workplaces and occupational groups.[16] A key concern, for example, has been to outline within communities how different forms of power relations overlap, such as the relationship between gender or ethnic discrimination and labour market segmentation; or the lowering of worker rights in the public sector and the deteriorating provision of services within communities. In short, social movement unionism seeks to break down traditional barriers between workplace and community, production and social reproduction, and trade unions and social movements.[17]

Perhaps nowhere exemplifies this tradition of an expansive vision of labour organization more than the struggle for social justice in South Africa. In the 1970s, increased labour militancy and community support in the movement against apartheid led to the successful 1973 strikes in Durban, which in turn inspired strikes elsewhere and the Soweto uprising of 1976. By the early 1980s, anti-apartheid forces had coalesced into a nonviolent, informal alliance of civic, church, students' and workers' organizations calling for a multiracial democracy. Throughout those years, they developed international networks of solidarity. International labour organizations such as the International Confederation of Free Trade Unions (ICFTU), International Trade Secretariats (ITSs) and the World Federation of Trade Unions (WFTU) played a key role in helping to build international momentum by campaigning against the regime, notably through a worldwide boycott campaign aimed at putting pressure on the pro-apartheid government. Civil and students' organizations were also essential in supporting the boycott campaign. They were later joined by national governments, which, from Australia to Ghana and from Egypt to Indonesia, condemned the apartheid government. By 1989, South Africa, isolated, had to begin to lift the ban on black liberation parties, release political prisoners and allow freedom of the press. Institutionalized racial discrimination and oppression officially came to an end with the election to the presidency of Nelson Mandela in 1994. What makes the campaign against the apartheid stand out is the dual process by which it created, nurtured and expanded across labour and civil organizations in South Africa, and rescaled this coalition through international networks of solidarity where both labour movements and social movements were called on to play a significant role. In short, it brought social movement unionism and labour internationalism together through politics of space and politics of scale.

Social movement unionism also makes explicit the great diversity of working conditions, employment relations and political identities that workers have. The position of women workers in global production networks, for example, is one important challenge that labour organizations must recognize, as patriarchal union structures exclude women workers by ignoring issues that are key to them.[18] Consider the effort to promote women's autonomous organizing and gender mainstreaming in Ukrainian public sector trade unions in the early 2000s. Initiated by the Public Services International's women committee, the collaborative project between UK-based public services unions and Ukrainian public service union partners aimed to give greater visibility to issues affecting women. It proposed to do this by promoting action on gender equality issues such as work–life balance and sexual harassment, working towards greater women's representation in union structures and leadership positions, and developing women's campaigning skills. Navigating between mainstream and women-only spaces, the project demonstrated how a masculinized discourse and gendered hierarchy were upheld by the male leaderships in the mainstream space, dominating as they did the agenda and trivializing issues that typically affect women, such as sexual harassment. While the project showed the necessity to bridge those spaces through gender mainstreaming, it also revealed the importance of having spaces where women could transcend gender politics through individual and collective empowerment. Many women workers noted how cross-union and cross-border solidarity had played an important role in helping them learn how to become active agents in the transformation of their own union structures. In short, bridging spaces and building the union as an inclusionary gender project demanded first that its members recognize the relations of power and the spaces of exclusion existing within it.

Women workers have also organized outside the traditional space of trade unions. The Self Employed Women's Association (SEWA), an informal workers' union founded in 1972 in India, counted close to 700,000 members by the mid-2000s. SEWA organizes poor, self-employed women in the Indian informal sector, including domestic workers, petty vendors, bidi workers, handcart pullers, laundry workers and weavers. SEWA promotes a holistic approach encompassing socioeconomic and political rights. It seeks to achieve two main goals. First, it strives to secure full-employment for its members so that they can ensure economic and social security. In order to do this, it provides its members with services such as childcare, healthcare, housing and access to drinking water. Second, the association promotes self-reliance by empowering informal workers both at the individual and the collective level, most notably through the SEWA Bank and the SEWA Academy, both of which seek to develop capacity building for its members, including job training and skills. Some services, such as childcare and savings and credit, are organized in cooperatives, promoting self-reliance and member participation. The association is thus made aware of the issues that affect women workers and strives to act on them. By privileging the mobilization of workers as the main driver of social change amongst poor and marginalized communities, SEWA seeks to empower its members and give them the capacity to influence and control at least part of their lives. Perhaps most impressive is SEWA's ability to work at multiple levels as a means to impact upon the complex structures and power relations that impact upon its members' livelihoods. It shows how empowered, dedicated and active members can produce creative solutions to complex problems by working together.

More largely, the SEWA experience demands that we recognize the central role played by informal labour in the global economy (see chapter 6). In Mozambique, a series of structural adjustment programmes introduced in the late 1980s and throughout the 1990s reduced the rights and size of industrial and public sector workforces, thereby increasing the size of the informal sector within the capital city of Maputo. Like most African cities, informal labour was (and remains) by far the most common form of employment, with street selling representing a substantial proportion of informal livelihoods. Because the government did not recognize these activities as legitimate, it failed to provide informal workers with proper infrastructures and services. Instead, street vendors occupied idle land and built unplanned markets, while being chased and harassed by government agents. In response, in 1999 street sellers founded the Association of Workers and Operators of the Informal Sector. The association provides basic infrastructure such as water and toilets, makes improvement to unplanned markets, and organizes security services and cleaning, all of which are financed by vendors. Its city-wide structure also promotes solidarity between sellers in different markets, which can be mobilized when vendors in an affiliate market are threatened with eviction by government authorities. Consequently, despite the informal nature of their work, street vendors are able to better defend themselves against the hostility of municipal agents. Organizing has also empowered street sellers' ability to defend their right to the city, seek the legalization of unplanned markets and promote their activities as a legitimate form of work. While informal vendors in Maputo do not enjoy the legal protection and rights conferred to formal work, they have nonetheless been able to carve out a collective space for political action aimed towards improving their conditions.[19]

The process of organizing informal workers typically seeks to transform their work conditions through collective empowerment and the provision of resources for more secure livelihood strategies. At a wider scale, a parallel strategy is to seek legal recognition for informal occupations to begin a process of formalization. Consider the case of Uruguay, which in 2012 was the first state to ratify ILO Convention 189 on domestic workers. The new law gave the 120,000 domestic workers in Uruguay the same rights as other workers, including the right to collective bargaining, a guaranteed minimum wage, rules on working hours, access to social security, and legal protection. Under this legislation, bargaining takes place before the Tripartite Wage Board, which comprises the union, the Housewives League (a group of activist housewives representing the employers' side) and the government.[20] The initiative in Uruguay is part of a much bigger movement supported by the International Trade Union Confederation (ITUC), the International Domestic Workers' Federation (IDWF) and many workers' and civil organizations across nations to defend and promote domestic workers' rights. So far, only twenty-two countries have ratified C189, twelve of which are from Latin America. The overwhelming majority of countries in Asia, Europe and North America, with established guest worker programmes for domestic workers, have shown no interest in ratifying the convention. There are an estimated 53–100 million domestic workers worldwide, the vast majority of whom are women, including many millions of girls and migrants. C189 is premised on the idea that domestic workers constitute a significant proportion of informal workers worldwide, especially in developing countries, where opportunities for formal work are scarce. While important progress has been made to organize informal domestic workers, there is still much to be done to ensure that the dozens of millions of workers who cook, clean and provide care enjoy the same rights as all other workers.[21]

New Forms of Labour Internationalism

In a world defined by capital mobility and global production networks, labour movements must increasingly pay attention to the politics of scale in an attempt to build labour organizations that can adapt to changing circumstances. In this respect, cross-border solidarity has a long and rich history. Of historical importance was the establishment in the 1890s and 1900s of International Trade Secretariats (ITSs). The latter were federations of national trade unions representing different occupational groups such as typographers and printers, shoemakers, miners, railway workers and carpenters that were networked across national borders. Although there had been initiatives in the 1970s and 1980s to mount transnational organizing activities and build countervailing power against multinational corporations, it was not until the 1990s that international trade union federations gained momentum and became more effective and relevant to an emerging global economy.[22] At the same time, the rise of neoliberalism and the end of the Cold War convinced many union leaders that stronger representation at the international level and a more active global labour movement campaigning for human and labour rights were essential to the pursuit of the movement's interests. In this respect, the ITSs evolved over the twentieth century to become – symbolically, in the year 2000 – the Global Union Federations (GUFs), thus sending a strong message that twenty-first-century labour internationalism would take the form of global trade unionism.

Global trade unionism represents a response to both the challenges and the opportunities created by the restructuring of global capitalism. It typically operates through transnational campaigns, solidarity networks and coordinated actions. One key initiative coming from global unions is the attempt to create a labour organization strategy that is able to match the formation of global production networks. This aim has resulted in a strategy to pressure corporations into negotiating International Framework Agreements (IFAs) that set common working conditions and worker rights across the company's supply chain, much like the labour codes of conduct we examined in the previous chapter. In contrast to labour codes of conduct, however, IFAs are not top-down decrees, but are negotiated directly between the corporation and organized labour, and both sides are to play a role in monitoring the agreement. They are therefore designed to work for transnational corporations such as Chiquita, BMW, DANONE, IKEA and Volkswagen, where unions already have a handhold across the corporate supply chain.[23]

The vast majority of such IFAs have been signed since 2000, and to date there are more than 100 of them. While some have argued that IFAs have the potential to positively impact efforts to revitalize local union politics, others have stressed that their impact is greatly hindered by the fact that they are normally nonbinding agreements lacking stringent enforcement mechanisms. Where they have been most successful is in maintaining core labour standards for permanent employees, yet their capacity to cover suppliers, subcontractors and informal labour has yet to be tested, and no one really knows how well IFAs can be upheld in countries without strong labour laws. Indeed, they are mostly a European feature, proliferating where unions already exist and where structures of coordination have already been established. Moreover, there is always the risk that companies might use IFAs as a public relations stunt to demonstrate their commitment to social dialogue or to prevent consumer-based campaigns from agitating for ethical production without really ensuring their application across the production chain. That being said, despite their limitations, IFAs give global unions the capacity to play a more active negotiating role in multinational companies so as to guarantee the protection of the ILO core labour standards, while charting new territories for global labour.[24]

If global framework agreements tend to be orientated primarily around the goals of European unions, an important counterpoint has been the development of South–South labour solidarity initiatives. A key example of this movement is the Southern Initiative on Globalization and Trade Union Rights (SIGTUR), an alliance of democratic unions in Africa, Asia, Australia and Latin America. Building on social movement unionism principles, SIGTUR promotes internal and new forms of participatory democracy, a mobilized, activist and action-oriented membership, and alliances with social movements. Rather than collaborate with international capital, as European and American trade unions do, SIGTUR challenges the existing social order through extensive network building between existing unions and social movements across the global South. While encompassing leading unions in Argentina, Australia, Brazil, South Africa and South Korea, SIGTUR nonetheless remains a loose organizational structure that primarily serves to link trade unions active at various scales. Some have argued that there are still too few examples of effective international solidarity leading to tangible gains. Others counter that

SIGTUR is a fresh, revitalizing force with growing capacity for global influence. At a time where the labour movement in the West is still recovering from the 2008 economic crisis and the subsequent imposition of austerity measures, southern trade unions have an opportunity to strengthen their presence at the international level. Meanwhile, the initiative seeks to continue to build a new labour internationalism by framing workers' collective problems within a southern perspective.[25]

As the many challenges facing global unions indicate, international solidarity and labour internationalism are hard to achieve. Cross-border solidarity may seem logical, but it is extremely difficult to put into practice because workers have vastly different working experiences and contrasting positions within global structures of production and consumption.[26] Informal workers struggling to survive, for example, might indeed find cross-border solidarity to be logical in theory, but quickly discover that different cultures and languages, as well as national sentiments, gendered biases and racial prejudices, can become massive roadblocks on the road to cohesion. Moreover, as labour geographer Andrew Herod argues, we should resist the idea that, because we live under global capitalism, labour movements must equally 'go global' to be effective.[27] While there is certainly a need for a renewed labour internationalism, we should not forget that the vast majority of labour struggles are specific to a region, a country or even a city, and that their particular nature must be considered in the mobilization and formulation of an effective strategy for success.

While one might expect that keeping the movement on a national scale would make it easier for workers to show solidarity, since they have more issues in common, recent experiences show that even within the same country, important distinctions exist that can create deep divisions, as shown in Jane Holgate's study of a failed attempt to organize migrant workers in a London processed-foods factory. To begin with, the union adopted a traditional industrial relations approach based on management/union negotiations instead of an organizing model tailored after workers' issues, particularly in the complex context of many workers being asylum seekers. Second, despite it being a core issue for many workers, the union refused to acknowledge many of the company's racialized employment practices. Even though a large number of migrant workers spoke very little English, the union made little effort to facilitate communication. The union also refused to organize outside the workplace, as union officials felt insecure about moving away from collective bargaining to dealing with issues of social justice. Finally, the union was unable to conceive of workers' identity in anything other than a work context. It did not adequately recognize that work is only one dimension of identity alongside others such as race and gender. The inability of the union to adapt itself to the reality of a workplace composed almost exclusively of migrant workers resulted in a lack of trust and respect. Indeed, most workers remained perplexed about the relevance of an organization that could not understand their lived experiences as workers.[28] While solidarity and collective action may often originate with union membership, this example shows that the former does not necessarily follow from the latter.

Labour Organization Moving Forward?

That solidarity within and across labour organizations is difficult to achieve should not be surprising. As the field of global labour studies has repeatedly indicated, workers operate in contexts closely structured by uneven relations of power, meaning that they face considerable obstacles, both structural and political, to the formation of effective collective organizations. As Piya Pangsapa has argued in her important study of collective resistance among female workers in the Thai garment industry, many workers follow strategies of adaptation and accommodation towards disciplinary factory regimes wherein the routines of daily factory life become normalized and instances of explicit resistance or opposition are not commonplace.[29] Notwithstanding these constraints, this chapter has charted how new forms of organizing labour have gained significant purchase in particular contexts. This is especially the case where labour movements have created innovative organizational strategies that explicitly recognize the variety of workplace experiences and the complex livelihoods strategies that workers must embrace. Whether or not this acknowledges that women workers often find it easier to organize outside the factory than within it, or that many informal sector workers experience no clear distinction between the workplace and the home, labour organization must continue to adjust to these pressing realities.

Further Reading

An excellent introduction to new forms of global labour organization and their challenges ahead is provided by Stephanie Luce in *Labor Movements: Global Perspectives* (Cambridge: Polity, 2014). A more explicitly radical sentiment can be found in the thematic collection edited by Andreas Bieler and Ingemar Lindberg, *Global Restructuring, Labour and the Challenges for Transnational Solidarity* (London: Routledge, 2010). For a comprehensive, interdisciplinary investigation of the challenges facing organized labour worldwide, see Craig Phelan, *The Future of Organized Labour: Global Perspectives* (Bern: Peter Lang, 2007).

Chapter 13
Conclusion: The Futures of Global Labour

As we saw at the beginning of this book, labour is best understood as work in its social context. To study labour is to engage in a whole series of questions concerning who is performing work, for whom and under what conditions. Critical to this endeavour is the need to explore how such work is embedded within the wider production and consumption of goods and services on a global scale. To this end, we have explored the world of work, employment and livelihoods across diverse social contexts, using a consistent set of analytical tools that help focus attention on the possibilities, unevenness and inequities of current trends. To draw this process towards a conclusion, we raise three interrelated themes extracted from the previous chapters that are likely to define the future of labour over the coming decades. These are, respectively, the perpetuation of stark global inequalities in wealth and income; the prospect of deepening automation and the creation of jobless growth; and the escalating tensions between a global economy that relentlessly scales up production and the straining ecological foundations that underpin human well-being. In highlighting these issues, we seek to assert once more the ways in which *Global Labour Studies* provides a compelling framework to pose key questions and conduct perceptive analysis when facing the core problems of our age.

Global Inequalities and the Persistence of Poverty among Plenty

Given the considerable excitement within the international community about reductions in global poverty within the Millennium Development Goals (MDGs) initiative, our emphasis here on the continued production of poverty among plenty may seem surprising. To be sure, there has been notable progress in addressing the condition of extreme poverty since the mid-1990s. These achievements, however, have been geographically concentrated, with socioeconomic change in China accounting for a large part of the recorded success. They also vary greatly depending on how we define poverty. The reduction in poverty highlighted within the MDGs, for example, relates to a particularly extreme form of poverty characterized by income levels that leave an individual unable to meet basic nutritional requirements. When we look beyond this category, we still find that, by 2011, some 50 per cent of the world's population had incomes that provide only basic material comforts.[1] Combined with those in extreme poverty, the majority of the world's population – somewhere around 60 per cent – comprise what we could term the working poor: households that range from extreme deprivation to a materially more comfortable yet basic existence strongly dependent on continued access to employment.

The persistence of deprivation among incredible wealth remains an enduring issue for global labour studies. This becomes vividly clear when we consider that, at the other end of the scale, incomes of the global rich have increased momentously over the same period. A provocative Oxfam report estimated that the top 1 per cent of the global population – those at the very pinnacle of the global economy – holds more than half the world's wealth.[2] In pinpointing wealth, we are not talking simply about income levels, but, rather, accumulated assets, including ownership of companies and financial assets such as stocks and shares. This is important, because such concentrated wealth indicates the narrowness of control over the world's productive capabilities. A small fraction of the global population possesses a highly concentrated ability to benefit from the wealth generated by productive activities worldwide. Pertinently, whether in the United States or Uganda, concentrated wealth is invariably translated into a large degree of political influence through either concerted lobbying or direct access to the levers of power.

Such inequalities reinforce the inherently political nature of work. Consider the case of Mohammed Bouazizi, a poor street seller in

Sidi Bouzid, Tunisia. One morning, Bouazizi was harassed and fined by local authorities seeking bribes, and his wares were confiscated. Angered, he went to the provincial headquarters to complain, but the governor refused to see him. Bouazizi returned moments later with a can of gasoline and set himself on fire. This tragic incident quite literally ignited one of the most significant political mobilizations of recent times. Like most street sellers who incur debts to buy their daily wares, the prospect of being fined, paying bribes or having wares confiscated represents a sure road to greater poverty and economic hardship. Helped by union mobilization, the anger and humiliation expressed by Bouazizi reverberated widely and galvanized the frustrations of a youth deprived of secure employment and social mobility. Massive street protests rapidly engulfed Tunisian cities, leading to the fall of a dictatorial government that had held power for twenty-three years. This Tunisian revolution then spread out across the Arab world, leading to insurgencies in Libya, Syria and Yemen, and civil uprisings in Bahrain and Egypt. The Arab Spring, as these waves of discontent came to be known, was anchored in the working experiences of millions of people like Bouazizi who faced an uncertain future with limited job prospects in a stifling political environment.[3]

Contemporary global wealth stratification is therefore a huge and enduring issue. This is because concentrations of wealth shape who works where, for whom, and under what conditions.[4] While we offer no easy solutions to this stratification, by exploring at a grounded level the socioeconomic processes that produce startling wealth alongside persistent poverty, global labour studies does provide core tools to help us understand the tangible ways by which individuals and households are able to work towards a more materially secure life, while also indicating the many barriers and constraints to such outcomes. In chapter 12, we opened the question of which new forms of labour organization might be pertinent in a changing global order to ensure that decent work conditions and living wages can be more easily accessed by a majority of the world's workforce. Given that the presence of labour organizations can moderate power imbalances both in labour markets and workplaces, the ability to analyse and potentially overcome the many barriers to organizing dispersed and fragmented workers remains a central task for ensuring more equitable distributions of wealth on both national and global scales.

Technological Change and the Spectre of Jobless Growth

A founding premise of global labour studies is that most of the world's population strives diligently to craft more secure lives through building robust livelihoods that can deliver higher or more reliable incomes and a better quality of life. For most people, this is to be achieved first and foremost through work as the means to earn money. What happens, however, if the jobs that people seek become increasingly hard to find? The pace of automation within the workplace that we raised in chapter 5 has many analysts predicting a secular decline in the demand for labour over the coming decades. Such trends, moreover, are projected to impact labour in both the global North and the global South. German footwear giant Adidas, for example, has recently announced the reshoring of two factories for the production of sports shoes from Asia back to Germany and the United States respectively. This seems counterintuitive, given that the formation of global production networks was aimed precisely at relocating the production of low-skilled labour intensive items to labour regimes in Asia and Latin America as a way to reduce costs. The new factories in Germany and the United States, however, will not require a cheap and disciplined workforce because they will be entirely automated. The implications are astounding: one of the most labour-intensive industries is exploring ways to make labour redundant.[5]

At a wider level, such technological changes are associated with an emerging Fourth Industrial Revolution, which brings together physical, biological and digital systems. The result is not only the blurring of the lines between natural and artificial spheres, but also the development of ever more complex and comprehensive digital networks of robots based on technological breakthroughs in nanotechnology, artificial intelligence, quantum computing and energy storage. One key dimension of this technological revolution is linked to autonomous vehicles. Multinational mining corporation Rio Tinto, for example, currently has sixty-nine autonomous trucks in operation at its Pilbara operations in Australia, and Suncor is hoping to replace its 800 heavy-haul drivers in the Canadian oil sands with driverless trucks by 2020. Yet the effects of autonomous vehicles go far beyond a few mining sites scattered across the globe, as dozens of millions of taxi drivers, public transit workers, truck drivers, delivery workers and parking attendants will be directly impacted by the introduction of driverless vehicles. The latter have lower operating costs, can work without rest, are not subject to labour regulations, and do not strike or bargain for better conditions. With international giants investing heavily in driverless research and development, including Apple, Ford, GM, Google, Honda, Intel, Lyft, Microsoft, Toyota, Uber and Volvo, autonomous vehicles are arguably the next major transportation revolution, one that combines economic growth with massive layoffs.[6]

What is the future of labour in an increasingly automated world? In theory, automation should lead to greater productivity and, therefore, to the production of more aggregate wealth that will make societies richer. However, such trends raise complex questions about the distribution of this wealth, particularly if work is no longer a feasible means by which a majority can earn the means to a livelihood. It raises the spectre of jobless growth, a phenomenon whereby economic expansion does not create new job opportunities but, rather, stagnates or reduces employment levels through technological change. Far from a future possibility, this trend is already occurring in some large newly industrializing nations such as South Africa and India. There, the accomplishment of relatively sustained economic growth has not translated into employment creation but has proceeded alongside stagnant labour markets.[7] The outcome is one of polarization and stratification: some new jobs pay well and provide a ticket to relative affluence and security. Others, however, are pushed into hugely competitive labour markets that exert downward pressure on wages and are predicated upon casualized labour relations. The automation question evidently links closely with the issue of inequality.

For some authors, this raises the pivotal question of whether struggles in the realm of work will remain the pivotal locus for social justice in the coming decades. Anthropologist James Ferguson, for instance, has argued that work is no longer the primary means by which many households secure their social reproduction in southern Africa. Political movements, he notes, are increasingly aimed at ensuring state redistribution through guaranteed cash transfers as the guarantee of household reproduction. Cash transfer programmes, he argues, have become increasingly commonplace and expansive, providing the basic income on which many rely.[8] This shift raises a key question: in a world of potentially greater wealth but fewer opportunities to claim a share through labour, are guaranteed entitlements a central cog in the future of progressive politics? At the very least, the perspective of global labour studies allows us to chart how such politics of distribution can interact with the politics of production, potentially opening new avenues for the productive alliance between labour movements and community-based social movements.

Global Environmental Change and the Ends of Production

If automation and increased productivity presents the hypothetical potential of an end to scarcity, our ability to produce ever greater quantities of goods is now widely recognized to conflict considerably with the ecological foundations of future prosperity. Resource depletion, environmental degradation and climate change are seemingly hardwired into the current functioning of the global economy, yet have very unequal impacts on different social groups. Those most vulnerable to climate change, for example, are frequently those who have scarcely contributed to the problem and have benefited least from the productivity revolutions that burning fossil fuels has underpinned. Given that the projects of modernity and development have been tightly wedded to increases in the productivity of labour through carbon-based energy forms, we are faced with troubling questions about the impacts of tightening ecological constraints upon different segments of the global workforce. Put simply, can the world continue to seek growth as a way to remedy questions of poverty and inequality if the means for doing so are increasingly fragile?

The prospect of a powering down of economic growth – either planned or unplanned – forces us to address whose consumption might be affected and how such a transition would impact upon livelihoods. Optimistic scenarios argue that a shift to 'green growth' can reconcile job creation, sustainability and open new pathways towards responsible economic growth.[9] The grounds for optimism, however, may be rapidly diminished as the extraction of finite resources such as oil continues apace while international commitments to address carbon emissions fail to offer a convincing framework to decarbonize the global economy within a proximate timeframe. At issue are intractable conflicts between countries over the responsibility to address climate change and the right of less-developed nations to maintain carbon-intensive development paths as a way to promote social development. In short, the climate question highlights in close relief the social question that *Global Labour Studies* has been interrogating: how are current patterns of work and production related to the uneven ability to consume the fruits of such labour on a global scale? In a world of tightening ecological constraints, these questions – and therein the key analytical tools we can use to address them – become ever more pertinent.

Notes

Chapter 1 Thinking Global Labour Studies

1 Ellis (2013).
2 Cavalcanti and Bendini (2014).
3 For a robust critique of labour conditions in Brazil's fruit sector, see the short film *Squeezed: The Cost of Free Trade in the Asia-Pacific* by a fruit worker advocate group called the Association of Conscientious Consumers, https://www.youtube.com/watch?v=7MmI1Vn6Fn4.
4 Pun (2007).
5 Cooper (2001).
6 Chan (2011).

Chapter 2 The Toolkit of Global Labour Studies

1 The above is an elaborative yet hypothetical example built from the work of Purkayastha (2005). To explore further the question of Indian IT workers in the United States, see Ong (2006).
2 For a discussion of political agency among Peruvian informal sector vendors, see Steel (2012).
3 For an incisive account of the many power imbalances within Walmart's Chinese supply chains, see Chan (2011).
4 Kim (2013).
5 Salzinger (2003).
6 Sneath (2006).
7 Williams (2005)
8 Mosse et al. (2002).
9 Harvey (2006).
10 Campbell (2013).
11 Chambers and Conway (1992).
12 Rigg et al. (2014).

Chapter 3 Labour Regimes

1 Al-Mahmood (2013). The *Guardian* also provides an interactive guide to conditions within Bangladeshi garment factories that is well worth reading: http://www.theguardian.com/world/ng-interactive/2014/apr/bangladesh-shirt-on-your-back.
2 Deyo (2001).
3 Polanyi (2001).

4 Mies (1986).
5 Peck (1996).
6 Upadhya (2009).
7 Edin and Schaefer (2015).
8 Clarke (1999).
9 Campling et al. (2016).
10 Pager (2003).
11 Bradley and Healy (2008).
12 Kabeer (1988); Hale and Wills (2005).
13 Heath and Mobarak (2015).
14 Kabeer (2002).
15 Coe and Kelly (2002).
16 Thompson (1967).
17 Gallagher (2004).
18 Salzinger (2003).
19 Edwards (1979).
20 Lee (1995).
21 Chan and Wang (2004).
22 Kelly (2002).
23 Burawoy (1985).

Chapter 4 Global Production Networks

1 Yeung (2009).
2 Gereffi et al. (2005).
3 Uzzi (1997).
4 See the account by Armitage (2013).
5 Kerr (2012).
6 Suarez-Villa (2015).
7 Arnold and Shih (2010).
8 Bair and Werner (2011).
9 See Merk (2008).
10 Taylor (2006).
11 Gereffi et al. (2005).
12 Sevastopulo (2014).

Chapter 5   Formal Work in Transition

1 Braverman (1974).
2 Harrington (1963).
3 Reich et al. (1973); Reich (2008).
4 Anglade and Fortín (1985).
5 Schultz (2000).
6 Pofeldt (2015).
7 Sussmann (2015).
8 NUS (2016).
9 Sparshott (2015).
10 Wacquant (2009).
11 Katz and Krueger (2016).
12 Breman and van der Linden (2014); Standing (2015).
13 Bakker (2003).
14 Gregg (2013).
15 Callaway (2015).
16 Osborne and Farrell (2016).
17 Asher-Schapiro (2014); Levine (2016).
18 Lambert (2015).
19 Dyer-Witheford (2015).
20 Check out the provocative video by the Moth Collective: 'The Last Job on Earth: Imagining a Fully Automated World', at https://www.theguardian.com/sustainable-business/video/2016/feb/17/last-job-on-earth-automation-robots-unemployment-animation-video.

Chapter 6   Labour in the Informal Economy

1 Vanek et al. (2014).
2 The ILO provides a wealth of statistical information on informality at http://laborsta.ilo.org/informal_economy_E.html.
3 Schneider (2013).
4 Hart (1973).
5 ILO (2002).
6 For a powerful collection of histories and analysis, see Wills et al. (2010).
7 BBC (2012).

8 Rostow's (1960) classic outline of the 'stages of development' is a prime example.
9 Vanek et al. (2014).
10 de Soto (1989, 2003).
11 Perry et al. (2007).
12 Leys (1974).
13 Breman (2009).
14 Nun (2000).
15 Sanyal (2007).
16 Davis (2006).
17 Chen et al. (2006).
18 Maloney (2004).
19 Kabeer et al. (2010).
20 Mezzadri (2016).
21 Tafere and Pankhurst (2015).
22 Meagher (2010).
23 Minoia (2015).
24 Bayat (2009).
25 Cross (1998).
26 For a vivid account of one such vendor association leader, see Dickerson (2007).

Chapter 7 Agrarian Labour

1 Lapegna (2016).
2 Pretty (2002).
3 MacDonald et al. (2013).
4 Cronon (1991).
5 For a deep account of agricultural transformation, racial segregation, migration and cultural change in Mississippi, see Woods (1998).
6 *The Economist* (2015).
7 Weis (2013).
8 Thompson (2010).
9 On the loss of topsoil, see the video by the Environmental Working Group: https://youtu.be/ehlUKkw69Dg. On energy usage, see Pelletier et al. (2011).
10 Weis (2013).
11 Binford (2013).
12 World Bank (2015a).

13 IFAD (2012, 2013).
14 Hussain (1988).
15 Cullather (2014).
16 Taylor (2015).
17 World Bank (2007).
18 Akram Lodhi (2013).
19 World Bank (2007), p. 26.
20 Rigg (2006).
21 Taylor (2015).
22 Razavi (2009).
23 Borras and Edelman (2015).
24 Wolford (2010).
25 Deininger and Byerlee (2011).
26 Vidal (2010).
27 The Oakland Institute (2015).
28 World Bank (2015b).
29 *The Economist* (2008).
30 Campbell et al. (2014).
31 Fraser and Charlebois (2016).

Chapter 8 Migrant Labour

1 United Nations (1990).
2 IOM (2015).
3 Crush et al. (2015).
4 Ravenstein (1889); Lee (1966).
5 Katz and Stark (1986); Massey (1990).
6 World Bank (2016).
7 The plight of South African former miners with silicosis is brought vividly, yet painfully, to life in photojournalist Thom Pierce's collection 'The Price of Gold', at http://thompierce.com/tpog. In China, the struggles of silicosis-affected workers for compensation is described in Nang and Pun (2013).
8 See Cohen (1987).
9 Cohen (2010).
10 Potts (1990).
11 Blackburn (2010); Solow (1993).
12 Northrup (1995); Behal and van der Linden (2007).

13 Kaur (2014).
14 Emmer (1992).
15 Cross (1983); Homze (1967).
16 World Bank (2016).
17 Acosta Arcarazo and Geddes (2014).
18 Piore (1979).
19 Jurje and Lavenex (2015).
20 Salazar Parreñas (2015).
21 Wills et al. (2010).
22 Rannveig Agunias et al. (2011).
23 World Bank (2016).
24 Takenaka et al. (2010).
25 ILO (2015).

Chapter 9 Forced Labour

1 See the full documentary as part of the excellent 21st Century Slavery series produced by Al Jazeera, at http://www.aljazeera.com/progra mmes/slaverya21stcenturyevil/.
2 Gibson (2016).
3 Robinson (1962), p. 45.
4 ILO (2012a).
5 Breman (2010), p. 345.
6 Sandy (2015).
7 LeBaron (2008).
8 Ashbrook (2016).
9 Zatz et al. (2016).
10 Lan (2007).
11 Consider watching the video from the International Dalit Solidarity Network, at http://idsn.org/caste-discrimination/.
12 Human Rights Watch (2014).
13 SOMO and ICD (2011).
14 Sandy (2012).
15 Smith (1999).
16 Ryan (2011); Payson Center for International Development and Technology Transfer (2011).
17 Breman (2010).
18 Allain et al. (2013).
19 Rioux (2015).
20 Hodal et al. (2014).
21 Brass (2011).
22 Shen (2016).

Chapter 10 Environment and Labour

1 Minter (2013) provides a compelling journey around North American and Chinese waste disposal practices, including an excellent chapter on Giuyu.
2 Guo et al. (2014). Daming (2010) provides an excellent summary of how the labour and environmental issues in Guiyu are closely intertwined.
3 Blaikie and Brookfield (1987).
4 Marx (1990).
5 Smith (2008).
6 Kloppenburg (2004).
7 Bridge (2004).
8 BBC Online (2016).
9 Gordon (2014).
10 Mordi (2008).
11 Adeniyi Ajonbadi (2015).
12 Kashi and Watts (2008).
13 Mitchell (2009).
14 Steffen et al. (2007).
15 Oreskes (2014).
16 Kolbert (2014).
17 See the Planetary Boundaries website operated by the Stockholm Resilience Institute, at https://www.sei-international.org/planetary-boundaries
18 Moore (2016).
19 Urry (2013).
20 Stern (2007).
21 Asafu-Adjaye et al. (2015).
22 European Environment Agency (2014).
23 Malm (2016).
24 Edwards (2013).
25 Taylor (2015).

26 The most comprehensive introduction to the theme of degrowth is provided by D'Alisa et al. (2015).
27 Shiva (2005).
28 Gudynas (2011).
29 Lalander (2014).

Chapter 11 Corporate Social Responsibility

1 Chan et al. (2013).
2 China Labor Watch (2010).
3 As Wells (2007) notes, given the estimates of 200,000–300,000 established garment factories worldwide – and probably a million if small workshops were included – only a tiny fraction of these will ever be audited.
4 Sharp and Ho (2013).
5 Klein (1999) is a foremost examination of the politics of branding and the anti-sweatshop movement attempts to leverage the brand within a politics of consumption.
6 Dirnbach (2014).
7 Armbruster-Sandoval (2005) provides an excellent account of four such anti-sweatshop movements in the 1990s, including a strong analysis of their strengths and weaknesses.
8 Bonacich and Appelbaum (2000).
9 Yu (2007).
10 H&M's statements on CSR can be accessed through their website, at http://about.hm.com/en/sustainability.html. A critique of their programme is presented in Clean Clothes Campaign (2015).
11 Pun (2007) offers a compelling account of this aspect of the labour regime in the factories of south China.
12 Foster and Harvey (2005).

13 Human Rights Watch (2015).
14 Seidman (2009).
15 Butollo (2015).
16 Bartley and Egels-Zandén (2015).
17 Leong and Ka-wai (2011).
18 Clifford and Greenhouse (2013).
19 McDougall (2007).

Chapter 12 Organizing Global Labour

1 Bengali (2016); Manuel (2016).
2 van der Linden (2008), p. 173.
3 For a powerful critique of the notion of the labour aristocracy, see Post (2010).
4 Wright (2000). See also Silver (2003).
5 Jenkins (2002).
6 Hale (2004).
7 Piazza (2005).
8 Burgess (2004).
9 Canadian Foundations for Labour Rights (2016).
10 Tanguy (2013).
11 Dix et al. (2009).
12 Robinson (2011).
13 Seidman (1994).
14 Lee (2007).
15 Friedman (2015).
16 Scipes (2014).
17 Webster (2008).
18 Ledwith (2007).
19 Lindell (2011).
20 Consider watching ILO's (2012b) excellent short video on the subject.
21 ITUC (2012).
22 Fairbrother and Hammer (2005).
23 Papadakis (2008).
24 Stevis and Boswell (2007); Blin (2011).
25 Dobrusin (2014).
26 van der Linden (2008), p. 261.
27 Herod (2003).

28 Holgate (2005).
29 Pangsapa (2007).

Chapter 13   Conclusion: The Futures of Global Labour

1 The statistical breakdown of global income figures by Kochhar (2015) is extremely illuminating. See also Hickel (2016).
2 Hardoon (2015).
3 Bayat (2015).
4 For an accessible examination of debates over different methodologies for calculating wealth inequalities, see Vara (2015).
5 On Adidas' automated factories, see Agence France-Presse (2016) and BI Intelligence (2016).
6 Kanter (2015); Grant (2015).
7 Punj (2016).
8 Ferguson (2015).
9 Asafu-Adjaye et al. (2015).

References

Acosta Arcarazo, Diego and Andrew Geddes (2014) 'Transnational Diffusion or Different Models? Regional Approaches to Migration Governance in the European Union and MERCOSUR', *European Journal of Migration and Law* 16(1), pp. 19–44.

Adeniyi Ajonbadi, Hakeem (2015) 'The Dynamics of Policies and Practices of Labour Contracting in the Nigerian Oil and Gas Sector', *Open Access Library Journal* 2(9). DOI:10.4236/oalib.1101756.

Agence France-Presse (2016) 'Reboot: Adidas to Make Shoes in Germany Again – but Using Robots', *Guardian*, 25 May. https://www.theguardian.com/world/2016/may/25/adidas-to-sell-robot-made-shoes-from-2017.

Akram-Lodhi, Haroon (2013) *Hungry for Change: Farmers, Food Justice and the Agrarian Question.* Halifax and Winnipeg: Fernwood Press.

Allain, Jean, Andrew Crane, Geneviève LeBaron and Laya Behbahani (2013) *Forced Labour's Business Models and Supply Chains.* York: Joseph Rowntree Foundation.

Al-Mahmood, Syed Zain (2013) 'Bangladesh's Garment Industry Still Offers Women Best Work Opportunity', *Guardian*, 23 May. http://www.theguardian.com/global-development/2013/may/23/bangladesh-garment-industry-women-opportunity.

Anglade, Cristian and Carlos Fortín, eds. (1985) *The State and Capital Accumulation in Latin America*, vol. 1. London: Macmillan.

Armbruster-Sandoval, Ralph (2005) 'Workers of the World Unite? The Contemporary Anti-Sweatshop Movement and the Struggle for Social Justice in the Americas', *Work and Occupations* 32(4), pp. 464–485.

Armitage, Jim (2013) '"Even Worse Than Foxconn": Apple Rocked By Child Labour Claims', *Independent*, 30 July. http://www.independent.co.uk/life-style/gadgets-and-tech/even-worse-than-foxconn-apple-rocked-by-child-labour-claims-8736504.html.

Arnold, Dennis and Toh Han Shih (2010) 'A Fair Model of Globalisation? Labour and Global Production in Cambodia', *Journal of Contemporary Asia* 40(3), pp. 401–424.

Asafu-Adjaye, John, et al. (2015) *An Ecomodernist Manifesto*. http://www.eco modernism.org/manifesto-english/.

Ashbrook, Tom (2016) 'American Prison Inmates, On Strike', *WBUR*, 28 September. http://www.wbur.org/onpoint/2016/09/28/prison-strike-prison-reform.

Asher-Schapiro, Avi (2014) 'Against Sharing', *Jacobin*, 19 September. https://www.jacobinmag.com/2014/09/against-sharing/.

Bair, Jennifer (2009) *Frontiers of Commodity Chain Research*. Stanford: Stanford University Press.

Bair, Jennifer and Marion Werner (2011) 'The Place of Disarticulations: Global Commodity Production in La Laguna, Mexico', *Environment and Planning* 43(5), pp. 998–1015.

Bakker, Isabella (2003) 'Neo-liberal Governance and the Reprivatization of Social Reproduction: Social Provisioning and Shifting Gender Orders', in Isabella Bakker and Steven Gill (eds.), *Power, Production and Social Reproduction*, pp. 66–82. Basingstoke: Palgrave Macmillan.

Bales, Kevin (2012) *Disposable People: New Slavery in the Global Economy*. Berkeley: University of California Press.

Bartley, Tim and Niklas Egels-Zandén (2015) 'Responsibility and Neglect in Global Production Networks: The Uneven Significance of Codes of Conduct in Indonesian factories', *Global Networks* 15(s1), pp. S21–S44.

Bayat, Asef (2009) Life as Politics: *How Ordinary People Change the Middle East*. Stanford: Stanford University Press.

Bayat, Asef (2015) 'Plebeians of the Arab Spring', *Current Anthropology* 56(S11), pp. 33–42.

BBC (2012) 'Welcome to Lagos', Episodes 1–3. http://www.bbc.co.uk/programmes/b00s3vdm/episodes/guide.

BBC Online (2016) 'Nigeria's NNPC "Failed to Pay" $16bn in Oil Revenues', 16 March. http://www.bbc.com/news/world-africa-35810599.

Behal, Rana and Marcel van der Linden (2007) *Coolies, Capital and Colonialism: Studies in Indian Labour History*. Cambridge: Cambridge University Press.

Bernstein, Henry (2010) *Class Dynamics of Agrarian Change*. Halifax and Winnipeg: Fernwood Press.

Bieler, Andreas and Ingemar Lindberg, eds. (2010) *Global Restructuring, Labour and the Challenges for Transnational Solidarity*. London: Routledge.

Bengali, Shashank (2016) 'Why Millions of Indian Workers Just Staged One of the Biggest Labor Strikes in History', *Los Angeles Times*, 14 September. http://www.latimes.com/world/la-fg-india-strike-snap-story.html.

BI Intelligence (2016) 'Adidas Will Open an Automated, Robot-Staffed Factory Next Year', *Business Insider*, 12 August. http://www.businessinsider.com/adidas-will-open-an-automated-robot-staffed-factory-next-year-2016-8.

Binford, Leigh (2013) *Tomorrow We're All Going to the Harvest Temporary Foreign Worker Programs and Neoliberal Political Economy*. Austin: University of Texas Press.

Blackburn, Robin (2010) *The Making of New World Slavery: From the Baroque to the Modern, 1492–1800*. London: Verso.

Blaikie, Piers and Harold Brookfield (1987) *Land Degradation and Society*. London: Methuen.

Blin, Dick (2011) 'Global Framework Agreements: Compliance', *International Union Rights* 18(2), pp. 3–4.

Bonacich, Edna and Richard Appelbaum (2000) *Behind the Label: Inequality in the Los Angeles Apparel Industry*. Berkeley: University of California Press.

Borras, Saturnino and Marc Edelman (2015) *Political Dynamics of Transnational Agrarian Movements*. Halifax: Fernwood Press.

Bradley, Harriet and Geraldine Healy (2008) *Ethnicity and Gender at Work: Inequalities, Careers and Employment Relations*. London: Palgrave Press.

Brass, Tom (2011) *Labour Regime Change in the Twenty-First Century: Unfreedom, Capitalism and Primitive Accumulation*. Leiden: Brill.

Braverman, Harry (1974) *Labor and Monopoly Capital: The Degradation of Work in the Twentieth Century*. New York: Monthly Review Press.

Breman, Jan (2009) 'Myth of the Global Safety Net', *New Left Review* 59, pp. 29–37.

Breman, Jan (2010) *Outcast Labour in Asia: Circulation and Informalization of the Workforce at the Bottom of the Economy*. Oxford: Oxford University Press.

Breman, Jan and Marcel van der Linden (2014) 'Informalizing the Economy: The Return of the Social Question at a Global Level', *Development and Change* 45(5), pp. 920–940.

Breman, Jan, Arvind Das and Ravi Agarwal (2000) *Down and Out: Labouring Under Global Capitalism*. Oxford: Oxford University Press.

Breman, Jan, Isabelle Guérin and Aseem Prakash (2009) *India's Unfree Workforce: Of Bondage Old and New*. New Delhi: Oxford University Press.

Bridge, Gavin (2004) 'Gas, and How to Get It', *Geoforum* 35(4), pp. 395–397.

Burawoy, Michael (1985) *The Politics of Production: Factory Regimes Under Capitalism and Socialism*. London: Verso.

Burgess, Katrina (2004) *Parties and Unions in the New Global Economy*. Pittsburgh: University of Pittsburgh Press.

Butollo, Florian (2015) 'The Impact of Industrial Transformation on Labour in Guangdong's Garment and IT Industries', in Anita Chan (ed.), *Chinese Workers in Comparative Perspective*, pp. 85–104. Ithaca: Cornell University Press.

Callaway, Andrew (2015) 'Instaserfs, Part 1–3', *Benjamen Walker's Theory of Everything*. https://toe.prx.org/2015/06/instaserfs-i-of-iii/.

Campbell, Bruce, Philip Thornton, Robert Zougmore, Piet van Asten and Leslie Lipper (2014) 'Sustainable Intensification: What Is Its Role in Climate Smart Agriculture?', *Current Opinion in Environmental Sustainability* 8(1), pp. 39–43.

Campbell, Stephen (2013) 'Solidarity Formations Under Flexibilisation: Workplace Struggles of Precarious Migrants in Thailand', *Global Labour Journal* 4(2), pp. 134–151.

Campling, Liam, Satoshi Miyamura, Jonathan Pattenden and Benjamin Selwyn (2016) 'Class Dynamics of Development: A Methodological Note', *Third World Quarterly* 37(10), pp. 1745–1767.

Canadian Foundations for Labour Rights (2016) 'Restrictive Labour Laws in Canada'. http://labourrights.ca/issues/restrictive-labour-laws-canada.

Cavalcanti, Josefa Salete Barbosa and Mónica Izabel Bendini (2014) 'Globalization and Change in Labor Relations in Fruit Regions of Brazil and Argentina', in Alessandro Bonanno and Josefa Salete Barbosa Cavalcanti (eds.), *Labor Relations in Globalized Food* (Research in Rural Sociology and Development, vol. 20), pp. 3–32. Bingley: Emerald.

Chambers, Robert and Gordon Conway (1992) 'Sustainable Rural Livelihoods: Practical Concepts for the 21st Century', *IDS Discussion Paper*, 296. Brighton: IDS.

Chan, Anita, ed. (2011) *Walmart in China*. Ithaca: Cornell University Press.

Chan, Anita and Hong-zen Wang (2004) 'The Impact of the State on Workers' Conditions: Comparing Taiwanese Factories in China and Vietnam', *Pacific Affairs* 77(4), pp. 629–646.

Chan, Jenny, Ngai Pun and Mark Selden (2013) 'The Politics of Global Production: Apple, Foxconn and China's New Working Class', *New Technology, Work and Employment* 28(2), pp. 100–116.

Chen, Martha, Joann Vanek and James Heintz (2006) 'Informality, Gender and Poverty: A Global Picture,' *Economic and Political Weekly* 41(21), pp. 2131–2139.

China Labor Watch (2010) *Code of Conduct is No More than False Advertising: Disney Suppliers Continue Exploiting Chinese Workers*. Report No. I00404E. Hong Kong: CLW.

Clarke, Simon (1999) *The Formation of a Labour Market in Russia*. Cheltenham: Edward Elgar.

Clean Clothes Campaign (2015) 'H&M's Sustainability Promises Will Not Deliver a Living Wage', 9 April. http://www.cleanclothes.org/news/press-releases/2015/04/09/h-ms-sustainability-promises-will-not-deliver-a-living-wage.

Clifford, Stephanie and Steven Greenhouse (2013) 'Fast and Flawed Inspections of Factories Abroad', *New York Times*, 1 September. http://www.nytimes.com/2013/09/02/business/global/superficial-visits-and-trickery-undermine-foreign-factory-inspections.html.

Coe, Neil and Philip Kelly (2002) 'Languages of Labour: Representational Strategies in Singapore's Labour Control Regime', *Political Geography* 21(2), pp. 341–371.

Coe, Neil and Henry Yeung (2015) *Global Production Networks: Theorizing Economic Development in an Interconnected World*. Oxford: Oxford University Press.

Cohen, Robin (1987) *The New Helots: Migrants in the International Division of Labour*. Aldershot: Gower Publishing.

Cohen, Robin (1991) *Contested Domains: Essays in the New International Labour Studies*. London: Zed Books.

Cohen, Robin, ed. (2010) *The Cambridge Survey of World Migration*. Cambridge: Cambridge University Press.

Cooper, Frederick (2001) 'What is the Concept of Globalization Good For?', *African Affairs* 100(1), pp. 189–213.

Cronon, William (1991) *Nature's Metropolis: Chicago and the Great West*. New York: W. W. Norton.

Cross, Gary (1983) *Immigrant Workers in Industrial France: The Making of a New Laboring Class*. Philadelphia: Temple University Press.

Cross, John (1998) *Informal Politics: Street Vendors and the State in Mexico City*. Stanford: Stanford University Press.

Crush, Jonathan, Abdel Chikanda and Caroline Skinner, eds. (2015) *Mean Streets: Migration, Xenophobia and Informality in South Africa*. Ottawa: IDRC.

Cullather, Nick (2014) *The Hungry World: America's Cold War Battle Against Poverty in Asia*. Cambridge: Harvard University Press.

D'Alisa, Giacomo, Federico Demaria and Giorgos Kallis, eds. (2015) *Degrowth: A Vocabulary for a New Era*. London: Routledge.

Daming, Zhou (2010), 'Environmental Problems and Electronic Waste: Anthropological Research into Working Conditions of Migrants in Guiyu,

Guangdong', in Bettina Gransow and Zhou Daming (eds.), *Migrants and Health in Urban China*, pp. 28–39. Münster: Berliner China-Hefte.

Davis, Mike (2006) *Planet of Slums*. London: Verso.

Deininger, Klaus and Derek Byerlee (2011) *Rising Global Interest in Farmland: Can It Yield Sustainable and Equitable Benefits?* Washington, DC: World Bank.

de Soto, Hernando (1989) *The Other Path: The Economic Answer to Terrorism*. New York: Harper.

de Soto, Hernando (2003) *The Mystery of Capital*. New York: Basic Books.

Deyo, Frederic (2001) 'The Social Construction of Developmental Labour Systems: South-East Asian Industrial Restructuring', in Garry Rodan, Kevin Hewison and Richard Robinson (eds.), *The Political Economy of South-East Asia: Conflicts, Crises and Change*, pp. 259–282. Oxford: Oxford University Press.

Dickerson, Marla (2007) 'In Mexico City, A Great-Grandmother Defends Street Vendors' Turf', *Los Angeles Times*, 13 August. http://www.latimes.com/world/mexico-americas/la-trw-mexicocityqueen13aug13-story.html.

Dirnbach, Eric (2014) 'Truth in Labelling: Towards a Genuine Multistakeholder Apparel Social Label', in Jennifer Bair, Doug Miller and Marsha Dickson (eds.), *Workers' Rights and Labor Compliance in Global Supply Chains: Is a Social Label the Answer?* pp. 282–302. London: Routledge.

Dix, Gill, Keith Sisson and John Forth (2009) 'Conflict at Work: The Changing Pattern of Disputes', in William Brown, Alex Bryson, John Forth and Keith Whitfield (eds.), *The Evolution of the Modern Workplace*, pp. 176–200. Cambridge: Cambridge University Press.

Dobrusin, Bruno (2014) 'South–South Labor Internationalism: SIGTUR and the Challenges to the Status Quo', *WorkingUSA: The Journal of Labor and Society* 17(2), pp. 155–167.

Dyer-Witheford, Nick (2015) *Cyber-Proletariat: Global Labour in the Digital Vortex*. London: Pluto Press.

Edelman, Marc, Carlos Oya and Saturnino Borras, Jr. (2014) *Global Land Grabs: History, Theory and Method*. London: Routledge.

Edin, Kathryn and Luke Schaefer (2015) *$2.00 a Day: Living on Almost Nothing in America*. New York: Houghton Mifflin Harcourt.

Edwards, Richard (1979) *Contested Terrain: The Transformation of the Workplace in the Twentieth Century*. London: Basic Books.

Edwards, Terrence (2013) 'Mine-Dependent Mongolia to Push Renewables as Climate Change Bites – President', *Reuters*. http://www.reuters.com/article/mongolia-mining-idINDEE95408920130605.

Ellis, Hattie (2013) 'With Love From Brazil: The Mango's Journey to Britain', *The Telegraph*, 10 October. http://www.telegraph.co.uk/foodanddrink/10367303/With-love-from-Brazil-the-mangos-journey-to-Britain.html.

Emmer, Pieter (1992) 'European Expansion and Migration: The European Colonial Past and Intercontinental Migration; An Overview', in Pieter C. Emmer and Magnus Mörner (eds.), *European Expansion and Migration: Essays on the Intercontinental Migration from Africa, Asia and Europe*, pp. 1–12. New York: Berg.

European Environment Agency (2014) *Progress on Resource Efficiency and Decoupling in the EU-27*. EEA Technical Report 7-2014. Copenhagen: European Environment Agency.

Fairbrother, Peter and Nikolaus Hammer (2005) 'Global Unions: Past Efforts and Future Prospects', *Industrial Relations* 60(3), pp. 405–31.

Federici, Silvia (2012) *Revolution at Point Zero: Housework, Reproduction, and Feminist Struggle*. Oakland, CA: PM Press.

Ferguson, James (2015) *Give a Man a Fish: Reflections on the New Politics of Distribution*. Durham: Duke University Press.

Foster, Lauren and Alexandra Harvey (2005) 'Why Ethical Sourcing Means Show and Tell', *Financial Times*, 22 April. http://www.ft.com/cms/s/0/203674f2-b2cd-11d9-bcc6-00000e2511c8.html?ft_site=falcon&desktop=true#axzz4Z4ge1N1D.

Fraser, Evan and Sylvain Charlebois (2016) 'Automated Farming: Good News for Food Security, Bad News for Food Security?', *Guardian*, 18 February. http://www.theguardian.com/sustainable-business/2016/feb/18/automated-farming-food-security-rural-jobs-unemployment-technology.

Friedman, Eli (2015) *Insurgency Trap: Labour Politics in Postsocialist China*. Ithaca: Cornell University Press.

Gallagher, Mary (2004) '"Time is Money, Efficiency is Life": The Transformation of Labor Relations in China', *Studies in Comparative International Development* 39(2), pp. 11–44.

Gereffi, Gary, John Humphrey and Timothy Sturgeon (2005) 'The Governance of Global Value Chains', *Review of International Political Economy* 12(1), pp. 78–104.

Gibson, Owen (2016) 'Migrant Workers Suffer "Appalling Treatment" in Qatar World Cup Stadiums, says Amnesty', *Guardian*, 31 March. https://www.theguardian.com/global-development/2016/mar/31/migrant-workers-suffer-appalling-treatment-in-qatar-world-cup-stadiums-says-amnesty.

Goldberg, Stephen, Ashley Gist and Stanton Lindquist (2011) 'Auditor's Guide to Corporate Social Responsibility', *Journal of Corporate Accounting & Finance* 22(4), pp. 51–59.

Gordon, Orin (2014) 'Nigeria's Growing Number of Female Oil Bosses', *BBC News Report*. http://www.bbc.com/news/business-29127436.

Grant, Tavia (2015) 'Driverless Trucks Could Mean 'Game Over' for Thousands of Jobs', *Globe and Mail*, 26 July. http://www.theglobeandmail.com/report-on-business/autonomous-trucks-could-transform-labour-market-eliminate-driver-jobs/article25715184/.

Gregg, Melissa (2013) *Work's Intimacy*. Cambridge: Polity.

Gudynas, Eduardo (2011) 'Buen Vivir: Today's Tomorrow', *Development* 54(4), pp. 441–447.

Guo, Pi, et al. (2014) 'Blood Lead Levels and Associated Factors among Children in Guiyu of China: A Population-Based Study', *PLoS ONE* 9(8), pp. –12.

Hale, Angela (2004) 'Beyond the Barriers: New Forms of Labour Internationalism', *Development in Practice* 14(1/2), pp. 158–164.

Hale, Angela and Jane Wills, eds. (2005) *Threads of Labour: Garment Industry Supply Chains from the Workers' Perspective*. Oxford: Blackwell Press.

Hardoon, Deborah (2015) *Wealth: Having It All and Wanting More*. http://policy-practice.oxfam.org.uk/publications/wealth-having-it-all-and-wanting-more-338125.

Harrington, Michael (1962) *The Other America: Poverty in the United States*. New York: Simon & Schuster.

Hart, Keith (1973) 'Informal Income Opportunities and Urban Employment in Ghana', *Journal of Modern African Studies* 11(1), pp. 61–89.

Harvey, David (2006) 'Space as a Key Word', in *Spaces of Global Capitalism:*

Towards a Theory of Uneven Geographical Development, pp. 119–148. London: Verso.

Heath, Rachel and A. Mushfiq Mobarak (2015) 'Manufacturing Growth and the Lives of Bangladeshi Women', *Journal of Development Economics* 115(1), pp. 1–15.

Herod, Andrew (2003) 'Geographies of Labor Internationalism', *Social Science History* 27(4), pp. 501–523.

Herod, Andrew (2010) *Scale*. London: Routledge.

Hickel, Jason (2016) 'The True Extent of Global Poverty and Hunger: Questioning the Good News Narrative of the Millennium Development Goals', *Third World Quarterly* 37(5), pp. 749–767.

Hodal, Kate, Chris Kelly and Felicity Lawrence (2014) 'Revealed: Asian Slave Labour Producing Prawns for Supermarkets in US, UK', *Guardian*, 10 June. http://www.theguardian.com/global-development/2014/jun/10/super market-prawns-thailand-produced-slave-labour.

Holgate, Jane (2005) 'Organizing Migrant Workers: A Case Study of Working Conditions and Unionization in a London Sandwich Factory', *Work, Employment and Society* 19(3), pp. 463–480.

Homze, Edward (1967) *Foreign Labor in Nazi Germany*. Princeton: Princeton University Press

Human Rights Watch (2014) *Cleaning Human Waste: 'Manual Scavenging,' Caste, and Discrimination in India*, 25 August. https://www.hrw.org/report /2014/08/25/cleaning-human-waste/manual-scavenging-caste-and-discriminati on-india.

Human Rights Watch (2015) *'Work Faster or Get Out': Labor Rights Abuses in Cambodia's Garment Industry*. http://features.hrw.org/features/HRW_2015_ reports/Cambodia_Garment_Workers/index.html.

Hussain, Akmal (1988) *Strategic Issues in Pakistan's Economic Policy*. Karachi: Progressive Publishers.

IFAD (2012) *Sustainable Smallholder Agriculture: Feeding the World, Protecting the Planet*. Rome: IFAD

IFAD (2013) *Smallholders, Food Security and the Environment*. Geneva: IFAD / UNEP.

ILO (2002) *Resolution Concerning Decent Work and the Informal Economy*. Geneva: ILO. http://www.ilo.org/public/english/standards/relm/ilc/ilc90/pdf/ pr-25res.pdf.

ILO (2012a) *ILO Global Estimate of Forced Labour: Results and Methodology*. Geneva: ILO.

ILO (2012b) 'Uruguay Takes the Lead to Protect Domestic Workers'. https:// www.youtube.com/watch?v=tDZoOjS38MM.

ILO (2015) *ILO Global Estimates of Migrant Workers and Migrant Domestic Workers: Results and Methodology*. Geneva: International Labour Office.

ILO and WTO (2009) *Globalization and Informal Jobs in Developing Countries*. Geneva: ILO.

IOM (2015) *World Migration Report 2015. Migrants and Cities: New Partnerships to Manage Mobility*. Geneva: International Organizations for Migration.

ITUC (2012) '12 by 12 Campaign: Uruguay First Country to Ratify C189'. https://www.ituc-csi.org/12-by-12-campaign-uruguay-first?lang=fr.

Jenkins, Steve (2002) 'Organizing, Advocacy, and Member Power: A Critical Reflection', *WorkingUSA* 6(2), pp. 56–89.

Jurje, Flavia and Sandra Lavenex (2015) *ASEAN Economic Community: What Model for Labour Mobility?* NCCR Working Paper No. 2015/02. Bern: Switzerland.

Kabeer, Naila (1988) 'Subordination and Struggle: Women in Bangladesh', *New Left Review* 1(168), pp. 95–121.

Kabeer, Naila (2002) *The Power to Choose: Bangladeshi Women and Labour Market Decisions in London and Dhaka.* London: Verso.

Kabeer, Naila, Khawar Mumtaz and Asad Sayeed (2010) 'Beyond Risk Management: Vulnerability, Social Protection and Citizenship in Pakistan', *Journal of International Development* 22(1), pp. 1–19

Kanter, Zach (2015) 'Autonomous Cars Will Destroy Millions of Jobs and Reshape the US Economy by 2025', *Quartz.* 13 May. http://qz.com/403628/autonomous-cars-will-destroy-millions-of-jobs-and-reshape-the-economy-by-2025/.

Kashi, Ed and Michael Watts (2008) *The Curse of Black Gold.* New York: powerHouse Books.

Katz, Eliakim and Oded Stark (1986) 'Labor Migration and Risk Aversion in Less Developed Countries', *Journal of Labor Economics* 4(1), pp. 134–149.

Katz, Lawrence and Alan Krueger (2016) 'The Rise and Nature of Alternative Work Arrangements in the United States, 1995–2015', *NBER Working Paper* 22667. www.nber.org/papers/w22667.ack.

Kaur, Amarjit (2014) 'Plantation Systems, Labour Regimes and the State in Malaysia, 1900–2012', *Journal of Agrarian Change* 14(2), pp. 190–213.

Kelly, Philip (2002) 'Spaces of Labour Control: Comparative Perspectives from Southeast Asia', *Transactions of the Institute of British Geographers* 27(4), pp. 395–411.

Kerr, Dara (2012) 'Apple's iPad Mini Said to be Made by Pegatron, Foxconn', CNET, 17 September. https://www.cnet.com/news/apples-ipad-mini-said-to-be-made-by-pegatron-foxconn/.

Kim, Jaesok (2013) *Chinese Labor in a Korean Factory: Class, Ethnicity, and Productivity on the Shop Floor in Globalizing China.* Stanford: Stanford University Press

Klein, Naomi (1999) *No Logo! Taking Aim at the Brand Bullies.* Toronto: Knopf Canada.

Kloppenburg, Jack (2004) *First the Seed: The Political Economy of Plant Biotechnology.* Madison: University of Wisconsin Press.

Knocke, David (2012) *Economic Networks.* Cambridge: Polity.

Kochhar, Rakesh (2015) *A Global Middle Class Is More Promise than Reality*, Pew Research Center. Washington, DC: Pew Research Center.

Kolbert, Elizabeth (2014) *The Sixth Extinction: An Unnatural History.* New York: Henry Holt Press.

Lalander, Rickard (2014) 'Rights of Nature and the Indigenous Peoples in Bolivia and Ecuador: A Straitjacket for Progressive Development Politics?', *Iberoamerican Journal of Development Studies* 3(2), pp. 148–173.

Lambert, Craig (2015) *Shadow Work: The Unpaid, Unseen Jobs That Fill Your Day.* Berkeley: Counterpoint.

Lan, Pei-Chia (2007) 'Legal Servitude and Free Illegality: Migrant "Guest" Workers in Taiwan', in Rhacel Parreñas and Lok Siu (eds.), *Asian Diasporas: New Formations, New Conceptions*, pp. 253–277. Stanford: Stanford University Press.

Lapegna, Pablo (2016) *Soybeans and Power: Genetically Modified Crops,*

Environmental Politics and Social Movements in Argentina. Oxford: Oxford University Press.

LeBaron, Geneviève (2008) 'Captive Labour and the Free Market: Prisoners and Production in the USA', *Capital & Class 95*, pp. 59–81.

LeBaron, Genevieve and Jane Lister (2015) 'Benchmarking Global Supply Chains: The Power of the "Ethical Audit" Regime', *Review of International Studies* 41(5), pp. 905–924.

Ledwith, Sue (2007) 'The Future as Female? Gender, Diversity and Global Labour Solidarity', in Craig Phelan (ed.), *The Future of Organized Labour: Global Perspectives*, pp. 91–134. Oxford: Peter Lang.

Lee, Ching Kwan (1995) 'Engendering the Worlds of Labor: Women Workers, Labor Markets, and Production Politics in the South China Economic Miracle', *American Sociological Review*, 60(3), pp. 378–398.

Lee, Ching Kwan (2007) *Against the Law: Labor Protests in China's Rustbelt and Sunbelt*. Berkeley: University of California Press.

Lee, Everett (1966) 'A Theory of Migration', *Demography* 3(1), pp. 47–57.

Leong, Apo and Chan Ka-wai (2011) 'Critical Reflection of CSR: A Labour's Perspective', *Asian Monitor Resource Centre*, 9 September. http://www.amrc.org.hk/content/critical-reflection-csr-labours-perspective.

Levine, Dan (2016) 'Uber Drivers Remain Independent Contractors as Lawsuit Settled', *Reuters Technology News*, 22 April. http://www.reuters.com/article/us-uber-tech-drivers-settlement-idUSKCN0XJ07H.

Leys, Colin (1974) *Underdevelopment in Kenya: The Political Economy of Neo-colonialism, 1964–1971*. Berkley: University of California Press.

Lindell, Ilda (2011) 'Informal Work and Transnational Organizing', in Andreas Bieler and Ingemar Lindberg (eds.), *Global Restructuring, Labour and the Challenges for Transnational Solidarity*, pp. 75–86. London: Routledge.

Luce, Stephanie (2014) *Labor Movements: Global Perspectives*. Cambridge: Polity.

MacDonald, James M., Penni Korb and Robert A. Hoppe (2013) *Farm Size and the Organization of U.S. Crop Farming*, ERR-152. US. Department of Agriculture. https://www.ers.usda.gov/webdocs/publications/err152/39359_err152.pdf?v=41526.

Maddison, Angus (2003) *The World Economy: Historical Statistics*. Paris: OECD.

Malm, Andreas (2016) *Fossil Capital: The Rise of Steam Power and the Roots of Global Warming*. London: Verso.

Maloney, William (2004) 'Informality Revisited', *World Development* 32(7), pp. 1159–1178.

Manuel, Thomas (2016) 'The Labour Story that Big Media is Not Telling You', *The Wire*, 2 September. http://thewire.in/63622/labour-trade-unions-strike/.

Marx, Karl (1990) *Capital: A Critique of Political Economy*, vol. 1. London: Penguin.

Massey, Douglas (1990) 'Social Structure, Household Strategies, and the Cumulative Causation of Migration', *Population Index* 56(1), pp. 3–26.

McDougall, Dan (2007) 'Child Sweatshop Shame Threatens Gap's Ethical Image', *Guardian*, 28 October. https://www.theguardian.com/business/2007/oct/28/ethicalbusiness.india.

Meagher, Kate (2010) 'The Politics of Vulnerability: Exit, Voice and Capture in Three Nigerian Informal Manufacturing Clusters', in Ilda Lindell (ed.), *Africa's Informal Workers: Collective Agency, Alliances and Transnational Organizing*, pp. 46–64. London: Zed Books.

Merk, Jeroen (2008) 'Restructuring and Conflict in the Global Athletic Footwear Industry: Nike, Yue Yuen and Labour Codes of Conduct', in Marcus Taylor (ed.), *Global Economy Contested: Power and Conflict across the International Division of Labour*, pp. 79–97. Routledge, New York.

Mezzadri, Alessandra (2016) 'The Informalisation of Capital and Interlocking in Labour Contracting Networks', *Progress in Development Studies* 16(2), pp. 124–139.

Mies, Maria (1986) *Patriarchy and Accumulation on a World Scale: Women in the International Division of Labour*. London: Zed Books.

Minoia, Glulia, Wamiqullah Mumtaz and Adam Pain (2015) 'Peeling the Onion: Social Regulation of the Onion Market, Nangarhar, Afghanistan', *Economic and Political Weekly* 50(9), pp. 75–83.

Minter, Adam (2013) *Junkyard Planet*. London: Bloomsbury Press.

Mitchell, Timothy (2009) 'Carbon Democracy', *Economy and Society* 38(3), pp. 399–432.

Moody, Kim (1997) *Workers in a Lean World: Unions in the International Economy*. London: Verso.

Moore, Jason (2015) *Capitalism in the Web of Life*. London: Verso.

Moore, Jason, ed. (2016) *Anthropocene or Capitalocene? Nature, History, and the Crisis of Capitalism*. New York: PM Press.

Mordi, Chima (2008) 'Segmented Work and Ethnic Divided Workers in the Nigerian Oil Sector', *International Africa Academy of Business and Development Journal* 9, pp. 533–537.

Mosse, David, Sanjeev Gupta, Mona Mehta, Vidya Shah, Julia Rees and the KRIBP Project Team (2002) 'Brokered Livelihoods: Debt, Labour Migration and Development in Tribal Western India', *Journal of Development Studies* 38(5), pp. 59–88.

Munck, Ronaldo (1988) *The New International Labour Studies*. London: Zed Books.

Nang, Leung Pak and Ngai Pun (2013) 'Radicalization of the new Chinese Working Class: A Case Study of Collective Action in Gemstone Industry', in Marcus Taylor (ed.), *Renewing International Labour Studies*, pp. 251–265. London: Routledge Press.

Northrup, David (1995) *Indentured Labor in the Age of Imperialism, 1834–1922*. Cambridge: Cambridge University Press.

Nun, Jose (2000) 'The End of Work and the "Marginal Mass" Thesis', *Latin American Perspectives* 27(1), pp. 6–32.

NUS (2016) *Double Jeopardy: Assessing the Dual Impact of Student Debt and Graduate Outcomes on the First £9k Fee Paying Graduates*. http://www.nus-connect.org.uk/resources/double-jeopardy/download_attachment.

Oakland Institute (2015) *Breaking the Silence Against Forced Displacement in Ethiopia*. San Francisco: Oakland Institute. http://www.oaklandinstitute.org/we-say-land-not-yours-breaking-silence-against-forced-displacement-ethiopia.

Ong, Aihwa (2006) 'Labor Arbitrage: Displacements and Betrayals in Silicon Valley', in *Neoliberalism as Exception: Mutations in Citizenship and Sovereignty*, pp. 157–175. Durham: Duke University Press.

Oreskes, Naomi (2014) 'The Scientific Consensus on Climate Change: How Do We Know We're Not Wrong?', in Joseph DiMento and Pamela Doughman (eds.), *Climate Change: What it Means for Us, Our Children and Our Grandchildren*, pp. 65–99. Cambridge: MIT Press.

Osborne, Hilary and Sean Farrell (2016) 'Deliveroo Workers Strike Again Over

New Pay Structure', *Guardian*, 15 August. https://www.theguardian.com/ business/2016/aug/15/deliveroo-workers-strike-again-over-new-pay-structure.

Pager, Devah (2003) 'The Mark of a Criminal Record,' *American Journal of Sociology* 108(5), pp. 937–975.

Pangsapa, Piya (2007) *Textures of Struggle: The Emergence of Resistance Among Garment Workers in Thailand*. Ithaca: Cornell University Press.

Papadakis, Konstantinos, ed. (2008) *Cross-Border Social Dialogue and Agreements: An emerging Global Industrial Relations Framework?* Geneva: ILO.

Payson Center for International Development and Technology Transfer (2011) 'Oversight of Public and Private Initiatives to Eliminate Worst Forms of Child Labor in the Cocoa Sector in Côte d'Ivoire and Ghana', *Tulane University*. https://issuu.com/stevebutton/docs/tulane_final_report?e=1162575/3403846.

Pearson, Ruth, Gill Seyfang and Rhys Jenkins, eds. (2002) *Corporate Responsibility and Labour Rights: Codes of Conduct in the Global Economy* (London: Earthscan).

Peck, Jamie (1996) *Work-Place: The Social Regulation of Labour Markets*. London: Guildford Press.

Peck, Jamie (2001) *Workfare States*. London: Guilford Press.

Pelletier, Nathan, Eric Audsley, Sonja Brodt, Tara Garnett, Patrik Henriksson, Alissa Kendall, Klaas Jan Kramer, David Murphy, Thomas Nemecek and Max Troell (2011) 'Energy Intensity of Agriculture and Food Systems', *Annual Review of Environment and Resources* 36, pp. 223–46.

Perry, Guillermo, William Maloney, Omar Arias, Pablo Fajnzylber, Andrew Mason and Jaime Saavedra-Chanduvi (2007) *Informality: Exit and Exclusion*. Washington, DC: World Bank.

Phelan, Craig (2007) *The Future of Organized Labour: Global Perspectives*. Bern: Peter Lang Press.

Piazza, James (2005) 'Globalizing Quiescence: Globalization, Union Density and Strikes in 15 Industrialized Countries', *Economic and Industrial Democracy* 26(2), pp. 289–314.

Piore, Michael (1979) *Birds of Passage: Migrant Labor and Industrial Societies*. Cambridge: Cambridge University Press.

Pofeldt, Elaine (2015) 'Shocker: 40% Of Workers Now Have "Contingent" Jobs, Says U.S. Government', *Forbes*. http://www.forbes.com/sites/elainepofel dt/2015/05/25/shocker-40-of-workers-now-have-contingent-jobs-says-u-s-gove rnment/#3daedbd52532.

Polanyi, Karl (2001) *The Great Transformation: The Political and Economic Origins of Our Time*. Boston: Beacon.

Post, Charles (2010) 'Exploring Working-Class Consciousness: A Critique of the Theory of the "Labour-Aristocracy"', *Historical Materialism* 18(4), pp. 3–38.

Potts, Deborah (2012) 'The Urban Informal Sector in Sub-Saharan Africa: From Bad to Good (and Back Again?)', *Development Southern Africa* 25(2), pp. 151–167.

Potts, Lydia (1990) *The World Labour Market: A History of Migration*. London: Zed Books.

Pretty, Jules (2002) *Agri-Culture: Reconnecting People, Land and Nature*. London: Earthscan.

Pun, Ngai (2007) 'Gendering the Dormitory Labor System: Production, Reproduction, and Migrant Labor in South China', *Feminist Economics* 13(3), pp. 239–258.

Punj, Shweta (2016) 'Where Are the Jobs?', *India Today*, 20 April. http://india

today.intoday.in/story/employment-scenario-job-crunch-jobless-growth-econo my/1/647573.html.

Purkayastha, Bandana (2005) 'Skilled Migration and Cumulative Disadvantage: The Case of Highly Qualified Asian Indian Immigrant Women in the US', *Geoforum* 36(2), pp. 181–196.

Rannveig Agunias, Dovelyn, Christine Aghazarm and Graziano Battistella (2011) *Labour Migration from Colombo Process Countries: Good Practices, Challenges and Ways Forward*. Bangkok and Washington, DC: International Organization for Migration.

Ravenstein, Ernst (1889) 'The Laws of Migration', *Journal of the Statistical Society* 52, pp. 214–301.

Razavi, Shahra (2009) 'Engendering the Political Economy of Agrarian Change', *The Journal of Peasant Studies* 36(1), pp. 197-226.

Reich, Michael (ed.) (2008) *Segmented Labor Markets and Labor Mobility*. Cheltenham: Edward Elgar.

Reich, Michael, David Gordon and Richard Edwards (1973) 'Dual Labor Markets: A Theory of Labor Market Segmentation', *American Economic Review* 63:2, pp. 359–365.

Rigg, Jonathan (2006) 'Land, Farming, Livelihoods, and Poverty: Rethinking the Links in the Rural South', *World Development* 34(1), pp. 180–202.

Rigg, Jonathan, Tuan Anh Nguyen and Thi Thu Huong Luong (2014) 'The Texture of Livelihoods: Migration and Making a Living in Hanoi', *Journal of Development Studies* 50(3), pp. 368–382.

Rioux, Sébastien (2015) 'Food Retailers, Market Concentration and Forced Labour', openDemocracy, 25 February. https://www. opendemocracy.net/beyondslavery/s%c3%a9bastien-rioux/ food-retailers-market-concentration-and-forced-labour.

Robinson, Bruce (2011) 'Making Connections: Transnational Solidarity Through the Internet', in Andreas Bieler and Ingemar Lindberg (eds.), *Global Restructuring, Labour and the Challenges for Transnational Solidarity*, pp. 193–205. Abingdon: Routledge.

Robinson, Joan (1962) *Economic Philosophy*. London: Aldine Press.

Rostow, Walt (1960) *The Stages of Economic Growth: A Non-Communist Manifesto*. Cambridge: Cambridge University Press.

Routh, Supriya and Vando Borghi (2016) *Workers and the Global Informal Economy: Interdisciplinary Perspectives*. London: Routledge.

Ryan, Órla (2011) *Chocolate Nations: Living and Dying for Cocoa in West Africa*. London: Zed Books.

Salazar Parreñas, Rhacel (2015) *Servants of Globalization: Migration and Domestic Work*. Stanford: Stanford University Press.

Salzinger, Leslie (2003) *Genders in Production: Making Workers in Mexico's Global Factories*. Berkeley: University of California Press.

Sandy, Larissa (2012) 'International Politics, Anti-Trafficking Measures and Sex Work in Cambodia', in Michele Ford, Lenore Lyons and Willem van Schendel (eds.) *Labour Migration and Human Trafficking in Southeast Asia*, pp. 41–56. London: Routledge.

Sandy, Matt (2015) 'The Fight Against Slavery in Brazil', *Al Jazeera*, 1 August. http://projects.aljazeera.com/2015/07/slavery-brazil/slaves-fight-back.htm.

Sanyal, Kalyan (2007) *Rethinking Capitalist Development: Primitive Accumulation, Governmentality and the Post-Colonial Capitalism*. New Delhi: Routledge.

Sayer, Derek (1990) *Capitalism and Modernity*. London: Routledge.

Schneider, Friedrich (2013) *The Shadow Economy in Europe*. Geneva: A. T. Kearney.

Schultz, T. Paul (2000) 'Labour Market Reforms: Issues, Evidence and Prospects,' in Anne O. Krueger (ed.), *Economic Policy Reform: The Second Stage*, p. 295. Chicago: University of Chicago Press.

Scipes, Kim (2014) 'Social Movement Unionism or Social Justice Unionism? Disentangling Theoretical Confusion within the Global Labor Movement', *Class, Race and Corporate Power* 2(3), Article 9.

Scoones, Ian (2015) *Sustainable Livelihoods and Rural Development*. Halifax: Fernwood Press.

Seidman, Gay (1994) *Manufacturing Militance: Workers' Movements in Brazil and South Africa, 1970–1985*. Berkeley: University of California Press.

Seidman, Gay (2009) 'Labouring Under an Illusion? Lesotho's 'Sweat-Free' Label', *Third World Quarterly* 30(3), pp. 581–598.

Sevastopulo, Demetri (2014) 'China: Delt Blues', *Financial Times*, 22 January. https://www.ft.com/content/a60413c2-7c46-11e3-9179-00144feabdc0.

Shalla, Vivian and Wallace Clement (2007) *Work in Tumultuous Times: Critical Perspectives*. Montreal: Queen's-McGill Press.

Sharp, Alastair and Solarina Ho (2013) 'Joe Fresh Maker to Stay in Bangladesh – Loblaw Chief', *Reuters South Asia News*, 2 May. http://in.reuters.com/article/bangladesh-building-loblaw-idINDEE93T00R20130502.

Shelvy, Toby (2007) *Exploited: Migrant Labour in the New Global Economy*. London: Zed Books.

Shen, Andy (2016) 'Financing Forced Labor: The Legal and Policy Implications of World Bank Loans to the Government of Uzbekistan', *International Labor Rights Forum*. http://laborrights.org/sites/default/files/publications/Financing_Forced_Labor_1.pd.

Shiva, Vandana (2005) *Earth Democracy: Justice, Sustainability, and Peace*. London: South End Press.

Silver, Beverly (2003) *Forces of Labor: Workers' Movements and Globalization since 1870*. Cambridge: Cambridge University Press.

Smith, Adam (1999) *The Wealth of Nations*. London: Penguin.

Smith, Neil (2008) *Uneven Development: Nature, Capital, and the Production of Space*. Athens: University of Georgia Press.

Solow, Barbara, ed. (1993) *Slavery and the rise of the Atlantic System*. Cambridge: Cambridge University Press.

SOMO and ICD (2011) *Captured by Cotton: Exploited Dalit Girls Produce Garments in India for European and US Markets*. http://www.indianet.nl/pdf/CapturedByCotton.pdf.

Sneath, David (2006) 'Transacting and Enacting: Corruption, Obligation and the Use of Monies in Mongolia', *Ethnos* 71(1), pp. 89–112.

Sparshott, Jeffrey (2015) 'Congratulations, Class of 2015. You're the Most Indebted Ever (For Now)', *Wall Street Journal*, 8 May. http://blogs.wsj.com/economics/2015/05/08/congratulations-class-of-2015-youre-the-most-indebted-ever-for-now/.

Standing, Guy (2015) *The Precariat: The New Dangerous Class*. London: Bloomsbury.

Steel, Griet (2012) 'Whose Paradise? Itinerant Street Vendors' Individual and Collective Practices of Political Agency in the Tourist Streets of Cusco, Peru', *International Journal of Urban and Regional Research* 36(6), pp. 1007–1021.

Steffen, Will, Paul Crutzen and John McNeill (2007) 'The Anthropocene: Are Humans Now Overwhelming the Great Forces of Nature?', *Ambio* 36(8), pp. 614–621.

Stern, Nicholas (2007) *The Economics of Climate Change: The Stern Review*. Cambridge: Cambridge University Press.

Stevis, Dimitris and Terry Boswell (2007) 'International Framework Agreements: Opportunities and Challenges for Global Unionism', in Kate Bronfenbrenner (ed.), *Global Unions: Challenging Transnational Capital through Cross-Border Campaigns*, pp. 174–194. Ithaca: Cornell University Press.

Soederberg, Susanne (2014) *Debtfare States and the Poverty Industry: Money, Discipline and the Surplus Population*. London: Routledge.

Suarez-Villa, Luis (2015) *Corporate Power, Oligopolies, and the Crisis of the State*. New York: SUNY Press.

Sussmann, Anna (2015) 'Inside the Fight Over Productivity and Wages', *Wall Street Journal*, 8 September. http://blogs.wsj.com/economics/2015/09/08/inside-the-fight-over-productivity-and-wages/.

Tafere, Yisak and Alula Pankhurst (2015) 'Can Children in Ethiopian Communities Combine Schooling with Work?', *Young Lives Working Paper*, no. 141. http://www.younglives.org.uk/sites/www.younglives.org.uk/files/YL-WP141-Combining%20Schooling%20and%20Work.pdf.

Takenaka, Ayumi, Karsten Paerregaard and Ulla Berg (2010) 'Peruvian Migration in a Global Context', *Latin American Perspectives* 37(5), pp. 3–11.

Tanguy, Jeremy (2013) 'Collective and Individual Conflicts in the Workplace: Evidence from France', *Industrial Relations* 52(1), pp. 102–133.

Taylor, Marcus (2006) *From Pinochet to the Third Way*. London: Pluto Press.

Taylor, Marcus (2015) *The Political Ecology of Climate Change Adaptation: Livelihoods, Agrarian Change and the Conflicts of Development*. London: Routledge.

The Economist (2008) 'The New Face of Hunger', 17 April. http://www.economist.com/node/11049284.

The Economist (2015) 'Milking taxpayers: As crop prices fall, farmers grow subsidies instead', 14 February. http://www.economist.com/news/united-states/21643191-crop-prices-fall-farmers-grow-subsidies-instead-milking-taxpayers.

Thompson, Edward (1967) 'Time, Work-Discipline, and Industrial Capitalism', *Past & Present* 38, pp. 56–97.

Thompson, Paul (2010) *The Agrarian Vision: Sustainability and Environmental Ethics*. Lexington: University of Kentucky Press.

United Nations (1990) 'International Convention on the Protection of the Rights of All Migrant Workers and Members of Their Families', Office of the High Commissioner for Human Rights. http://www2.ohchr.org/english/bodies/cmw/cmw.htm.

United Nations Environment Programme (2007) *Labour and the Environment: A Natural Synergy*. Geneva: UNEP.

Upadhya, Carol (2009) 'Controlling Offshore Knowledge Workers: Power and Agency in India's Software Outsourcing Industry', *New Technology, Work and Employment* 24(1), pp. 2–18.

Urry, John (2013) *Societies Beyond Oil: Oil Dregs and Social Futures*. London: Zed Books.

Uzzi, Brian (1997) 'Social Structure and Competition in Interfirm Networks: The Paradox of Embeddedness', *Administrative Science Quarterly* 42(1), pp. 35–68.

van der Linden, Marcel (2008) *Workers of the World: Essays toward a Global Labor History*. Leiden: Brill.

Vanek, Joann, Martha Alter Chen, Françoise Carré, James Heintz and Ralf Hussmanns (2014) *Statistics on the Informal Economy: Definitions, Regional Estimates & Challenges*. Manchester: WIEGO.

Vara, Vauhini (2015) 'Critics of Oxfam's Poverty Statistics Are Missing the Point', *The New Yorker*, 28 January. http://www.newyorker.com/business/currency/critics-oxfams-poverty-statistics-missing-point.

Vidal, John (2010) 'How Food and Water are Driving a 21st-Century African Land Grab', *Guardian*, 7 March. https://www.theguardian.com/environment/2010/mar/07/food-water-africa-land-grab.

Wacquant, Loïc (2009) *Punishing the Poor: The Neoliberal Government of Social Insecurity*. Durham: Duke University Press.

Webster, Edward (2008) 'Recasting Labor Studies in the Twenty-First Century', *Labor Studies Journal* 33(3), pp. 249–254.

Webster, Edward, Rob Lambert and Andries Bezuidenhout (2008) *Grounding Globalization: Labour in the Age of Insecurity*. Oxford: Blackwell.

Weis, Tony (2013) *The Ecological Hoofprint: The Global Burden of Industrial Livestock*. London: Zed Books.

Wells, Don (2007) 'Too Weak for the Job: Corporate Codes of Conduct, Non-Governmental Organizations and the Regulation of International Labour Standards', *Global Social Policy* 7(1), pp. 51–74.

Williams, Alex (2005) 'Wheels and Deals in Silicon Valley', *New York Times*, 4 December. http://www.nytimes.com/2005/12/04/fashion/sundaystyles/wheels-and-deals-in-silicon-valley.html?_r=0.

Wills, Jane, Kavita Datta, Yara Evans, Joanna Herbert, Jon May and Cathy McIlwaine (2010) *Global Cities at Work: New Migrant Divisions of Labour*. London: Pluto Press.

Wolford, Wendy (2010) *This Land Is Ours Now: Social Mobilization and the Meanings of Land in Brazil*. Durham: Duke University Press.

Woods, Clyde (1998) *Development Arrested: The Blues and Plantation Power in the Mississippi Delta*. London: Verso.

World Bank (2007) *World Development Report 2008: Agriculture for Development*. Oxford: Oxford University Press.

World Bank (2015a) *Climate-Smart Agriculture in Peru*. Washington, DC: IBRD.

World Bank (2015b) *Future of Food: Shaping a Climate-Smart Global Food System*. Washington, DC: World Bank.

World Bank (2016) *Migration and Remittances. Factbook 2016*. Washington, DC: World Bank.

Wright, Erik Olin (2000) 'Working-Class Power, Capitalist-Class Interests, and Class Compromise', *American Journal of Sociology* 105(4), pp. 957–1002.

Yeung, Henry (2009) 'Regional Development and the Competitive Dynamics of Global Production Networks: An East Asian Perspective', *Regional Studies* 43(3), pp. 325–351.

Yu, Xiaomin (2007) 'Impacts of Corporate Code of Conduct on Labor Standards: A Case Study of Reebok's Athletic Footwear Supplier Factory in China', *Journal of Business Ethics* 56(1), pp. 43–53.

Zatz, Noah, Tia Koonse, Theresa Zhen, Lucero Herrera, Han Lu, Steven Shafer and Blake Valenta (2016) *Get To Work or Go To Jail: Workplace Rights Under Threat*. UCLA Institute for Research on Labor and Employment. http://www.irle.ucla.edu/publications/documents/Get-to-Work324.pdf.

Index